WESTMAR COLLEGE

Anthony de Jasay is the author of *The State* (1985).

SOCIAL CONTRACT, FREE RIDE

SOCIAL CONTRACT, FREE RIDE

A Study of the Public Goods Problem

Anthony de Jasay

CLARENDON PRESS · OXFORD

1989

Oxford University Press, Walton Street, Oxford OX2 6DP
Oxford New York Toronto
Delhi Bombay Calcutta Madras Karachi
Petaling Jaya Singapore Hong Kong Tokyo
Nairobi Dar es Salaam Cape Town
Melbourne Auckland
and associated companies in
Berlin Ibadan

Oxford is a trade mark of Oxford University Press

Published in the United States
by Oxford University Press, New York

© Anthony de Jasay 1989

All rights reserved. No part of this publication may be reproduced,
stored in a retrieval system, or transmitted, in any form or by any means,
electronic, mechanical, photocopying, recording, or otherwise, without
the prior permission of Oxford University Press

British Library Cataloguing in Publication Data
De Jasay, Anthony, 1925–
Social contract, free ride: a study of the
public goods problem.
1. State. Theories: Social contract
I. Title   320.1'01
ISBN 0–19–824474–6

Library of Congress Cataloging in Publication Data
De Jasay, Anthony, 1925–
Social contract, free ride: a study of the public
goods problem / Anthony de Jasay.
p.   cm.   Bibliography: p.   Includes index.
1. Public goods.   2. Social contract.   I. Title.
HB846.5.D4 1989   363—dc19   88–7647   CIP
ISBN 0–19–824474–6

Printed and bound in Great Britain by
Biddles Ltd, Guildford and King's Lynn

CONTENTS

INTRODUCTION

'You get what you pay for.' As often as not, however, you do not. If you did, the world would be a simpler place. It would be wholly ruled by exchange relations. All would bear the full consequences of their actions and nobody would suffer or profit from 'spillovers' he[1] did not cause. Politics would be a redundant activity, and as a subject of study it would be swallowed up by economics. All social co-operation would be regulated by contracts, none by commands. Individuals would be sovereign, each deciding all matters for himself.

Yet it is of the essence of social coexistence that a person can get more than he pays for, and also that he can be made to pay for more than he gets. When this is the case, the advantage of mutually agreeable exchanges fails to explain fully why co-operation takes the forms it does. Certain acts and forbearances, goods and services are bought and sold; others are 'provided'. It is believed that there are goods, such as national defence, traffic lights, clean air, or union bargaining, whose intrinsic characteristics predestine them to be collectively provided, for they cannot be doled out in driblets to individuals willing to buy them nor be withheld from those who will not pay for them. However, the dividing-line between public provision and private exchange does not run according to the textbook distinction between public and private goods. Intrinsically private goods, like health care and education, are in large part publicly provided in most societies that are regarded as democratic, and in some that are not. Both individual exchange and collective provision require contributions of resources, efforts, good conduct, and good sense. Contributions give rise to benefits to be enjoyed. But the relation governing how contributions are transformed into benefits is different between 'exchange' and 'provision'. In the realm of exchanges, value is received for value rendered; some firm

---

[1] Wherever I say 'he' or 'man', I really mean 'she' or 'woman'.

nexus links any single individual's benefit to his own contribution. He gets a good if he pays its price. In the realm of public provision, however, the individual nexus is relaxed or uncoupled altogether; only aggregates remain firmly linked. For the group, the town, or the nation, total contributions match total benefits. Within such communities any individual can be a free rider as long as at least one other will be a sucker. Only by sheer accident does one's contribution 'fairly' match one's benefit and it is not the purpose of public provision that it should. If anything is intended it is the contrary, for non-market provision is as much an exercise in making selected goods and services freely available as in helping some members of a 'public' at the expense of others. The uncoupling of individual benefit from contribution which is intrinsic in 'publicness' designates it as the redistributive engine *par excellence*—an engine that keeps churning away unstoppably, impervious to sporadic attempts to throttle it back.

Social anthropology is in two minds about the institution of private property and the historical evidence, such as it is, of 'what came first' (or mattered more)—exchange and giving in the firm expectation of receiving a due return, or provision according to some principle of sharing. The balance at any time between the two ways of going about getting what one wants determines the character of a society in more ways and probably more decisively than anything else in the political culture. It suffices to conjure up the ideal image of the classical liberal market order at one Platonic extreme and full communism at the other, to size up the potential effect of the balance shifting one way or the other, as it appears to have done from time to time since our earliest days. It is a curious and imperfectly understood feature of modern societies, however, that when the balance does shift it now shifts only one way, towards wider and more diverse collective provision by central and local governments and quasi-voluntary associations, leaving a shrinking relative role to private exchanges. This tendency, discernible for at least the last century or so, is one no political regime of any persuasion has yet reversed, though more than one have proclaimed the vital need to try. One of the puzzles the present book seeks to unravel is why contemporary societies end up with 'more government' both when they seem to want more and when they claim to prefer less.

Harder to unravel, though of the same design, is the puzzle of why groups of interdependent persons seem unable to attain certain outcomes that are perfectly within their reach and that each member of the group would prefer. Public provision has long been held to be such an outcome. The diagnosis dates back at least to Hobbes, who taught us that it is impossible to assure civil order by way of voluntarily agreed mutual respect for life and property, for covenants to keep the peace would be but 'vain breath' in the absence of an all-powerful, sole contract-enforcer. All would like civil peace, but each would like it better still that all others should keep it while he remained free to breach it. Hence, none could have civil peace unless all laid down their arms and submitted to the threat of public coercion in the enforcement of agreements. Their willingness to submit—essentially, their acceptance of the social contract—is the direct consequence of their want of a good that can be provided out of mandatory contributions or not at all.

What Hobbes deduced from the preference for a single good— civil order—later theorists have extended to any good from which an individual can benefit without contributing to the cost of producing or maintaining it. The implied incentive structure gives rise to a dilemma in that contribution is both advantageous and irrational. Contributing to public goods is interpreted as a particular case of the notoriously destructive 'prisoners' dilemma', in which the pursuit of self-interest is an insurmountable obstacle to its own success, and rational conduct leads to needlessly poor and wasteful outcomes. If so, people would naturally rather be forced into individually unappealing conduct permitting better outcomes than accept the inferior ones that would perversely result from their free choices. On this reasoning is founded the legitimacy of the social contract and the related proposition that, generally, without mandatory contributions there can be no publicly provided goods (or, in a variant of the proposition, only inefficiently small supplies).

It is by taking this proposition as self-evidently true that public goods theorists from Wicksell and Lindahl to Samuelson have felt free to treat the Hobbesian problem of the unenforceable covenant as one that could be dealt with in terms of optimum taxation and optimum allocation of state expenditures. In their hands, a conundrum of political philosophy became a technical question of welfare economics. There is, of course, no call to object to this reduction on the ground that it is 'reductionist'. It is by successful reduction of problems that, with luck, we solve them. This particular reduction, however, is not successful, depending as it does on an underlying interpretation of the alternatives confronting men in the state of nature that does not stand up to scrutiny. The point of this book is to demonstrate that there is no public goods dilemma in Hobbes's fatal sense—a sense adopted by subsequent thought in law, politics, and economics (impoverishing each)—for voluntary contribution to shared benefits can be fully consistent with the successful pursuit of narrow self-interest. Willing surrender of free choice in the matter, as social contract theory would have us do, cannot be accounted for by our desire to attain purportedly better states of affairs than our uncoerced self-seeking could bring about.

The antithesis between building social co-operation on free contracts and on obedience to legitimate commands lies at the base of the cleavage between individual and social choice. It is only when his benefit is matched by his contribution and he 'pays for what he gets and gets what he pays for' that an individual's choice is solely, or at least predominantly, his own business and no proper concern of others. When, in co-operative situations, his benefit exceeds or falls short of his contribution he plays a *de facto* free-rider or sucker role, bound up with either the tolerance or the pressing encouragement of others who, by right or force, get a say in the matter. Unless they are fatuous (a redundant adding together of identical wishes), collective decisions involve the will, preference, or interest of one part of a collectivity overruling those of the rest. Who overrules whom depends on the decision rule or constitution. By being more or less democratic, plutocratic, aristocratic, or whatever, or simply by virtue of its more or less agile or sluggish nature, a given kind of constitution is predisposed to produce a corresponding kind of social decision, biased in favour of an identifiable interest. This is conspicuously the case in matters of public goods production, taxation, property and other minority[2] rights. Hence, no non-fatuous constitution can be adopted without in advance overruling those whose interest would have been, on the average, predictably better served by a different one. The social contract is a hypothetical

---

[2] A property right is a minority right of a particularly vulnerable type, since it is in its nature that there is generally a potential majority coalition that would benefit by depriving the holder of the right. Other minority rights do not necessarily entail the adversarial interest of a majority. For further discussion, see Appendix to ch. 5.

agreement which no sane person would have good reason to reject; it is legitimate because it overrules no one. The point of a 'constitution' or decision rule, by contrast, is precisely to overrule dissent and produce choices in the face of non-unanimity. Unlike the social contract 'upstream' of it, the very nature of a social decision rule contradicts the requirement that no one should have a justifiable reason to reject it. It cannot derive legitimacy from unanimity, since the choices it is biased or 'programmed' to produce 'downstream' are themselves neither unanimous nor randomly unpredictable. At best, such a rule can be legitimate on the ground of acquiescence—a logically different and ethically questionable if not downright inferior status.

Hence, anything that expands the domain of social choice *ipso facto* enlarges both the scope for free riding and the call for commands of contestable legitimacy to cope with it. The passage from exchange to public provision, taking both in a wide sense, is by the same token a passage from contracts to commands, whether the latter are intended to force some to accept unpalatable sucker roles, or to suppress the free riding in which others would be tempted to indulge.

Both these intentions are misconceived. It is part of the central thesis presented in this book that most of the commands of social choice are redundant to their ostensible purpose. They are not necessary for realizing the advantages of public provision by compelling people to contribute the required efforts and resources. Nor do they create a regime of fairness by suppressing free riding. What they accomplish is the replacement of what would be willingly adopted, social roles—some accepting to act as suckers on a prudential calculation of the alternatives, and others taking the risk of free riding in the expectation that there will be enough suckers to carry them—by centrally assigned taxpayer and tax-beneficiary roles. Instead of self-selected subsets of free riders and suckers, they divide the public into 'socially' designated subsets fulfilling analogous functions. The quest for fairness that inspires this substitution of the conscript for the volunteer may or may not be held to bring greater fairness, but it is certain to bring what it does by greater constraint and reduced autonomy. In retrospect, the bargain is hardly one reasonable men could *not* refuse.

Nevertheless, they might easily have blundered into it by a series of perhaps avoidable, but certainly tempting, errors of foresight and judgement. Wanting firm assurances that 'essential' public goods will be available (for, as Hobbes has it, the mere lack of certainty of peace is war), going for tidy certainties where probabilities would serve nearly as well in some ways and better in others, might be the original sin, the fruit of the tree of knowledge that is the social contract. Suspicion of the sin keeps raising its head in our probings into subjects as diverse as contract enforcement, civil peace in the state of nature, motives for contributing to public provision, and the selection of goods to be provided.

Around the supposed public goods dilemma there is a genuine, but altogether non-fatal, public goods problem. In sorting out the purported from the practical, one goes to the heart of the antagonism of the great rival principles of liberalism and democracy. If, after the grotesque mid-Atlantic misuse the word has long been subjected to, liberalism still means anything, it means a broad presumption in favour of deciding individually any matter whose structure lends itself, with roughly comparable convenience, to both individual and collective choice. There are, to be sure, indivisible matters of common concern which no one can decide for himself without also deciding them for others, and which it would be arbitrary to entrust to any one individual's will or subject to his veto. Fluorization of water, noise at night, billboards or speed limits are some of the more prosaic cases in point, public worship a more exalted one. Other matters are divisible. They can be equally well arranged so that each individual can decide them for himself without his decision greatly affecting others (as is the case, for example, when everybody in the office buys his own lunch), or so that a whole group of people is jointly concerned and should seek to deal with them collectively (as would be the case if a free lunch with a set menu of dishes not all liked equally were served to all in the office cafeteria). How the latter sort of inherently divisible matter is in effect divided up into small bits or gathered into large lumps, being as a consequence assigned either to individuals or to groups for decision, is a question of social institutions. Liberal institutions tend to give rise to divisions where each individual is able to choose for himself, with the consequences of his choice accruing mostly to him and only minimally to others (unless the latter are willing to be compensated for effects that impinge on them).

It is this distinction which, to my mind, is the best rationalization of the inarticulate (and contested) belief that privacy, private property, and freedom of contract are the essential determinants of the 'liberalness' or otherwise of a society, in that they help set up alternatives for choice in properly subdivided structures suitable for individual decisions, and minimize occasions for collective ones. Contrary to likewise inarticulate beliefs, this does not suffice to make liberalism a good thing; more extensive support is needed for that judgement. But the defects of social choice provide something of a base for it.

On the face of it, democracy is a characteristic that defines a class of collective decision rules (constitutions). As such, it seems irrelevant to the question of liberalism, which is logically prior to it, concerning as it does the drawing of the frontier between the individual and the collective domain. The individual domain, exempt from collective decisions, may be staked out generously ('liberally') or not. Within it, each individual agrees with himself and needs no decision rule, democratic or otherwise, to do it. It is only on the collective side of the frontier that decision rules can be democratic or not. In reality, however, there is no fixed frontier and no prior and posterior question. Democracy in the strict sense, as in 'a democratic political system', is an attribute of a procedure and not of the outcome reached by it. However, like other procedures, it is visibly predisposed to produce one kind of outcome, 'democracy' in the loose sense, as in 'a democratic society' and in 'economic democracy'. Democratically reached collective decisions usually aim at eroding privilege, levelling out rewards and making the more widely accepted notions of fairness prevail over less popular principles in the distribution of burdens and benefits. Under a democratic decision rule, all those who count count equally in the common decision, regardless of their different possessions, abilities, and concerns. Each can better his chances of attaining his preferred state of affairs by using collective decisions for committing the resources and energies of others to the uses he prefers; yet none can afford to let others do this to him without trying to do it to them.

Whether the result is sheer inconclusive churning or whether a majority succeeds to bend collective outcomes in its own favour, the attempt by each either to reap free-rider gains or to protect himself from the like attempts of others acts to broaden the scope of collective resource allocation. A democratic social-choice rule consequently tends to produce decisions that enlarge its own domain, breaking down the domain restrictions that liberal institutions erect. Its bias is to reduce the relative role of exchange, where each gets what he pays for, and to increase that of public provision, where some can get more than they contribute. Beneath the many *ad hoc* reasons that apply to particular cases, this bias is a constant in each, helping to explain the works canteen serving a free lunch, state and communal schools providing free tuition, diverse entitlements, unrelated to contributions, unfunded pension schemes, all manner of services sold at less than their cost, and, last but not least, endemic budget deficits. In each such case, the uncoupling of individual benefit from contribution creates *de facto* 'public goods' as a matter of explicit or implicit social choice, transferring the relevant resource allocation decision from the private to the public domain.

Contrary to the orthodox theory which sees the root causes of publicness in the intrinsic logistics of supplying particular goods (can a lighthouse be run for profit? can justice be bought and sold? can passers-by be charged for looking at the statue in the square? can the market hold up a 'social safety net'?), we discover a more potent and extensive principle: it is the public that decides what shall be a public good. In doing so, it creates indivisibilities. It requires that contributions to a good and the benefits it can yield should come in critical-sized aggregate lumps fitting their relevant public. Large indivisible units come about even if there is no technical obstacle to divisibility, small doses, private exchange, and hence to the operation of liberal institutions.

If it were true that there is a fatal public goods dilemma such that voluntary contribution to shared benefits is irrational and self-interest is condemned to be self-defeating, little would be left to say. At best, we could restate, with some gain in conciseness, why a self-sustaining sequence with a steadily expanding role of public provision, marked by the advance of democracy and the retreat of liberalism, must be held to be the best, and ethically least objectionable path for social evolution to take. Political science and economics could each go its own increasingly dreary way, pursuing technicalities of dubious import, as few or no large questions would be worth asking.

Since, however, strong arguments suggesting that the public-goods dilemma is false can be found, at the very least there is some hope for the revival of non-dreary political philosophy and political economy. Beyond that, there is the more sanguine hope that the future need be no drearier than the past.

PART ONE
THE SURRENDER OF AUTONOMY

'New discoveries are not to be expected in these matters'
DAVID HUME, *Of the Original Contract*

1

COMMITMENT TO CO-OPERATION

Peaceful, mutually agreeable coexistence of persons is tantamount to a measure of social co-operation whether or not such is their conscious intent. Both by design and by spontaneous emergence, their interactions tend severally or jointly to produce results— 'positive' but also 'negative' man-made variations in the orderliness, agreement, and riches of their own and other people's lives. The results may accrue wholly or in part to those who co-operate, though not necessarily to all who do, nor to only those who do, for there are 'externalities', spillovers benefiting or harming bystanders. Production of private goods for exchange and the provision of public goods (including under 'goods' as much as we decently can of what people want[1] for themselves or for others) are the areas of activity where co-operation owes least to affective ties between persons and where contract, command, or both tend to be relied on to ensure reliable commitment to co-operative acts. The diversity of possible relations, including the absence of any discernible relation, between contributions and benefits in these domains is one of the central themes of ethics, economics, and politics, and an anxious preoccupation of this book.

People of course co-operate informally by making unspoken-for and unrequited contributions to the endeavours of others. They 'lend a hand', or a tool, or money; they help out, chip in, give advice, share knowledge, await their turn, give way, go to the end of the queue, refrain from littering in public, and so forth. Unilateral contributors may or may not share in the richer life they help in some measure to bring about. If they do, their share may not perceptibly vary with their own contribution. In any event,

---

[1] It is not obvious that all that people want for themselves or for others should or can be drawn into the concept of 'goods'. There may be normative reasons for denying that certain entities are goods however much they are desired, or methodological reasons against letting in, as the arguments of a utility function, all that serves as a *de facto* motive for action. We shall be concerned with such restrictions in ch. 8.

expectation of a benefit may not always or wholly explain a contribution which is made unilaterally. By the same token, people may stop contributing without losing much, or any, of their share in the richer life. However, noticeable non-co-operation, unless it is widespread enough to pass for normal, exposes a person to a range of possible sanctions from blame through ostracism, reciprocal non-co-operation in some other endeavour, to positive retaliation. These sanctions obviously involve some opportunity cost to administer, and therefore constitute, so to speak, a second-order co-operation problem on top of the first-order problem involved in the indeterminate nexus between contribution and benefit.

Behind the informal, spontaneous, and ostensibly sanction-free character of unilateral contribution there lurk tacit understandings, quid pro quos, and probable if uncertain penalties, conferring upon it the features of an incipient, incomplete contract. For all its roots in social history and its potential for teaching people about reciprocity without explicit commitment, this form of co-operation has obvious weaknesses in being indefinite, uncommitted, and (at least formally if not always in fact) unenforceable. Consideration of its weaknesses is of some help in grasping the functions and structure of fully fledged contracts, which *commit* two parties to agreed courses of action that promote the purposes of both, and of command–obedience relations which *commit* subordinates to contribute to the purposes of superiors.

Custom

An avowedly 'reductionist' manner of calling reality to some sort of order is to treat the indefinitely many forms of social co-operation as if they all fell into two uniform classes: contract and command. In opting for this, we claim that at least in non-affective contexts the inclusive binary relation whereby all that is not contract-compliance is command–obedience can describe and explain all commitment to social interactions well enough, though next to the fully fledged specimen each class must be understood to include the incipient, the imperfectly enforced, and the embryonic. Where, then, is the place of custom in this structure?

The substantive content of any contract is a matter of agreement between the parties within the 'frame' (broad or narrow as dictated by exogenous factors) of contractual freedom. The frame is exogenously fixed simply in the sense that it is independent of the will of the parties to the agreement, who have to stay within it or not agree at all. Formally, the same statement explains the substantive content of contract and of custom. Custom would not be what it is if those adhering to it preferred no agreement to the agreement embodied in the custom, e.g. if people would rather not marry than agree to some customary property settlement.

The sense of custom as a special case, a subclass of the general class of contracts, is that where a custom rules there is usually no room within the 'frame' for terms of agreement other than those embodied in the custom. Keep narrowing the frame of contractual freedom within which the terms of agreement may vary and once negotiation has fallen into disuse, contract becomes custom. A 'time-honoured custom' carries the authority conferred by repeated agreement over time, one that has proved acceptable to successive generations. Whatever its historical origin, the rational-choice explanation of a custom has its least unpromising start in a range or frequency distribution of freely negotiated agreements, whose central core gradually solidifies into custom embodying unvarying terms, for a host of reasons having to do with 'face',[2] the difficulties of negotiation, and the greater convenience of dispute-resolution and enforcement when terms are standard.

The part of custom which, at least in the Germanic cultures, has little by little found its way into the law carries evidence of its consensual origin. The (albeit factually somewhat inaccurate) notion of an evolution from free agreements to custom, from custom to law, explains the high public regard for the common law which, unlike statute law, did not have to be enacted before it was accepted. The same sort of evolution seems to explain the rise of criminal law out of tort law, and of tort law out of agreements to compensate, to buy off revenge—an explanation which is adequate, logically whole, regardless of its contested historical accuracy. Customary terms of the service tenure of land, rents, tolls, wages, professional fees, customs regulating early forms of banking and marine insurance and, of course, above all the prices and

---

[2] One merit of fixed prices, customary terms, stereotyped agreements is that, as there is no negotiation, no one yields and no one has to lose face. Nor does any party suffer the anguish and self-reproach that often accompanies the difficult and inconclusive drive for the *best* terms.

specifications of traded goods all bear plausible traces of earlier contractual or para-contractual origin. Unless we resign ourselves to the idea of an endless chain stretching into the past where every custom is born of another earlier custom, or to the idea that customs can be decreed into existence by command, contract is the only residual hypothesis to account for them. We can then look upon custom as ossified contract whose terms have become standardized. In the case of the just price and the more general scholastic category of the just contract (conceived as the sole morally deserving case of 'zero-sum' transactions, where 'neither party gains' instead of one losing what the other gains), standard terms have even been invested with moral value.

There is a demonstrable advantage to any two parties in not having to adhere to custom but having the broadest possible frame within which the terms of a contract can be adjusted to their particular 'circumstances'.[3] Offsets against the advantage of adjustability are provided by the reduced transaction and information costs, and the greater peace of mind associated with customary terms. If such offsetting advantages predominate, the spontaneous rise and survival of a custom are broadly consistent with rational choice and it can be explained as if it were itself a result of agreement.

The significant particularities of custom are that terms are standard rather than *ad hoc* (though, as the great diversity of 'customary' medieval and early modern terms and conditions for property holding, inheritance, marriage, master-and-servant relations, commercial ventures, etc. demonstrate, there was usually some room for negotiated agreement about *which* custom would apply); that a reciprocal promissory obligation to perform often remains inexplicit, or is made explicit only in some weak form; and that sanctions to ensure conformity to the custom are of widely varying reliability and strength. While bearing these features in mind, I see

[3] The 'circumstances' (tastes, endowments, etc.) of the parties to a potential exchange define, to use technical language, a 'contract curve' between them. It is the locus of the points, representing terms of exchange, at which for given levels of well-being for one party, the other party can advantageously trade with him. A change in terms that represents a move from a point off the curve to a point on the curve can, by definition, make at least one party better off without making the other worse off. Hence, the imposition of a narrow 'frame' of contractual freedom, e.g. one limited to 'just' prices only, which rules out segments of many people's contract curves, reduces their potential well-being; it remains to be demonstrated that it increases that of others. Limiting the freedom of contract is usually advocated on grounds of fairness and not of well-being.

no harm in letting custom submerge under contract in what
follows.

Contract is not Command

Implicit in social criticism, much of normative political theory, and
much of economics outside the neo-classical mainstream is the
position that the contract–command dichotomy is at best verbal
and empty of real empirical content, and at worst a tendentious
semantic fraud.

The contract–command distinction is upheld in everyday discourse
by the imprecise but robust connotation that seems inseparable from
the two concepts: contract is understood as being freely entered
into, hence compliance is by voluntarily assumed obligation; while
command is obeyed under coercion or, of course, the probable
threat of it. The arguments denying that such a distinction is
possible have roughly the following form.

1. Contracts are generally not entered into freely, though it is
just possible to claim that unimportant ones may be. The
consequence of not entering into a given contract is to incur an
opportunity cost, which is the difference between the value a
would-be contracting party places on the expected consequences of
entering into *this* contract and the expected consequences of taking
the *next-worse* alternative available to him. The next-worse
alternative may be quite bad. There may be, in everyday language,
'no alternative'. The opportunity cost of declining the best
alternative in favour of the next-worse one may be such that he 'just
can't afford it'; '. . . being free to choose . . . has got to include the
idea that not going along with the deal that is being offered is *an
acceptable state of affairs*'.[4] Unless society is just or rich (beyond
scarcity) or both to begin with, so that it does not put people before
unacceptable alternatives, the contracts that really make a difference
to one's well-being *cannot* be refused, i.e. they are 'unfree'. A
related though different claim is that a society of scarcity and
injustice will not, in general, be made richer and juster by letting
contracts take their course.

2. Admittedly, it is easy to dismiss as naïve the idea of a binary

---

[4] Barry (1986) 26, my italics.

division between 'acceptable' and 'unacceptable', for one does not end and the other does not begin at a particular line or point in the universe of states of affairs. Must 'unacceptable' mean starvation, or is 'relative deprivation' bad enough? And when is it 'acceptable' to be humbled by yielding in a negotiation? A state of affairs can be 'unacceptable' only in the sense that another one within reach is more acceptable to a particular person. If we must at all costs seek a binary relation of either/or, 'acceptability' is not going to furnish a generally recognizable dividing-line.

A more sophisticated account of free choice might replace preferences for *available* states of affairs by preferences for states of affairs of varying degrees of *probability*, so that 'not going along with a deal' could be interpreted as evidence, not or not only of the definite availability of a (more) acceptable alternative but also of certain probabilities, 'hopes' of more acceptable ones. Such an interpretation, by making room for error of probability judgement and wishful thinking, could at least give coherent meaning to a person 'not going along with a deal' although he actually *prefers* it to the 'unacceptable' next-worse alternative that is 'being offered'— for taking his chances on the probability distribution of yet other 'deals', not 'offered' but possible, ranks higher than either of the offered deals in his preference order. Whichever way we turn and refine the notion, however, 'acceptability' is hardly a promising test of the freedom of entering into a contract.

3. It could be held, instead, that the idea of freely entering into a contract suffers from the same conceptual weakness as the idea of free acts in general. Not entering into a given contract entails an opportunity cost in the same way that an act runs into a constraint; if we would rather not incur the cost, or not bump against the constraint, we will (trivially speaking) 'choose' not to do so. We will do the other thing instead, but what is the sense of calling the other thing, namely our resulting alternative action, 'free'? On this view, it is senseless to speak about choice, with the overtone of freedom that the word carries, once a complete preference-ranking of alternative courses of action is supposed to exist, since the preferred one must *ex hypothesi* be taken. At worst, this is complete determinism; at best, it shifts the domain of freedom from the choice of actions to the choice of the preferences which wholly prejudge the action that must be taken in conformity with them. At the level of actions, however, 'freedom' is a useless attribute for

distinguishing contract from command, since one is just as 'unfree' as the other.

4. Instead of putting another inclusive binary relation, 'either free or unfree', in the place of 'either acceptable or unacceptable', a continuity argument may be used. It may reasonably be held that while all acts—except perhaps unimportant ones—are unfree, the unfreedom of accepting or refusing contractual and command–obedience relations, as well as of the acts of subsequent compliance, is a function of opportunity cost. Unfreedom of an act decreases as the opportunity cost of *not* doing it diminishes, i.e. as the value or utility difference between the consequences of doing one thing and doing the next-worse thing gets smaller, and hence the reason for doing the more valuable of the two acts becomes less compelling. In the limit, there *are* free acts. They are the ones that have *no* sufficient reason, that are *gratuitous* in the literal sense of being costless, of having *no* opportunity cost because the next-worse, forgone alternative was just as worthwhile or just as worthless as the one actually taken. All other non-gratuitous acts are unfree[5] to a degree depending on the alternatives, i.e. on the facts of the case. *A priori*, in abstraction from the circumstances, nothing valid can be said about contract being more (or less) free than command.

The arguments we have sketched ('unacceptable' alternatives cannot be said to leave room for 'free' acceptance of less unacceptable ones; there are no free acts anyway; freedom varies inversely with opportunity cost, so that the better the reason for an act, the less free it is) underpin two special pleas.

One arises out of the Marxist view of proletarian existence, of wage labour. The wage contract, despite its outward form, is ostensibly agreed to but in reality it is imposed and functions as if it were command. For the proletariat as a class or for labour as a factor there is no acceptable alternative to selling itself to capital. Capital does have an acceptable alternative to buying labour, namely not buying it, for it does not starve while it abstains. All the great contracts governing the 'relations of production' under capitalism—those between capital and labour, the industrialized and the underdeveloped, the centre and the periphery, whites and

---

[5] This was the position expressed by Gide in *Les Caves du Vatican*. If nothing else, such a reference should incite us to look at the position with a degree of moral and intellectual suspicion.

coloureds, urban ghetto and suburbia—are of this unequal sort
with no 'real' choice but acceptance on the part of the weaker
party. This argument draws its logical coherence from the holistic
definition of the parties. If 'capital' and 'labour' are each a single
contracting party, it is much easier to see the terms of a contract
between them as being primarily a result of bargaining, hence
favouring 'bargaining power', than if both capital and labour are
merely conventional expressions standing for a multitude of parties
who can, in the nature of things, hardly avoid competing among
themselves.

However, objections to rigging the terms of the debate by holistic
definition will unleash other, unanswerable arguments about
domination and the use of the political, legal, and cultural
'superstructure' to ensure that the predetermined result is in fact
produced. The terms of social co-operation will end up being what
they must, not matters of free argument but the commands of
historical necessity.

The other plea for the contract–command identity is contractarian.
It claims that legitimate command whose authority is, however
indirectly, derived from valid law must, for its proper understanding,
be taken as if it were contracted for. Command to suppress socially
destructive conduct, to make free rides costly or otherwise
unattractive, to overcame myopia, perversity and irrationality, falls
most clearly into the 'as if contracted for' category. People freely
obey such commands, or would do so if made to face the
consequences of massive disobedience, because they realize their
beneficial effects, because the commands emanate from recognized
authority, or, at worst, because they are backed by reserve powers
of coercion. However, if there were no such authority, it would be
constituted anew and equipped with coercive power, 'as if' by
unanimous consent. All prudentially motivated persons would
want to be mutually assured that none of them could upset or
frustrate the expected advantages of everybody else's command-
obedience. This *als ob* result, which would be reached by free and
unanimous agreement if it had not been reached by some other
'real-time', historical process, is of course the social contract as an
explicatum arising from rational choices. Its terms reflect the
general will. 'Particular general wills' have to submit to the post-
contract commands ('social choices') of the general will. If they
preferred to disobey and face sanctions, they could actually be

forced into specific performance. Such coercion is essentially contract–enforcement, voluntarily agreed to in the social contract because implicit in its logical structure.

It also follows from the contractarian analysis of terms that interest–antagonism, let alone domination–subjection between state and civil society, is a contrived misstatement of post-contract states of affairs. Conflicts between the propertied and the property-less, taxpayers and tax beneficiaries, are negotiable in a political market-place where certain exchanges can make some better off without having to make others worse off. They are part and parcel of consensual adjustment processes and fully consistent with unanimity about the terms of the social contract itself.

Both the Marxist plea that 'unequal' contract is really command, even if technically it has been agreed to, and the contractarian plea that command which it is in our prudential interest to obey is really contract, even though it has not been formally agreed to, are of course heavily normative. They operate through a reinterpretation of social arrangements and through a classification of the actions of the parties involved as being either 'ostensibly' free or 'really' free, according to the result required for the plea to be successful.

Avoiding Freedom-Talk and Rights-Talk

There is no need to seek a foolproof distinction between contract-based and command-based social co-operation by references to the freedom, or degrees of unfreedom, of entering into the relevant commitments and of acting in compliance with them. On the contrary, there are reasons against trying to base robust concepts upon frail ones. Avoidable recourse to concepts of freedom can only too easily lead to the graveyard of philosophical reputations, due to a person's freedom being an awkward function of constraints set both by nature and by the acts and omissions of other free persons. Nature is a datum, but how to deal with the freedom of others? Are there not more unknowns than equations?

Circularity or an infinite regress is involved in defining the freedom of each in terms of the freedom of others: witness the vacuous formulae 'equal freedom' (Kant, Herbert Spencer), or 'greatest freedom compatible with like freedom for everybody else'

(Rawls)[6]. As freedom cannot be grasped and explicated by reference to itself, freedom-talk invariably spills over into rights-talk, 'rights' defining freedoms and serving as the exit from circularity to a firm fulcrum on which to rest freedom concepts. A person's freedom, then, is confined within his rights; his rights, in turn, are constrained by the rights of others. Why, however, should a person have a particular right to begin with? Why should his rights (assuming he has any) stop, and those of others start, at a particular borderline? Rights can only serve as an Archimedean firm stopping-point if they do not themselves suffer from the logical disability which makes freedom-talk circular. Barring recourse to a transcendental, ultimate stopping-point in God's will or in a natural order, it seems to me hard to feel much optimism on that score.

The other reason for not getting involved in unpromising and intractable issues of freedom and rights has to do with Occam's razor. There is a simple, minimal way of establishing and using the contract–command distinction in terms of the minimum amount of explanation needed by each.

Let the object of a contract be some entity, whether money, utility, or concord, of which both parties would rather have more than less, i.e. which is a good for both, and let there be forms of possible co-operation between them which are expected by each to result in more of the good to the two of them taken together, and in not less of it to each separately. Minimal rational-choice assumptions help establish the probability, or make it greater than it would have been otherwise, that a contract will be concluded committing the two parties to the co-operative acts needed to produce the expected incremental surplus good, as well as settling in advance its distribution between them. An additional, relatively easy, assumption of no deceit, no entrapment, can exclude any solution of the bargaining problem involved in the distribution of the surplus which does not leave any of the parties at least as well off as if he had not entered into the contract.

The crucial difference in a command–obedience relation compared to contractual co-operation is that the former always requires some *additional* explanation; the surplus good expected to result from

---

[6] With all the respect due to Kant, it seems to me doubtful that one can provide a general definition of freedom (as distinct from the freedom to exercise a specific right), in terms of which *A*'s freedom is 'equal to' *B*'s or 'like' *B*'s.

the giving and carrying out of commands is an insufficient reason for the existence of the relation. Unlike the contract, the object of the command is not always a good for both the superior and the subordinate; often it serves the superior alone. (Nor, incidentally, is the distribution of the surplus between superior and subordinate a matter of the two of them solving a bargaining problem.) Historical explanations of command would discover real-time causes, such as the residual effects of conquest, authority springing from inherited status, or the sheer force of character, and perhaps above all the 'threat potential' inherent in uneven distributions of force. Functional explanations would furnish reasons drawn from the contribution or benefit structure of a potential co-operative arrangement which would set obstacles to contractual agreement and call for command. Regulating city traffic, keeping a classroom silent, cultivating sugar-cane in an impossible climate, fighting a war on foot-and-mouth disease might not lend themselves to contract at all or only with very indifferent success. The functional explanation will in some cases complement the historical, explaining the longevity and resistance to wear and tear of a command–obedience relation originating in history. Explanations of the state are often of this latter kind.

Reliance on minimal explanation for contract and the need for non-minimal ones for command seem to me a simpler, less unsatisfactory way of dividing non-affective co-operative social arrangements into contract and command than the recourse to slippery notions of freedom and rights. Even so, the dividing-line remains blurred.

2

PROMISE, PERFORMANCE, AND ENFORCEMENT

Unless there is specific occasion for proceeding otherwise, I shall argue as if all contracts were bilateral, two-sided. (Lawyers sometimes call a contract 'bilateral' only if it still involves two unexecuted performances, or duties, in satisfaction of two promises, or rights; while if one has been already executed, leaving only one outstanding, they call it 'unilateral'. This usage is misleading and should, I think, be avoided.) Although there may be several persons to a side, for the moment it will do to suppose one person or 'party' on either side. The essential elements of bilateral contracts are:

1. two promises; each party is both promisor and promisee;
2. two sets of performances, one by each promisor. They have two configurations:
   (a) one performance set is contingent on the other;
   (b) the two performances or performance-sets are mutually contingent.

The decisive dimension of the structure is the timing of its elements relative to each other. Following Hobbes,[1] one can distinguish three timing patterns. A given pattern must first and above all be looked at to see whether fulfilling its terms represents an 'equilibrium-point'[2] in the sense that, faced with the choice between 'perform' and 'default', each party will prefer to perform unless the other party defaults first. A contract having such an equilibrium-point is self-enforcing. Non-self-enforcing contracts pose various enforcement problems.

1. *The spot contract.* Two actions are promised and performed with little or no time elapsing between promise and performance,

---

[1] Hobbes (1651; 1968 edn.), ch. XIV.
[2] The pioneer game theorist J. F. Nash first formulated the concept of equilibrium points in 1950. At such points, the position of each party is that which would serve him best if the other party adopted the position that would best serve *him*.

and with the two performances being for all practical purposes simultaneous. An ordinary exchange is the standard case, where an offer and its acceptance constitute the two promises, delivering against the agreed consideration the two performances. The element of reciprocal promise may even be lost sight of if it is literally simultaneous with execution. However, the delivery of X against Y is logically always posterior to an exchange of promises to give X for Y and Y for X, respectively, even if in a functioning market, with goods on offer at given prices, promises to buy and sell, and their executions, are instantaneous and merge into each other.

A spot contract is *intrinsically self-enforcing* since, by the definition of a contract, neither party values what he has to *give up* by performing more highly than what he stands to *get* by inciting the other party to perform his half of the bargain.

2. *The half-spot, half-forward (also known as part-executed) contract.* Two promises are made, as for a spot contract. However, they are not to be executed simultaneously. The second or forward performance is contingent on the first or spot one, but *not*, as in the spot contract, vice versa. The second performance is typically deferred consideration, e.g. the repayment of a debt resulting from a first performance such as a loan or the delivery of goods on credit.

A half-spot, half-forward contract is *intrinsically not self-enforcing*, for once the promised first act has been performed its desirability no longer provides the incentive to perform the second act—though there may well be other incentives, such as keeping one's good name and credit intact for *other* contracts. However, they are external to the contract in hand.

3. *The forward (also known as wholly executory) contract.* Two simultaneous deferred performances are promised, i.e. two parties commit themselves to execute a 'spot' exchange at a future date. As the two performances are mutually contingent, this contract has *some tendency to enforce itself* without being intrinsically self-enforcing. For what is the parties' purpose in committing themselves today to a future exchange of performances, instead of biding their time?

3.1 The classic reason is a divergence of expectations; the two parties both believe they can get better terms from each other today than at the future date foreseen for the actual exchange, and indeed better than at any future date between then and now, working backwards from the date of exchange towards today. Each party, in other words, expects the available terms of exchange to be moving against him over this period. But if this expectation turns out to be true for one party, it must prove to have been false for the other. When the date set for the actual performance comes round, the party whose expectation was proved false would be better off if he had not made the contractual commitment and may have an incentive to default.

3.2 A less classic and less clear-cut reason for contracting forward has to do with the possible value (convenience, assurance, complementarity with some other contract) attaching to the perfect foreknowledge of the terms on which a future exchange will be carried out. This value, if there is one, is eroded over time at a rate which reduces it to zero on the day the exchange is to take place. If on this day the terms that happen to be available for the exchange in question differ from the ones that had earlier been contractually fixed, one of the parties will have a definite incentive to default even if no specific expectation of his has been falsified by events.

3.3 Lastly, there are reasons for forward contracts derived from transactions costs in a wide sense. It may pay, in terms of search, information, and negotiating costs, to hire a man for a whole month rather than to hire one (even if he were the same man) by the day every working day of the month. Likewise it may (but probably does not) pay to own a motor car instead of forever calling taxis. 'Vertical integration' instead of *ad hoc* recourse to bought goods and services, a household's installed equipment, a firm's owned and leased factors of production, are explained in these terms. Contracts concluded to economize search and bargaining costs tend to provide not for two mutually contingent *discrete* performances in the future but more typically for two mutually contingent *streams* of performances (e.g. work, and wage payments in return for work) running concurrently.

Thanks to simultaneity, they have a *strong tendency to enforce themselves*, yet remain vulnerable to a marked deviation between newly available terms of exchange and the terms that had been originally contracted for—a deviation which makes default attractive to one of the parties.

In sum, no forward, wholly executory contract is intrinsically self-enforcing. Item 3.1 has some bias to default, 3.2 may go either way, while 3.3 appears strongly biased towards self-enforcement. However, whether every forward contract is tendentially self-enforcing or not cannot be readily detected from its *form*—the configuration in time of promises and performances that it stipulates—but depends on the parties' motives relative to the facts of the case.

Defaults

It is now readily apparent that 'default' means two radically different events. Default in the half-spot, half-forward contract configuration means that performance by one party is not reciprocated by performance by the other. The first performer has made an unrequited delivery. He parted with the 'consideration' (promise fulfilled, service rendered, goods handed over). By the default of the second performer, he loses *both* the consideration *and* the advantage he expected to derive from the execution of the contract (the surplus good, the 'gains from trade'). In the fully forward configuration, the contract (or in the case of performance-streams, the part of the contract left to run, i.e. that is still to be fulfilled) remains 'wholly executory'. There is no first and second performer. Neither party gives up any consideration without simultaneously receiving its counterpart in discrete 'lumps' or in a continuous flow, lump matching lump, flow matching counter-flow. One's loss if the other defaults is limited to the expected 'gains from trade' that he forgoes, or, if he had discounted them, that he must surrender.

The difference between the two kinds of default is fundamental, so much so that one wishes separate words existed to denote each. As the next-best thing, I will refer to default involving loss of the consideration by the first performer as 'first-degree default', while calling that involving solely the loss of contractually secured expectations of advantage 'second-degree default'. The particularity of the half-spot, half-forward contract is that it carries risk of a greater order—for it is open to first-degree default—and a higher probability of the risk turning into actual loss—for the contract is intrinsically non-self-enforcing.

Hobbes calls half-spot, half-forward contracts 'pacts' or 'covenants', referring to wholly forward contracts as 'covenants of mutual trust'. His main interest is in the latter, where two continuing streams of mutually contingent performances are promised—'I promise to keep the peace as long as you keep your promise to do likewise'—the very contract configuration which, next only to the spot contract, has the best chance of enforcing itself. Strangely enough, Hobbes seems relatively unworried about the intrinsic risk of first-degree default in mere 'pacts', yet he is deeply concerned about the much more conjectural risk of second-degree default in 'covenants of mutual trust'[3] so much so that he deduces the rationale of the social contract from it. It is because he conceives of covenants of mutual trust, i.e. forward contracts, as intrinsically non-self-enforcing in the state of nature that he can represent the surrender of arms to the contract-enforcing sovereign, and willing obedience to him, as the sole rational and moral solution to human coexistence.

It would be fascinating to speculate about the shape Hobbes's theory, and subsequent contractarian arguments, might have assumed had he not confounded the two types of default risk and the intrinsic tendencies of two distinct types of contract to be, or not to be, self-enforcing. We will revert to a somewhat different form of much the same question in Chapter 4.

Enforcement

Non-self-enforcing contracts 'need enforcement' in two senses. In the first, the defaulter must be forced to fulfil his promise by specific performance, repair the harmful consequences of his non-performance, or possibly both, depending on circumstances. In the second sense, there must be some general presumption in favour of keeping promises as a matter of prudential policy on the part of promisors.

---

[3] Cf. Oakeshott's account of the Hobbesian position: 'And it is in respect of these that "reason" gives its most unmistakable warning and in which the true predicament of men in a state of nature is revealed': Oakeshott (1962), 257. In an otherwise masterly analysis, Oakeshott accepts without dispute Hobbes's strange characterization of these contracts as involving a first and a second performance, and being for that reason 'increasingly risky undertakings for the first performer' (p. 295), needing to be transformed into a new, different contract to which the sovereign is a party. In reality it is what Hobbes calls 'pacts' or 'covenants' that do involve a first and a second performer, while his 'covenants of mutual trust' do not; in the latter, the two performances are *simultaneous*, concurrent, *mutually contingent*, each party performing only as long as the other does.

Enforcement of some random sample of contracts is a prudential argument against default in all others, for it lengthens the odds, if only subjectively, against being able to default with impunity. The mere probability of successful enforcement, and the ensuing liabilities, will act as a general deterrent to default and contribute to a climate of respect for contractual obligations. This deterrent is an 'externality'. It is generated by one's *contribution* (effort, trouble, cost) devoted to the enforcement of certain contracts, while the *benefit* accrues both to the contributor and to others, in that all default becomes a little less likely and *reliance* on contracts more acceptable to everyone. Reliance on the 'practice' of contracting is a classic case of *public good* created for all by the contributions of some.

Enforcement is a blanket term, standing for a wide spectrum of alternative means, of varying efficiency and cost. At one end of the continuum, there is basic self-help ('If you break your word, I and my friends will make you regret it') and the help of bystanders who are not directly concerned with the contract in hand, but who have a general interest in discouraging default ('If you break your word, the people of goodwill who know of your promise will make you regret it'). Beyond this, there is enforcement by systematic, at least tacitly pre-arranged mutual aid; a perhaps quite small and informal coalition can advance its specific interest in the reliability of contracts in some field by acts of solidarity against promise-breakers. It can contribute to a precedent-based local climate of respect for promises, where a would-be defaulter must take some account of the probability of sanctions ('If you break your word, you will come to regret it, as did X'). Contract law and tort law are, of course, in this manner jointly enforced by the same powers, applied in response to the same incentives. 'Enforced' in its second sense, as an extenality, must be understood throughout as a matter of degree, as an *increased probability* of defaults being sanctioned, specific performances extracted from the defaulters, and torts repaired.

A special case of self-help is bought help, the purchase from specialized providers of protection against default and torts; debt-collectors, insurance adjusters, guard services fulfil some of these functions. More special still, protection rackets not only protect their clients' selected property and contracts (notably labour contracts and loans) in exchange for ransom, but they also try to suppress the 'externality', the free-rider benefit non-payers of ransom derive from the ransom-financed activity of the racketeer when he discourages interloper banditry, theft, arson, default on debts, and strikes. The protection racketeer will actually attack the non-client, burn him out, organize a strike by his employees, etc., to induce him to become his client by denying him the free-rider benefit.

Self-help, bought help, and mutual aid involve being judge and judgement-enforcer in one's own cause, or, in the cause of a member of one's coalition, *vis-à-vis* a non-member. This is generally condemned, though often it is a lesser evil or simply unavoidable. Manorial jurisdiction in matters between the lord and his serfs, and royal and republican jurisdiction in matters between the state and its subjects, have throughout history seldom produced quite the monstrously unjust results *a priori* reasoning would lead one to expect. The judge's temptation to find merit in his own cause is generally tempered by the risks of abusive behaviour. High-handedness always involves a danger, whether or not accurately gauged, of provoking tit-for-tat retaliation, hostile coalition-forming, and disproportionate reactions, from hayrick-burning and sabotage to 'exit' (the flight of serfs, the emigration of taxable subjects) damaging to the abusive judge, and possibly even to revolt, though the latter raises special problems.

Further along the range of what one might call private, decentralized or micro-means of enforcement there is, at least conceptually, some room for institutions that are recognizedly not the instruments of one party, but are meant to stand between litigants. A neutral stance lends them some authority, hence they regain, or more than regain, in efficiency of enforcement what they lost in motivation, in incentive to enforce. History has in fact had a large place for such institutions, from councils of elders to parish priests, until they were gradually undercut and pushed aside by the agencies of the sovereign state. In many parts of pre-feudal Europe there were peasant guilds which impartially assumed their members' duty of revenge against other members in cases of homicide, mutilation, or harm to livestock, awarded damages, and sanctioned tricky dealings. Where, as in the core area of post-Carolingian Europe, feudalism had a chance to develop properly and its justice has superseded the co-operative justice of the peasantry, the lord was technically neutral when dealing with disputes among tenants, though of course he was judge and party in matters affecting manorial rights. In enforcing the basic medieval contract of service tenure, however, feudal justice was bound by the 'custom of the manor' which the unjust lord could not transgress without some peril to his own interests. In commerce, fair courts and staple courts stood between the parties, settling disputes and enforcing bargains with a power and efficiency we moderns are surprised to find in non-sovereign, co-operative institutions.

Guild, town, and merchant jurisdictions spread the general benefit of an increased probability of contract enforcement and hence of observance; in this they acted as *providers* of a public good. In addition, they were *selling* the private good of justice in civil cases to individual litigants, the profits of the latter helping to 'finance' the emergent general benefits of the former. It was above all the revenue derived from selling justice in matters of property, source of the fattest fees, both in the narrow field of contracts and in unrequited transfers by marriage and inheritance, that most excited the competition between rival communal, ecclesiastical, manorial, and royal jurisdictions, and whose end-result was the emergence of the near universal monopoly of a single public, sovereign agency of law-enforcement. Within this trend there was, at least in England from the fourteenth century onwards, a secondary but none the less portentous development, namely the rise in importance of Chancery as opposed to the common-law courts—a development which, through a few ups and downs, has continued to this day on both sides of the Atlantic, and is giving us the benefits of social policy-making by judicial discretion.

One should perhaps tentatively set down a few markers at this point. The more 'micro', decentralized, and private is contract enforcement:

1. the greater is the share of the total cost of enforcement contributed by those for whom it is a private good, paid for in proportion to their recourse to it;
2. the smaller is the unrequited benefit non-contributing free riders derive from enforceability, hence, from the public good of safe reliance on contracts in general

The polar case of privateness is that where the seller of enforcement succeeds in completely shutting out non-contributors from the benefits of safe reliance on contracts. The labour racketeer who makes sure that an employer who does not pay him ransom will have his plant struck can be said to accomplish this to the full; he ensures that *only* those promises are kept whose promisee has paid enforcement costs.

The opposite extreme is purely public enforcement, where recourse to it is costless to the litigant and every promisee benefits from the general reliability of contracts as a free ride.

Generalizing the concept of enforcement over a range from the wholly private to the purely public, involving an unspecified variety of means and practices, a variable does of externality, and no doubt a varying degree of imperfection and injustice, is perhaps unusual and calls for an apology. The object is to dissipate two facile notions that seem to pervade all discussion of these matters.

One is that contracts are either enforceable or not, instead of enforceability and reliance being stochastic, more or less probable. The other is that only the sovereign state is capable of enforcing contracts. The same unproven and gratuitous supposition underlies the idea of the rule of law being a necessary condition of a 'market order'. If this were the case, the political authority would be logically prior to the institution of contract. It would then be difficult, to put it no higher, to view contract as one of the two elementary building-blocks of social co-operation. But perhaps neither is logically prior to the other. Perhaps such causal relation as there is between them is diffuse and roundabout. The more general approach, for which the present book is groping, allows us to stay uncommitted as to the priority, in history and in logic, of contract or society, the chicken or the egg.

Grounds for Enforcement

What reason is there for fulfilling non-self-enforcing contracts? If it is wrong to lie, it must also be wrong to lie about our future conduct, though the wrong is possibly lessened by the lapse of time between the contractual undertaking to perform an action and the failure to honour the undertaking. If I say 'I will do X', have I made a promise or a forecast? And if I do not in fact do X, have I lied, have I broken my promise, or has my forecast about the future conduct of the person 'I' was going to become, and about the circumstances 'I' was going to face, turned out to be mistaken? When did my statement about the future become a promise, and when did my promise become a contract or, more precisely, a half of one? The analogy between two formally not dissimilar requirements— that a statement be true and that a promise be kept—is not complete. If there are white lies, are there harmless breaches of promise? And can a promissory obligation be justified on other than consequential grounds? Or is the only ethical reason why a promise is binding the difference it makes to others if it is not honoured? A different question, straddling ethics and social theory, that is of obvious practical import is as follows. What reason is there, apart from the price he may be willing to pay for justice, for assisting a promisee to obtain the performance due to him from the promisor? More stringently, are there good arguments that he is in fact entitled to assistance without having to pay whatever it takes to call it forth—that it is incumbent upon certain or all others not party to his contract to see that it is fulfilled?

Under enforcement by self-help and bought help, and albeit much less clearly under mutual aid, the reason for enforcing can be reduced to some sort of probabilistic cost–benefit calculus, involving the chances of successful action, its costs, and the benefits of reparation. The question whether the contract ought to be enforced, and the validity of the ground on which a particular promissory obligation can be justified, need not arise. When, however, help in enforcement is requested from some putatively impartial institution, other grounds than the promisee's own interest, and his resulting capacity and willingness to pay for help, become relevant to the response.

There are then basically only two jurisprudential alternatives. Greatly simplified, one leads to pure rule-application, the other to discretion. The former, sometimes called Formalism and congenial to 'classical' liberalism, is content with adequate evidence that a contract of stated terms has come into being. Free of duress and misrepresentation, a contract that is recognized to exist is *eo ipso* binding and entitles the promisee to enforcement,[4] almost entirely

---

[4] Our use of the word 'contract', implying that each party is both promisor and promisee, excludes wholly gratuitous promises. These may be binding for independent reasons but not because *contracts* create binding obligations. Under the Formalist doctrine, there has to be some consideration, some reciprocity in performance, but the *adequacy* of the consideration is not a factor in determining whether a binding contract exists. Selling a kingdom for a horse or a soul for a smile are probably valid contracts.

regardless of its substantive content; the sale of children and slaves, Shylock's 'pound of flesh', and Faust's contract with Mephisto are some of the few culturally bound exceptions.

The contrary doctrine, sometimes called Realism, once a rival of, but for the last half-century the clear victor over, Formalism,[5] rejects the claim that promises, however reciprocal, are capable of creating enforceable promissory obligations without being supported by the *merits* of the case which alone can earn them the socially bestowed rank of enforceability.

'Merits', in turn, can be more general or more specific, both requiring validation but capable of being validated by different routes. Two routes admit a general presumption in favour of enforceability; the third is rigorously *ad hoc*, taking notice of specific merits only.

1. Hume formulated a sort of aggregate social cost–benefit view of the presumption in favour of enforcing contracts. Since the ability to rely on such agreements is convenient for society,[6] it makes good sense for it to help out with enforcement. Rule-utilitarianism has, of course, found this idea thoroughly to its taste. The point of the argument is not that a promisee should be able to get a contract enforced because it constitutes an obligation of the promisor, nor that all formally valid contracts constitute an entitlement to enforcement. Strictly what the argument implies is that it is rational for society to balance the incremental utility of greater respect for contracts against the incremental cost of more perfect enforcement. A sterner attitude to obligations should then be taken if greater strictness has 'net marginal social utility' or some equivalent index of what we should want to maximize. Not altogether unrelated to this way of justifying public enforcement is the 'efficiency' theory. For the contemporary American 'law and economics' school, in particular, the merit of a contract is proportional to the contribution its observance makes to some *maximand* of an economic nature, such as Pareto-optimal resource allocation, the gains from exchange, or (in bold contempt of the surrounding conceptual minefield where angels fear to tread) 'wealth'.

2. The other way of making a presumptive case for enforcement

---

[5] Gilmore (1974) and Atiyah (1979), chs. 19–22.
[6] Hume (1739), book III.

PROMISE, PERFORMANCE, AND ENFORCEMENT   33

out of the merits of contracts in general, is deceptively like
Formalism while being poles apart from it. There is in this
approach some limited recognition of the power of contracting
parties to create enforceable obligations by their mere *intent*.
In its boldest version, the promise to perform specific acts, expressed in
contract X, signifies adherence to an implicit and more general
contract Y always to perform as promised, always to keep one's
word. Contract Y standing behind contract X is 'a convention
whose function it is to give grounds . . . for another to expect the
promised performance'.[7] Contract Y, however, is in no better shape
than was contract X to constitute an enforceable obligation; if X
needed a more general Y to back it up, Y needs an even more
general Z, and so forth. What constitutes a satisfactory stopping-
point behind which we need not go in order to establish that
promises of a certain form and context are morally binding can
perhaps be made a matter of metaphysical agreement. However,
agreement to regard the nth back-up contract-to-respect-contracts
as the ultimate, irreducible source of the obligation does not really
meet the question why 'society' should use force to ensure
conformity to it.

In place of a regress of implicit secondary, tertiary, etc. contracts,
cut off somewhere by agreement, one can proceed by putting a
different construction on what being a party to the primary, overt
contract X signifies. Respect for contracts in general is conducive
to the public good of safe reliance on them; respect is produced by
enforcement. Anyone becoming party to a contract benefits from
the public good. By accepting the benefit, he *effectively incurs a
liability*[8] to contribute to its production. Consequently, not only
must he recognize the binding character of his promise and if need
be submit to its enforcement, but he must also do his best to help
enforce the contracts of others. All doing their bit, e.g. by paying
taxes to finance it, adds up easily enough to public enforcement by
'society'.

This doctrine declares the inadmissibility of free riding. There are
places in the subsequent argument of this book where this question

---

[7] Fried (1981), 36.
[8] This is the nub, or what I take to be the nub, of Herbert Hart's anti-free-rider
'principle of fairness', which is crucial to contractarian political philosophy; cf. Hart
(1955). The implications of holding that acceptance of a benefit can create a liability
to contribute to its cost of reproduction are, of course, extremely far-reaching.

plays a more central part; I will not pursue it here. Suffice it to note in passing that whatever the weight of the anti-free-rider argument in the case made for contract enforcement, it amounts to little as a reason for indiscriminately enforcing all formally valid contracts regardless of the substantive merits of each. If a particular party to a particular contract derives little or no benefit from the social institution of contracts, he should, on grounds of the fairness principle, neither have to submit nor be asked to contribute to maintaining the public enforcement apparatus. The working class is presumably a massive case in point. Marxist thought would seem to lead to the claim that while it is a party to the wage contract, the proletariat derives no benefits from bourgeois law in general and from the enforceability of contracts in particular; it is not a free rider on the social co-operation practised in capitalist society, it should not sumbit to enforcement, and still less should it be required to contribute to it. The very imperfect enforceability of labour contracts and the legal immunities of trade unions, though usually supported by other types of arguments, square well with such a principle of fairness, as does the reluctance of the courts to order poor tenants to be evicted. The anti-free-rider principle of fairness cannot be applied without answering questions of fact about the limited capacity of a perhaps helpless, plodding pedestrian—if not positively downtrodden—contracting party to free-ride on the enforceability of contracts; general in intention, it ends up dealing with cases on their merits.

3. The legal doctrine which avowedly treats each case on its merits is guided by the requirement of upholding one of a number of other fairness principles, each more private than Hart's general anti-free-riding, public-goods-type of fairness. Contracts must be enforced if, but only to the extent that, default by the promisor gives him an unfair advantage or constitutes unfair treatment of the promisee. This is the case in two kinds of circumstances.

Under the circumstances of what I propose to call first-degree default, the unfairness is 'benefit-based'. To be complete, the relevant fairness principle must posit a theory of consideration. The formal requirement that 'a bargain must have two sides', that there is no due performance without consideration, and neither party stands to get something for nothing, is an insufficient test of fairness. It must be shown, in addition, that in terms of the theory the consideration was adequate, that it provided full justification of the performance called for under the contract. It is unfair to the promisee to receive unrequited benefit from him by defaulting. Yet the promisor's obligation goes no further than the 'real' benefits conferred by the consideration—whatever else the contract may say. Whether the consideration is a fair match for the performance is a matter of separate judgement on merits and not an analytic consequence of the agreement of the parties to the terms of the contract. The terms are enforceable if they were fair, equal and not contrary to public policy. It is obvious enough that in becoming subject to judgements of this nature contract enforcement ceases to be a relatively straightforward, invariant practice of rule-application. It passes into the realm of judicial discretion and becomes in fact a motive force in the expansion of this realm.

Under the circumstances of second-degree default, the 'benefits-based' doctrine of fairness might well point to unenforceability, for if no consideration changed hands there was no unrequited benefit. However, an unconsummated, wholly 'forward' contract can nevertheless give rise to unfairness under the 'reliance-based' doctrine of fairness if one party has effectively discounted in advance the anticipated performance of the other party *and* suffered actual demonstrable damage as a result of the latter's default. Once again, by the recourse to fairness, a field is opened up to judgements of merits and to the application of discretion. It is perfectly possible to hold that discretion offers a greater likelihood of attaining just judgements than do blind rules; it is not unreasonable to believe the contrary. Our concern is not to weigh such beliefs against one another but to deduce, if we can, the influence of alternative doctrines and practices of contract-enforcement upon the social structure.

How Contract Breeds Command

Modern legal theory takes the view that if pure Formalism in contract law ever existed (which is doubtful, for if common law leaned to formalism it was always and everywhere checked in its leanings by the competing royal justice in Equity and by the natural-law doctrines of the Church), it is gone for good and cannot be brought back due to its own inherent weaknesses, which, now that we know better, we could not tolerate. Those who call for indiscriminating enforcement of formally valid contracts betray their incomprehension of what good law should be like and could do. 'To a lawyer acquainted with the difference between expectation, reliance and restitution damages',[9] the very meaning of redress for default in a wholly executory forward contract can be puzzling. Where neither party has performed and neither has suffered from reliance on the other's expected performance, where is the basis for prescribing a remedy?

To a layman observing what changes in legal doctrine do to the way society functions, this sort of argument merits little patience. Lawyers, modern or ancient, have never been long at a loss to specify remedies in civil law when it suited them to do so, however problematical the basis for it may have been. A more effective reason cited by certain authors for being at a loss to find a basis to repair default in forward contracts is their intrinsic bias. This type of contract, being a device for risk-redistribution, favours the shrewd, the strong, the clever at predicting the future—hence its enforcement would be anti-egalitarian.[10]

Once again, the point with which my argument takes issue is not how justice is best served. It is perhaps pertinent to say all the same that if the equal distribution of income, wealth, or anything else that is both desirable and transferable is to be the set objective, there must be more direct ways of achieving it than by indifference to the observance of contracts that are thought to favour the rich—however laudable a by-product of modern contract law it may be to make them poorer. Regardless of this by-product, however, how should we assess the doctrine on the merits of its main bias? It may be unjust to a class of contract parties who fail to get the performance that was agreed to be due to them. With this aspect we are not concerned. It may also little by little distort, if not undermine, the institution of contract, the manner in which it helps promote social co-operation. In particular, contract law and its application are bound to affect the 'dynamics' of the balance between contract and command. This is very much our concern here.

Why is the contract–command balance what it is at any time? At least for Western civilizations, there has for long been a pat answer. The origins very likely go back to the dissolution of the *polis*, the

[9] Atiyah (1979), 653.
[10] Atiyah (1979), 6.

Aegean city-state which introduced the clear division of human affairs into a private and a public sphere. It comes to us directly from Roman law, under which there is a manifest frontier, contract belonging to civil, and command to public life and public law. However, to escape the evident danger of circularity, such an answer needs definitions of private and public life which are themselves independent of the manner, contractual or coercive, in which social co-operation is cemented. Otherwise we would be asserting that the proper place of command is in public affairs, and public affairs are those ruled by command.

Whatever else it may be, it is at least not circular to say that the place of contract is in those situations of co-operation which do not require anything stronger for commitment to a common endeavour than the attraction of the surplus expected to be produced and divided. Command comes into its own when this expectation alone is insufficient to call forth the required conduct; when the way the surplus would naturally fall ('the incentive structure' or 'payoff structure') or the bargaining problem involved in dividing it differently is such that the threat of coercion is needed. Though these definitions are far from watertight, they are at least independent and do not coincide with the conventional private–public division. There is non-coerced, voluntary co-operation now and then in certain affairs that are indisputably public, and uncontracted-for subordination to command is not altogether unknown in private ones. None the less, the imputation of 'private' to 'contract', 'public' to 'command' has the ring of 'simple truths' and is worth pursuing.

Some important types of contracts, as we have seen, are by their structure not self-enforcing. Enforcement in turn is not *sui generis* public or *sui generis* private. It can be one or the other and sometimes one may supplement the other. The reasons why one or the other predominates are difficult to state concisely at the best of times, and especially so without a prior base of public goods theory. Some work in that direction will be presented in Part Two of this book. Meanwhile, we may at least note the following. There are two influences arising from the practice of contracting (one primary, the other secondary), tending to make the relative sphere of command grow.

1. The primary influence is the competitive advantage of contract-enforcement by the sovereign political authority over

self-help, bought help, or the agency of other non-sovereign institutions.

  (a) *Appeal.* Once a state exists, there are cost–benefit type incentives for the losing party in any action in private non-sovereign enforcement not to submit to his loss. He may have much to gain if he takes his case in appeal to the state, which may choose to assume jurisdiction and, if it does, can override non-sovereign instances. There are incentives for the state to assume jurisdiction. A given non-zero probability that the sovereign will on appeal override the non-sovereign in a random case would engender a given volume of appeals; the greater the probability, the better it pays to appeal. The process can feed on itself and have a debilitating effect on the lower instances. The decline of self-help, communal, ecclesiastical, and professional (peer) jurisdiction and enforcement is not altogether unrelated to this sort of process.

  (b) *Cost allocation.* The civil adjudicating and contract-enforcing functions of the state may obtain a free-ride on its functions in defence and public order. If the king has dragoons and gendarmes, the relative authority of royal justice gains from the existence of this back-up force, whose cost is borne by general revenue and need not be borne by individual litigants. Moreover, the cost of enforcing a judgment against a very powerful litigant is the more easily financed the more 'averaging' is taking place among cases, which gives an advantage to the large centralized enforcing authority, i.e. in practice the all-inclusive state.

2. The secondary or induced influence erodes the quality and acceptability of non-sovereign enforcement.

  (a) *From common law to equity.* One may assume for simplicity that the *authority* of non-sovereign, decentralized enforcement, by which I mean the extent to which it can enforce its judgments over and above what could be explained solely by the *force* at its disposal, is rooted in the regard for the customary law it applies. Customary law offers little scope for discretion. The state acting as sovereign contract-enforcer has important interests flowing from its vastly more substantial role as the tenant of political power, charged with maximizing some definition of the public good. Applying common law is mostly neutral, Equity often useful in furthering these interests. Both by overt legislation and by more surreptitious judicial law-making, the state has 'natural' tendencies, explicable in terms of rational choice, to introduce considerations of public policy and social justice into contract law. Rival jurisdictions cannot remain entirely indifferent to these developments; yet as they move away from (or adjust) common law, they lose, and the state gains, relative authority.

(b) *Judge in own cause.* Suppose, once more for simplicity, that with all other things equal judgments are the easier to enforce the more impartial the judge seemed in the eyes of the parties; his impartiality as presumed by them would increase with his distance from the case. Self-help, bought help, and mutual aid by coalition members would then be regarded as the least impartial, and the agents of the state as the most impartial, of possible judges. The importance of impartiality is obviously the greater the stronger is the element of discretion, or the less automatic is the 'formalistic' rule-application associated with customary law. Hence, by causing, in one way and another, Equity to prevail over the common law and discretion over rule-application, the state enhances the weight of its own comparative advantage in impartiality and the disadvantage of those who, in their smaller jurisdictions, are in the nature of things both judge and party.

3
STATE-OF-NATURE
CO-ORDINATION

For a pure intellectual construct which need have little regard for the messiness of historical reality, the state of nature is not always treated as consistently as its conceptual simplicity would permit. It is variously represented in the classic contractarian literature as a state of affairs where life and property are not protected by any collective effort; where man is judge in his own cause; where there is war of all against all, and contracts are but 'a vain breath'; where untamed man is too short-sighted and feckless to sustain the effort of lasting social co-operation; where there can be only non-produced public goods but no man-made ones; and so on. These characterizations, even if they were all mutually consistent, do not easily reduce to a single easy definition of a state of affairs. It seems to me worth while to try to work towards one and see what implications and consequences would follow from it.

Dr Johnson, musing about the English fearing the French and the French fearing the English, advanced this theory of the state of nature:

Were one half of mankind brave, and one half cowards, the brave would always be beating the cowards. Were all brave, they would lead a very uneasy life; all would be continually fighting: but being all cowards, we get on very well.[1]

It is always good policy to pay close attention to Dr Johnson's every hint, without being overawed by him to the point of stopping where he has led you. If braves are sensible, what makes them attack cowards is that they can subdue them. If cowards are sensible, what makes them get on with other cowards is that by fighting they would hurt themselves and might not even beat the others. If braves continually fight other braves without getting anywhere, they are

[1] Boswell (1791, 1793; 1924 edn.), iii. 46.

not being sensible—which is entirely possible, but then we must stop reasoning as if they were, i.e. we cannot rely on rationality as an aid to predicting people's conduct.

In order to get all the benefit from Dr Johnson's metaphor about the cowardly English getting on so well with the cowardly French, it must not be gratuitously assumed that braves would always fight other braves and cowards would never fight other cowards; this would make war or peace a simple matter of the *distribution of given dispositions*, 'bravery' or 'cowardice', among men. Without ruling them out, it is more instructive to suppose that if dispositions are what they are,[2] the likelihood of fighting would still vary with how the parties concerned saw the net effects or 'payoffs' to them of attack, defence, and surrender.

If the available 'technology' of fighting were neutral, i.e. if it favoured neither attack nor defence, and all were endowed with roughly equal force, the odds of one beating the other would be near enough even, the probability of getting seriously hurt in the process would be high, and the expected payoff from the first use of force would tend to be low and could be negative. This would only fail to be the case if it could be assumed that the second user would renounce defending himself. As we shall see presently, however, it would in most cases be unreasonable among foes of equal force for the attacked party not to use force, and it would be strange for the attacker to impute an unreasonable counter-strategy, i.e. surrender without a fight, to him.

There is an asymmetry between first use and second use, attack and defence. The opportunity cost of attack is the value ('utility') the would-be attacker places on his next-worse alternative, i.e. on keeping the peaceful status quo. The opportunity cost of defence, however, is not the value of the peaceful status quo; that is already lost. Given the attack, the opportunity cost of defence is the utility of a state of affairs created by surrender as the alternative to defence. The odds on successful defence are, under the assumption of equal forces, much the same as on successful attack, i.e. about even, and so is the likelihood and severity of getting hurt. Comparing the 'net payoffs' from attack and defence between equal forces, the reasonable *prima facie* estimate seems to be that there is

[2] Dispositions to fight may well be a variable, a matter of experience, a resultant of the good or bad *consequences* of a fighting disposition. 'Braves' may learn to be less brave, or risk extinction. Cf. Colinvaux (1978).

not much to choose in terms of expected orders of magnitude between the attacker's half-chance of beating the attacked party and the defender's half-chance of beating him back. Different orders of magnitude, however, prevail on the opportunity-cost side; the peaceful status quo, which the attacker forgoes, however unsatisfactory it may be, is yet less undesirable than the surrender without a fight which the defender forgoes if he decides to fight. The incentive structure under equal force is biased in favour of defence (nearly always better than surrender) and against attack (only sometimes better than keeping the peace), although attack may of course, be relatively commonplace if 'given dispositions' strongly incline to fighting. Whatever the *Deus ex machina* dispositions to bravery or cowardice and to fighting or keeping the peace, a more equal distribution of force at any given level—with all armed to the teeth or all disarmed—makes for a lower probability of first use, and consequently of all use, of force.

A corollary is that enforcing obedience is harder than getting away with disobedience to a command whose sanction is the use of force. If so, the predominant form of social co-operation in the state of nature is either unilateral co-operation or self-enforcing contract. Subordinating others to one's command is difficult to accommodate to the hypothesis of equal force; enforcement of non-self-enforcing contracts is less improbable, but still problematical.

Let us label the state of affairs that can be deduced from the assumption of equally distributed force the 'perfect state of nature'. Its polar opposite, familiar from Max Weber's overworked definition of the state, is the monopoly of the use of force.[3] Moving along the spectrum from the evenly spread, perfectly equal distribution of force towards the perfectly concentrated monopoly, we would pass through 'states of nature' of increasing imperfection. Successive degrees of it can, of course, be simply postulated, since we are engaging in a thought-experiment rather than investigating the presumable course of a real process. However, if such a process

---

[3] Weber adds the adjective 'legitimate'; this raises problems and calls for elaboration. In the legal–positivist tradition, the fact that it is a monopoly, not shared with anybody in a society, is both necessary and sufficient to confer legitimacy upon the use of force; consequently, an 'illegitimate monopoly' of it is nonsense and 'legitimate monopoly of the use of force' is a pleonasm. Use of the adjective 'legitimate' must be some anti-positivist declaration to the effect that legitimacy of the use of force within a society has some independent source in morals and culture, i.e. it is not simply a matter of effective sovereignty.

were thought to exist and its causes were to be discovered, one should first look for random events in the surrounding environment whose impact cannot, in general, fail to upset certain equalities, including the equality of force. One should next consider that coalitions can be formed and let some people be quicker and better at forming them than others. Either kind of cause would make for uneven distributions of force and might in fact do so in a self-reinforcing, cumulative manner.

If the latter were the case, a sufficiently imperfect state of nature could well be an unstable one. For once force-inequalities are large enough, the incentive structure no longer works against the first use of force. It may then often pay the strong to attack the weak and it may even pay the weak to surrender without a fight, since the alternative, the low probability of successful defence associated with the near certainty of getting hurt, has a still lower 'utility'. The resulting accentuation of force-inequalities would further reinforce the tendency to surrender, and the process would feed on itself. Failing some stabilizer, it could not stop short of the monopoly of force, the absolute non-state-of-nature.

Simplistic as this 'as if' account may be, it shows one manner in which state-of-nature theory can be used to provide a 'fact-deficient' account of the emergence of the state within the rational-choice tradition. Though we will conduct much of the argument in a setting devoid of the state, I have pencilled in its place here: partly because it flows naturally from defining the state of nature as a continuous function of the distribution of force (bounded by equal distribution and monopoly at its two ends); partly, however, because it is a useful foil for the great class of similarly 'fact-deficient' rational-choice theories in which it is dissatisfaction with various characteristics imputed to the state of nature (no civil peace, no enforceable agreements, no public goods, etc.) that leads men to agree to stop it and set up the state.

Co-ordination, Pure and Non-Pure

In what follows it will be convenient to use the term 'persons' to include both 'natural persons'—men, women, and the families they decide for—and 'legal persons', as well as coalitions, as long as they hold together and reach unique decisions that commit all their constituent members.

A possible interaction between two or more persons may be co-operative, in that it produces a positive sum of gains over losses,[4] as in exchange, in the division of labour, in the pooling of labour or other resources, in complementary conduct to beneficial effect as in queueing, not chattering in church, driving on the same side of the road, adopting standard electric voltage, and so forth. In some cases the net gain is confined to a few persons, some or all of whom may have contributed to bring it about; in others it may be a widely diffused externality with the contributors deriving little benefit themselves.[5] Despite its prima-facie attractiveness, the interaction may not take place of itself, due to a variety of possible obstacles. It may require co-ordination. Co-ordination is 'pure' when the benefit or 'payoff' accruing to any one participant in the successful interaction cannot be improved at the expense of another; it is 'impure' when it can.[6]

A pure co-ordination problem can have only one Pareto-optimal solution (all drivers end up driving on the same side), while a non-pure one can have indefinitely many, depending on how the positive 'sum' of the game is shared out among the participating players. Consequently, the co-ordinated solution requires prior resolution of an associated zero-sum bargaining game over the allocation of gains. The price of goods or the wage rate in the hiring of employees must normally be decided *before* the exchange of goods or the division of labour can take place and generate gains.

Many co-ordination problems are inherent in the human condition. Constantly recurring, they then tend to breed their standard solutions by a spontaneous process. Crowds waiting to board the bus every weekday at the rush-hour are best off if they form queues. The beginning of such a superior common 'strategy'

---

[4] With gains and losses accruing to different persons, 'positive sum' and 'negative sum' have a tongue-in-cheek quality; for a positive sum of gains over losses in terms of money or a commodity *numéraire* need not mean a positive sum of utility. We cannot even *have* a sum of utility, whether positive or negative, unless we can deduct one person's utility-loss from another person's utility-gain, i.e. unless we can compare interpersonally.

[5] J. S. Coleman, 'Norms as Social Capital', in Radnitzky and Bernholz (1987), 140.

[6] This is an adaptation of the terminology of Ullman-Magalit (1977), 78. She defines non-pure co-operation games as games where the players have both a common and a conflicting interest.

of waiting in a queue may once come about by chance, analogous in its function to the 'random mutation' of genetics. A 'critical mass' of conforming queuers may be required for the 'strategy' to start becoming attractive to non-queuers. However, once critical mass is attained and more join the queue, the chance configuration is little by little transformed into a recognized norm, part of civilized behaviour. Existence of the norm, in turn, causes possible gains from free-riding; if most people queue, it pays to push to the head of the queue, while if most of them jostle in disorder, there is no differential advantage in being disorderly. Hence, protection of the established norm typically requires a 'satellite norm' of sanctioning, whereby it is the done thing for those in the queue to take the trouble to discourage queue-jumpers. The satellite norm seems in practice often more difficult to establish than the main norm itself.

Both in the establishment and defence of beneficial norms and in non-standardized, one-off interactions which require some co-ordination to come about, the heterogeneity of the 'players' is of obvious significance. If all are exactly alike, co-ordination is likelier to happen and unlikelier to involve conflict, requiring pre-game bargaining. Heterogeneous 'players' seldom have *only* common interests. However, for any person before and during an interaction with others, the relevant consideration is not that the others are in fact like him in certain respects ('Are they going to back me up if I call this queue-jumper to order?'), but his 'subjective' belief that they are. Are they 'of the same tribe' or are they strangers? And what are the odds on their acting in certain ways?

Approaching Strangers

Take a person *A* about to join and 'interact' with a person *B*; to make the problem a little less dismal, let *B* be a 'coalition', say an organized community, having a friendly disposition to strangers and a preference for amiable ways of going about its affairs. *A* is a newcomer who ignores these dispositions. He has to choose an approach that will serve him best. His choice will help decide both his well-being and that of *B*, depending on how his choice fits in with *B*'s choice, which he can only guess. Given the things he knows, and the things he ignores, his situation can be represented by the two-person two-strategy game matrix in Figure 1. This is a

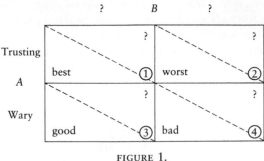

game with incomplete information. Moreover, such information as it contains is of A's own making, the product of the conjectures his ignorance of B forces him to make.

If A chooses to trust B, he stands to get either the best or the worst payoff. If he is wary of B, he stands to get either a merely good or a merely bad one. Since the pair 'best–worst' *straddles* the pair 'good–bad', 'trust' is neither obviously better nor obviously worse than 'wariness'. A has no dominant strategy; on the information shown in the matrix, his choice is indeterminate and cannot be predicted. (For such choices to be at least formally predictable, without assuming some *Deus ex machina* behaviour, their purpose must be utility-maximization; A's payoffs must lie on a cardinal scale of his utility; and A must attach numerically expressed probabilities to B's choices.) Suppose that instead of maximizing, he opts for an incompletely rational[7] rule of thumb, such as 'when faced with payoffs in a straddle, go for the inside pair', where the possible gain and loss are both smaller. He may choose to call this the prudential strategy. Given the dispositions of B, which are brought to light in Figure 2, A's prudence results in the joint payoff lying in square 3 and being sub-optimal for both players—it is the 'good' instead of the 'best' outcome.

For A to beware of B's ways is not being at an 'equilibrium-point'. A can improve his well-being by switching to 'trust'; he has nothing to fear from the switch since, regardless of how he approaches B, the latter will be friendly towards him, this being manifestly his best strategy regardless of how A approaches him. Once A realizes this

[7] The level on which rules of thumb (as opposed to maximization of expected utility) can be said to be rational is briefly discussed in Chapter 8.

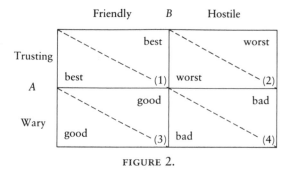

FIGURE 2.

(by getting to know B), he can unilaterally improve both their payoffs to 'best'. Co-ordination takes place by discovery, without a co-ordinator and unilaterally, without a contract being necessary— for there is no structural reason for one player's conduct to be made contingent on that of the other.

Pure Co-ordination by Contract

Once more, let us take a positive-sum game situation, where gains arise from co-ordinated moves. Two players must hit on the two strategies which bring about the best joint payoff, which also happens to be best for each individually, since there is no distributional conflict between them. Co-ordination, however, is not assured by the mere discovery, due to experience, intuition, or communication between the players, of the payoff structure and the potential gains it offers, but needs additional support.

Let A and B be two similarly situated players with symmetrical options (strategies) to choose from and symmetrical payoffs. Either can 'push' to help the other or 'pull' to help himself. Figure 3 depicts their difficulty. With 'push' promising either 4 or 0 and 'pull' promising either 3 or 2, the 'push' pair of payoffs straddles the 'pull' pair. A has no dominant strategy, and without additional utility and probability information his choice looks indeterminate. His 'prudential' rule-of-thumb choice would be to 'pull'. This would make his smallest payoff as great as possible—a result which is rightly prized in adversary play but has no particular merit where the other player cannot raise his own payoff by lowering that of the

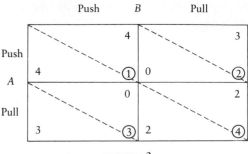

FIGURE 3.

first player, nor when he is simply indifferent (e.g. in games against 'nature'). It may well be, however, that even if A proceeded by Bayesian, fully rational choice, he would still decide to 'pull'. He could justify this to himself, arguing that he could not find reasons to assign more than an even chance to B 'sticking his neck out', going for the outer pair of the straddle and 'pushing'. If A has such reasons to opt for 'pull', he must attribute the same reasons to the similarly placed B and vice versa. The solution of the game is therefore in square 4, and both players get the relatively unattractive payoff 2. They are at an equilibrium-point; neither can improve it by unilaterally changing his strategy. A would land in square 2 and B in square 3 if either moved on his own, further reducing their payoff to 0. A co-ordinated switch of the two together from 'pull' to 'push' would, of course, enable them to reach the other, optimal equilibrium-point in square 1 with payoffs of 4 to each. Co-ordination here consists in reciprocity; the game which is characterized by the problem of passage from the sub-optimal to the optimal equilibrium-point is aptly called an 'assurance game'. How can the assurance required for the passage be provided? What would be the force of a contract to provide it? The answers we can lift from Chapter 2 are relatively comforting.

1. *A spot contract*. Performance of a single move is promised by each player and the two performances are exchanged, one against the other. If one fails to perform, the other does not perform either. As long as each prefers 4 to 3 to 2, each will seek to execute the exchange; default is irrational in the sense of non-correspondence between ends and means; the contract is self-enforcing.

2. *A spot-and-forward contract*. The parties may have some

STATE-OF-NATURE CO-ORDINATION   49

extra-game reason for agreeing that *A* will perform the agreed switch from 'pull' to 'push' immediately, *B* only at some future date. Such a contract, as we know, is structurally the most vulnerable to default. However, if *B* defaults he gets a payoff of 3 although he could get 4 by performing; though weaker than in the spot contract, his incentive will still be to perform.

For a contrary result, *B*'s 'end' must change. As a kind of dog in the manger, he may, for instance, be motivated by his own pay-off *directly* and by *A*'s payoff *inversely*. By defaulting, he worsens his own payoff from 4 to 3 and that of *A* from 4 to 0. He can thus inflict considerable harm on the other player at little cost to himself. If he is spiteful, or is setting out to wage war against an unwary victim, a default strategy would be attractive to him.

It may be worth stopping a moment to consider a default strategy as opposed to the tit-for-tat strategy which emerges as the winner in the widely remarked computer tournaments conducted by Axelrod.[8] Tit for tat is shown to be *score-maximizing*; it is utility-maximizing if scores are utility-indices. It is best for a player to play tit for tat if he does not mind the other player also maximizing *his* score. Wanting to win by maximizing one's *excess* over the score of the other player, which can be done both by scoring oneself and by stopping the other from scoring, does not enter into this type of contest. Tit for tat succeeds in maximizing both the *score* and its *excess score over other strategies*; a player playing tit for tat, however, would not beat another player who *also* played tit for tat. Presumably, he would not regard play with *that* player as a contest; the two of them would be helping each other maximize their scores, which is how they would pile up higher ones than players following other strategies. There is, in sum, a difference between a winner among competing strategies and a winner among competing players.

3. *A forward contract*. This provides for a single, discrete move to be performed by each party on the same future date. This contract is immune from first-degree default and is self-enforcing in the same way as a spot contract, except for the possibility of second-degree default if, during the time-lapse between commitment and execution, the payoffs or the utilities the players attach to them change.

---

[8] Axelrod (1984).

4. *A forward contract.* It promises streams of *continuous* performance over time. The likelihood of self-enforcement is formally the same as in 3.

Inequality of Character

Crediting Rousseau with its formulation in the parable of the hunters in his 'Discourse on the Origins of Inequality Among Men',[9] the assurance co-ordination problem discussed in the preceding section is sometimes misnamed a 'Stag Hunt', as if the problem set by Rousseau were a version of the 'assurance game' with only slightly modified payoffs. The real Stag Hunt as understood by Rousseau, however, is fundamentally different from an assurance game. In the latter, as was shown in the discussion of Figure 3, there is no obstacle to reaching the better of two equilibrium-points by self-enforcing contract, provided the players maximize their own payoffs. This is far from being the case in the genuine Stag Hunt, which must produce an inferior outcome.

Recall the parable. Its object is to convey the precariousness of co-operation in the (perfect) state of nature and the difficulty of the passage into civil society. Two (or more) hunters stalk a stag. They are sure to bag it before the hunting party ends if only each hunter will stand fast at his post. However, they lack forethought ('la prévoyance n'était rien pour eux'). If a hare runs past one of them, he will run off and catch it, letting the stag escape. The matrix of Figure 4 reflects their predicament.

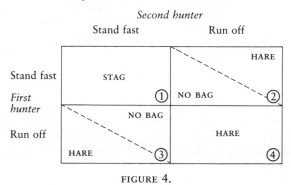

FIGURE 4.

[9] Rousseau (1755; 1964 edn.), 165–7.

In the misnamed, phoney Stag Hunt apocryphally ascribed to Rousseau, there is no real problem, for the stag to be had at the end of the day is clearly preferred to the immediate hare. Such time discount as the hunters may apply is not material; it will not make the stag smaller than a hare. For such hunters the game has two equilibrium-points in squares 1 and 4, and they prefer square 1. Several types of contract committing them to standing fast together are self-enforcing. There is no place for coercion and a social contract would be redundant. The superior outcome is capable of being reached without it. The situation does *not* represent Rousseau's idea of the state of nature. If it illustrates anything, it is the fruitfulness of co-ordination when it takes two to achieve a desired result, and the spontaneity of mutual commitment to it. Here, free private contract rules and enforces itself.

Rousseau creates the real Stag Hunt with its inferior outcome by having the hunters discount the end-of-the-day stag so heavily that it is now 'smaller' than (not preferred to) the immediate hare.[10] Square 1 is, therefore, no better than square 4. Strictly speaking, there *is* no co-ordination problem since it does not matter which square either hunter ends up in. If by mischance the hunters chose asymmetrically (one standing fast, the other running off), and found themselves in square 2 or 3, the one left with 'no bag' could always repair the mistake by unilaterally running off and getting his hare, without having to concert his move with his fellow. The converse, however, would not work; the one who ran off and got a hare would not want to reverse choices and unilaterally line up with his fellow on 'stand fast', since the stag in square 1 would not count as an improvement to him over the hare.

A special (and non-pure) co-ordination game—as Rousseau puts it, the desirability of respect for mutual engagements beyond 'present and palpable interest'[11]—can only exist if at least *somebody* in the state-of-nature population would prefer the stag,

---

[10] A further disconcerting possibility is that the stag and the hare are simply 'unconnected'. One should then fear that Rousseau's hunters would just wander about aimlessly, and commiserate with them as Sen does with Buridan's ass: 'The real dilemma would arise if the ass had an unconnected preference . . . There is very little doubt that Buridan's ass died for the cause of revealed preference, though—alas—he was not altogether successful since non-choice leading to starvation would have looked like the chosen alternative.' Sen, 'Behaviour and the Concept of Preference', in Elster (ed.) (1986), 63.

[11] Rousseau, (1755).

yet *not everybody* did so (for otherwise the hunters would land in square 1 and get the stag without particular difficulty). Appositely for Rousseau's title, the root of the problem is *inequality* of forethought, clarity of perception, patience, character. Inequality, too, provides the solution. Accepting for a moment the alleged equality of the hunters, a co-ordination game can be set up by postulating a third party, who has more 'character' than the hunters. He prefers the stag. If in the imperfect state of nature he is more powerful than they, he can impose on them his command to stand fast (though he may be unable to do so in the perfect state of nature). The longevity of the solution depends to some extent on the subsequent division of the stag. If the powerful third party keeps too much of it, the coerced arrangement may unravel as the hunters learn, by forced repetition, the lesson of the stag–hare comparison, and understand that they do not need any third party to co-ordinate them.

Instead of inequality of force, inequality of forethought may suffice for a solution yielding the highest joint payoff, i.e. the stag. It is only just possible to read into Rousseau's reference to the imperceptible acquisition of some notion of the advantage of keeping engagements a scenario in which one hunter acquires the notion and understands the advantage faster than the other. He now prefers the stag and grasps the manner of bagging it, but is frustrated by the other's unreliability when distracted by the passing hare. All he needs, however, is a pump-primer, an initial resource out of which to start a stream of side-payments by which to tempt his short-sighted fellow to stand fast. After the first successful hunt, he can renew this resource from his share of the stag, and the solution can become continuous and self-sustaining.

A fluke start-up (out of perhaps many botched hunting parties), where they had both happened to stand fast for lack of a passing hare and fortuitously caught the stag, might have provided the first hunter with the initial resource for the side-payment he needs to bind the second hunter. Superior in forethought to his fellow, he would save up part of his part, accumulating some starting capital by the classic recourse of the would-be capitalist to abstinence. He would then use the lesser character of his fellow hunter for harnessing him to a set purpose. Thus could the more advanced drag along the more backward and the tamer tame the savage. The analogy with the 'wage fund' and with the casting of persons into two kinds of social role, capitalists and proletarians, directors and directed, holders of residual claims and all prior claimants, is too obvious to be laboured.

Not Rocking the Boat

There is a sense in which even constant-sum games can be said to offer scope to profitable co-ordination (though purists could well object that if so, they are not really constant-sum games). Some important situations of social interdependence have an 'unwinnable' character of constant-sum futility in which it seems impossible for anyone to get anywhere and where co-ordination would provide relief. A dummy game, as in Figure 5, illustrates this feature of social life. Let there be a two-by-two game, the two strategies available to the two players A and B consisting of pushing the black or the white button, taking turns to push. A wins each time either player replies to the other's pushing a given button with pushing a button of the same colour (e.g. pushing black after black was pushed); B wins when either player changes colour. Both have a strongly dominant strategy. A must always copy what B has just done; B must always do the opposite of A. The dominant strategy of each always defeats that of the other. As a result, the 'solution' of the game moves cyclically, going round clockwise from square to square in an indefinitely repeated sequence.

Rivalry between two firms when one competitor innovates and the other copies the innovation; the transfer of power or money back and forth between two clans, coalitions, or classes; revolution

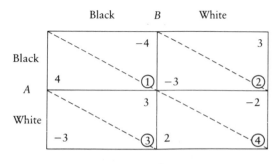

FIGURE 5.

and restoration; nationalization and privatization: if continued, these are all futile interactions neither party can win. All bear some resemblance to a cyclical constant-sum game that one might call 'rocking the boat', and that is pursued compulsively, without either player individually being able to stop and let be.

After each completed cycle round the four squares, both players just break even, but one would incur an opportunity cost if he left the other's last move without response. Hence, no completed cycle can be the final tour to be followed by a state of rest. If both players dislike the rocking motion, they could co-ordinate their moves and stop the cycle in a given square. But no square is neutral; each yields some gain to one player and some loss to the other compared to the square before or the square after. Choosing squares 1 or 4 as stopping-points would favour A, choosing 2 or 3 could leave B ahead. One player always gains by not stopping.

However, the players can 'neutralize' a square by a bargain between them over the redistribution of the gains and losses that accrue in that square, which is thus transformed into a mutually acceptable stopping-point. Square 4, where A gains only 2 and B loses only 2, involves the least inequality between their payoffs. This gives it a kind of 'salience' that might make it easier for the players to co-ordinate upon it than on other squares. The gainer would by a side-payment buy the loser's acquiescence to this particular status quo, at which the 'unfairness' of their relative positions is anyhow at its minimum.

The side-payment which A would make and B take rather than continuing to 'rock the boat' may actually be greater than 2. For instance, it may pay the non-innovative firm to offer the innovative one more than the latter's expected profit from its latest innovation, for the sake of suppressing *both* the latest innovation *and* the threat of future ones as well. Conversely, agreement may well be reached on a side payment of less than 2. One (albeit 'fact-deficient') example would be the much-lamented lack of class-consciousness of contemporary 'have-nots', whose militancy can be bought off (if indeed it has to be bought off) with a welfare-statist policy which leaves the 'haves' ahead of the game and still produces a stable status quo. There is no certainty of a bargain being struck, though there is obvious room for one. Assuming that one of several possible bargaining solutions is in fact reached, the status of a contract incorporating the bargain may be as follows.

1. *A half-spot–half-forward contract.* Under this *B* gets a side-payment immediately and promises not to 'rock the boat' for some period or ever. It is clearly not self-enforcing. *B*'s incentive to first-degree default may but may well not be offset by the likelihood of effective enforcement in a state-of-nature setting. There is little that theory can say about the longevity of such a solution, depending as it does on questions of fact, notably on the development of non-sovereign enforcement when there is no sovereign one.

2. *A forward contract.* Under this *B* desists from 'rocking the boat' as long as *A* keeps paying him an agreed bribe. The performances, whether two continuous or two series of discrete ones, are mutually contingent, there is no risk of first-degree default and the contract is self-enforcing except for intervening shifts in perferences or payoffs, which may provoke second-degree default.

There is, in sum, a reasonably good chance of state-of-nature solutions to co-ordination problems, some of which may be quite important, even though they involve conflicts over payoffs.

The Hardest Case

Without being as apparent as one might have wished, there was some rhyme or reason in the arrangement of the successive 'game' situations discussed so far. Starting with the discovery of favourable facts about the opposite 'player', moving on to the reciprocal recognition of the advantages of certain concerted moves among players, and finally to situations where concert presupposes the solution of a bargaining problem, successively steeper obstacles to useful co-operation were set. Co-ordinated moves of one kind or another by the players were seen to be necessary to scale them. Co-ordination required progressively more complex responses to the incentive structure built into each situation, moving from unilateral contribution on to reciprocal commitment, to mutually advantageous 'strategies' by the design of contracts with self-enforcing characteristics, and finally to agreements involving 'extra-game' side payments. Each game, chosen to stand for rising degrees of difficulty and falling certainty of the optimal solution, recalled at the same time the features of some important kind of real-life social interaction. This is how we inspected formalized representations of the approach to strangers, adaptation to their ways and 'socialization'; the mutually advantageous exchange of goods and the pooling of efforts; the interplay of unequal characters; innovation, restoration, and the buying off of competition and unrest.

If the exercise has yielded a result, it is to show that these types of problems are intrinsically capable of co-ordinated solutions. It appeared, too, that rational persons seeking only their own well-being have no good reasons to miss them. The solutions were broadly compatible with both the perfect and the imperfect state of nature, without reliance on a sovereign co-ordinator and contract-enforcer. A *fortiori*, no need was discovered for a social contract, considered as a means of creating and rendering legitimate a sovereign.

A somewhat extended aside is provoked by this provisionally negative finding before we can carry on the main argument. If co-ordination is, on the whole, no harder than this, conjuring up a co-ordinator to do it raises suspicions of civic laziness. A political theory, in turn, which postulates benefits from co-ordination in a general way, so as to deduce from it that rational persons would choose to create and submit to a co-ordinating sovereign, imputes civic laziness to them and indulges its own intellectual laziness. It is not good enough to cite the advantage of co-ordination on useful social norms such as the respect for life and property, the rule of law, the reliability of contracts, or, more vaguely and boldly still, 'playing by the rules'. It must also be proven, as Hobbes has set out to do, that co-ordination would fail without the sovereign. In this regard, both Locke and, albeit less obviously, Rousseau seem to me to content themselves with showing that submission has its uses, that it is a distinct convenience. Both touch upon state-of-nature problems, but neither looks seriously at state-of-nature solutions, let alone makes a case for their inferiority. Still less do they take account of the intriguing possibility that state-of-nature solutions may be superior for those who have learnt state-of-nature ways and inferior for those who have learnt civic laziness.

Hume, dismissing the social contract as a logically redundant fiction, has unerringly chosen firm ground instead. For him, people obey the commands of authority because it forces them to, and 'it is doing too much honour to lawful government' to assert that it arises from the consent of the governed.[12] (He does give some credit

[12]   Hume (1748; 1960 edn.), 158.

to contract notions in some contexts, not without sowing confusion but without admitting voluntary obedience.) In a striking turnabout, however, he then abandons firm ground and advances a *reason* (though not a cause), other than compulsion, for submitting to government: that 'society *could not* otherwise subsist'.[13]

It is not obvious why a *reason* is advanced for people to do what they must do for a different and sufficient *cause*, unless out of the characteristically contractarian desire, untypical of Hume, to render certain *de facto* situations *legitimate* by showing that they would have been freely chosen had there been occasion to choose. Hume's reason in this respect is on the same level of argument as Locke's and Rousseau's: government performs useful and important functions which *are not* performed by any other institution, but it is not shown why they, or substitute functions, *could not* be performed and institutions to perform them could not develop if the room for them were not pre-empted by a *de facto* sovereign, and society had not adapted its skills and habits to living with it. That society *could not* subsist is trivially true if by society Hume means a society already ruled by a sovereign government. The acid test, however, the deduction from rational choice in a hypothetical pre-contract situation, that one set of institutions would have been chosen rather than another because it is superior—the test applied by Hobbes and revived again by the public-goods theory of the Wicksell-to-Buchanan tradition—is not attempted in such discourse.

As we move to the hardest of the major co-ordination problems in society, the public goods 'dilemma', it may help to halt and inspect the way forward with some care. With public goods on the horizon, two approaches seem to be open. One is to take the more or less classic form of the dilemma, put it in a state-of-nature context, and find the conditions under which rational men would want to solve it by recourse to a social contract. This, and the required characteristics and clauses of such a contract, will hold our attention in the balance of Part One of this book. Here, we proceed in the mainstream of received contractarian theory. The second approach, which should at least have the merit, if it has no other,

---

[13] Hume (1748; 1960 edn.), 161, my italics. Buchanan has an apt phrase for illuminating the difference between the Hobbesian *cause* and the Humean *reason* for submission: 'one offers reasons for constraints, the other offers reasons for abiding with those that exist'. J. M. Buchanan, 'The Gauthier Enterprise' (unpublished MS, 1987), 34.

of improving our critical understanding of the first, is to recast the public-goods problem in what seem to me more general terms and infer the motivations that would lead people to adopt particular solutions, of which the social-contractarian formula is but one, to it. This will be the undertaking of Part Two.

This much having been promised, execution should start with a 'game' artificially representing the standard way of seeing the problem. Regrettably, a few more paragraphs must be added here to the over-abundant literature on the game in question, the somewhat hackneyed 'prisoners' dilemma', in order to seal off side-exits and bolt-holes and conserve the dilemma in a stark form. This will save us verbiage later. The bare bones of the game are as in Figure 6, with two players A and B each having the choice of two moves, black and white.

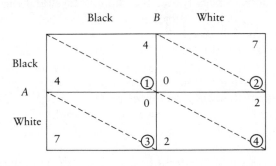

FIGURE 6.

A's and B's payoffs, produced by the interactions of their moves, appear in the corresponding triangles; the numbers are utility-indices. It is by getting the highest number that the players maximize utility; this is an empirically empty, formal view of utility, leaving the 'real' motivation that lurks underneath it unspecified. However, some restrictive conditions are needed. Taken together, I propose to call them 'single-mindedness'.

(a) Each player's move is determined solely by its expected payoffs.

(b) The game between any given players is played a known finite number of times.

The following interpretation of single-mindedness is suggested. Condition (a) means that moves are valued in terms of the two alternative payoffs they may bring and their binomial probability, and the move having the higher value is chosen. This excludes choosing the lower valued move on the ground that it is 'collectively' rational (i.e. maximizes the *sum* of two players' payoffs in a square, though not the payoff in a triangle). It excludes *pure* altruism and envy, i.e. any influence of the payoffs of the other player, whoever he is, on a player's choice of move, as well as *discriminating* altruism and envy, i.e. being influenced by another's payoff because he is who he is. By implication, it also excludes any other distributional consideration. One practical effect of this condition is that the willingness to assume burdens is independent of the burdens others look like having to bear as a consequence; we might call it the 'toleration of free riding', free riding being defined as intentional action or inaction whose effect is to redistribute payoffs (benefits) in the player's favour without redistributing burdens (contributions), or vice versa.

Condition (*b*) is the familiar one in games among strangers and makes collusion irrational. It tells the player to choose his move without allowing for any friendliness or hostility that his choice of move might induce in the other player's choice of moves in future games. Finally, this effect can also be induced by applying a high enough discount factor to the payoffs of future games, or a low enough probability of the same players meeting again in any future games; if neither the discount is high enough nor the probability low enough, 'incognito' may still achieve the same effect since, if the player cannot be identified, he cannot be rewarded or punished in a later game for his behaviour in an earlier one.

These conditions are not meant to be realistic or to resemble the conduct to be expected from some particular type of live person.

In the face of the payoff structure of Figure 6, single-mindedness in payoff maximization and no tentative or contingent moves being allowed, each player has 'white' as his dominant strategy; whatever the other player does, he will always get higher payoffs if he plays white (7 or 2) than black (4 or 0). The single equilibrium-point of the game in square 4 is strongly Pareto-inferior, for the players could both get higher payoffs in square 1 by both playing black. However, either player would further worsen his payoff by doing that unilaterally. A concerted, bilaterally co-ordinated move could get them to the Pareto-superior square 1. Once there, however, each could unilaterally improve his payoff and worsen that of the others by playing white and quitting square 1. It is this last option which singles out the prisoners' dilemma as a particularly hard-to-solve non-pure co-ordination game.

State-of-Nature Public Goods: The Standard Approach

Non-produced, everlasting, or self-renewing goods have the lucky property of not needing to be reproduced; until further notice, no public goods dilemma attaches to daylight. Some non-produced goods may be passing into the non-self-renewing category: urban air, lake water, and the English language are some of the usual suspects. Most produced goods, however, need to be reproduced lest they should become ever scarcer and finally disappear. How is the required contribution of resources, tangible and intangible, to be called forth?

If there is discriminating access to the good in question, so that some are in but others are excluded from the class that can enjoy it, there are ready-made solutions for linking inclusion in the benefit to contribution. Passage of a person from the excluded to the included class or, as they put it in 'rights-speak', the acquisition of property rights in the good, can be made contingent on a resource contribution. The basic case, often referred to as the 'cash nexus', is where a sufficiently divisible good has a price per unit; any 'excluded' person can 'include' himself by paying it. The excluded class is formed by implicit personal choices, while variations of the price reconcile the rate of reproduction of the good with the balance between the included and the excluded class; all get what they choose to pay for, and what they pay causes a sufficient quantity of the good to be offered. Markets operating with spot and forward contracts are the mechanism *par excellence* for arranging this.

Moreover, they do it in a manner which is reputed to have benign unintended effects upon the evolution and dissemination of useful knowledge (itself a factor in the reproduction of goods) and in the formation of a certain type of character. Historically, markets and their unintended effects have proved highly congenial to societies that were progressing materially and seemed keen to go on doing so. More controversially, markets are also held to allocate resources in the most efficient way feasible; under extremely strong assumptions, this can be proved deductively as an implication; under easier assumptions certain common-sense presumptions of efficiency subsist. Other mechanisms, such as lump-sum fees of admission to unrestricted enjoyment of a good, or cross-subsidization, deform or relax the nexus between enjoyment of a good and contribution to its resupply without, however, altogether severing it. They may, and in some cases blatantly do, involve loss of efficiency (they 'encourage over-consumption'), but stop short of doing away with all incentive to contribute in order to have access. Once discriminatory access ceases and the passage from exclusion to inclusion is set free, at least for the particular group of persons defined by the common interest they have in the good, none of that group needs to contribute in order to benefit, and a public goods 'dilemma' emerges.

It is usually treated as axiomatic that public goods are intrinsically non-excludable. In fact, 'non-excludability' is one part of their usual definition (the other part being 'jointness of supply'—we will defer consideration of this property). Whether any good is ever intrinsically non-excludable is doubtful; daylight is excludable by putting coin-operated automatic shutters on windows, allowing access to daylight to be bought by the hour;[14] exclusion schemes of comparable or lesser silliness and cost can be thought up for every reputedly public good. What the exercise teaches is that 'excludability' is a variable property of the universe of goods, being reflected in variable exclusion costs. This is a good reason to stop talking about the non-excludability of *public* goods and talk instead of the greater or lesser exclusion costs of goods *in general*.

There is, however, a more direct reason for steering clear of notions of intrinsic excludability. Public-goods problems arise not when a good is non-excludable (even if there were such a category) but when it is in fact not excluded, for whatever reason. Social mores may have as much to do with this as the awkwardness and high cost of exclusion; more than one reason may be at work. This is notably the case when an interest group, a community, or society as a whole attempts to provide X publicly—the proverbial night-watchman for any resident on his beat, free counselling for any pregnant woman, collectively bargained conditions for any wage-earner in an industry, traffic lights for anyone trying to cross a busy

---

[14] The window tax was a crude version of this. Those who would not or could not pay it practised self-exclusion from daylight by walling in some of their windows.

street, museums for any art-lover, and education for any school-age child; so that anyone in these classes of persons can seek to profit from the good suited to his interest and condition in life without contributing in proportion to his expected benefit, if at all.

There is manifest evidence, past and present, of successful and unsuccessful attempts at publicly providing a variety of goods for one group or another and increasingly for society as a whole, the chosen goods often having relatively easy and cheap 'logistics of exclusion' so that no technical obstacle would stand in the way of their provision on a private contractual, 'for profit' basis. Although 'excludable', they are not 'excluded'.

Recognizing that any problem that arises out of the disjunction of contribution and benefit is not rooted in the *intrinsic nature* of various goods which condemn them to be public, but in the *manner of their provision*, certain authors prefer to call it the 'problem of collective action' and even insist that it is different from the public-goods problem.[15] It seems to me a pity to invent two problems where one will do and looks hard enough; all that is needed to ensure the unity of the problem is to ban the notion of *excludability* and consistently deal with *de facto* exclusion, for which there can be a variety of sufficient reasons, high exclusion cost (though never 'non-excludability') being one of them.

Another way of looking at exclusion is to consider that for any good there is always a smallest viable, autarchic set of persons that includes both a subset of contributors and a subset of beneficiaries, such that the contributions are sufficient to produce the benefits. The smallest set may be as large as all humanity or the nation, though of course it may have any size. However, as long as this set is greater than one person, it is possible that some contribute and others benefit. The good concerned is then a *de facto* public good. If the set contains only one person, the good concerned is a private

[15] '. . . Since very few of the goals or goods that groups seek can accurately be described as pure public goods, it is probably best not to confuse the analysis of collective action by treating it as a problem in the provision of public goods.' Barry and Hardin (1982), 32. But whether goods can or cannot be described as 'pure public' or pure anything, is immaterial. It may be noted that 'collective action' seems too vague a term to describe the specific condition of non-proportionality, and in the limit *the absence of any functional relation between individual contribution and benefit*. Whichever is the right term to use, the main thing is not to treat one problem as two, one of collective action and one of public goods. The essential problem is *publicness*, the *possibility of benefiting without contributing*. Cf. Ch. 4 n. 12.

good. Private goods can be considered as the limiting case of public goods.

The exclusion problem is removed by making the two subsets overlap perfectly. Non-exclusion means that a person can be in the beneficiary subset without being in the contributor subset. It is possible to have imperfect exclusion, where all beneficiaries contribute, but some contribute more and others less than their 'share'—an ethically awkward continuity problem (how large is one person's fair share?) upon which we touch in Chapter 6 without resolving it.

Non-exclusion is purported to be sufficient to create a public-goods dilemma, and on Occam's principle we will not deal with its refinements, nor with other properties such as divisibility, until we have to.

The standard view of public provision, then, is that its incentive or 'payoff' structure is that of the prisoners' dilemma. A convenient visual representation is that in Figure 7. The two players A and B are natural or legal persons, or coalitions who, for extra-game reasons, play together. If A and B both contribute some fixed minimum of resources (money, effort, abstinence, etc.), the good in question is produced and made available to all non-excluded persons, including A and B. If both withhold their contribution, the good is not produced. If A contributes and B withholds, A becomes the sucker exploited by B the free rider, and of course vice versa. By implication, if one player contributes, enough of the good is produced to make free riding not only possible, but the most attractive among the possible payoffs. The upshot is that both

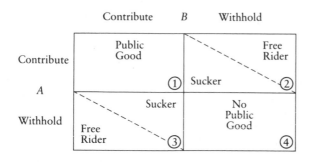

FIGURE 7.

players value the four payoffs in the following descending order: free rider, public good, no public good, sucker.

Under single-mindedness and no tentative moves, for the same reason as in the preceding section, the sole equilibrium-point is square 4 and the good will not be publicly provided. Square 1 is Pareto-superior and individually inaccessible. It is collectively inaccessible (or, if accessible by co-ordination, unstable and issuing in default) as long as the free-rider payoff is preferred. Either player's free riding relegates the other player to the role of sucker, the worst of all payoffs. Neither will, by contributing, knowingly offer the other the free-rider option.

Moral philosophers have, in recent years, developed ingenious arguments[16] to show an escape route from this dilemma without transgressing the confines of a rationality in which choice is motivated solely by the purpose of maximizing the chooser's own expected payoffs. In particular, they have shown why 'prudential' maximization, i.e. the choice consistent with the best probability-weighted outcome for oneself, does not (except in 'games against nature') coincide with 'straightforward' maximization where one's purpose is defeated by the straightforward maximization practised by the other player. Lest it be self-defeating, maximization by one must be considerate, constrained by regard for the interests of the other. It must aim at Pareto-superiority, seeking only such improvements in one's payoff as are compatible with no worsening in the payoffs of fellow players, since only such improvements will not be defeated by their predictable counter-moves.

These arguments would have great force if they could be reconciled with matters of fact. If it were the case that one player cannot, as a matter of fact, expect profitably to exploit the other because a blocking counter-move by the latter was certain or highly probable, squares 2 and 3 of the matrix would simply be wiped out. 'Selfish', 'straightforward' maximization and prudentially constrained, considerate maximization would dictate the same best choice, i.e. to contribute. But the empirical truth of this condition is far from evident; people do succeed to take advantage of others and to free ride on their contributions, especially in the multi-person 'games' of everyday social existence. It is easy enough to grasp that collectively it cannot be payoff-maximizing to do this, but not why individually

[16] Parfit (1984); Gauthier (1985).

it should not be, since patently 'it works', whereas if it were self-defeating it could not and would not.

The sort of individual-maximization calculus under which it works *even* better *not* to take advantage, for there are continuing interactions with the same players and self-restraint today pays returns tomorrow, is worth exactly what its 'numbers', its empirical data, are worth; if certain interactions are in fact like this (which may well be the case), it pays by definition to take the 'long-term' potential they offer, just as it pays by definition to 'take advantage' in interactions that are not like this. Living by the Kantian rule cannot possibly be the prudential policy if the coincidence of the two is contingent on the facts of each case, working in some but not in others.

For the present argument, the possibility that it may pay to be nice and that honesty is the best policy is ruled out by the second condition of single-mindedness. As there are, for practical purposes,[17] no continuing interactions with the same players, it always pays to 'take the money and run' if the other player offers you the free-rider option. As it is, in order for moral to be prudential, either some positive value would have to be assigned to the payoffs of others (which is ruled out by the first condition of single-mindedness) or some reliance would have to be placed on contractual agreements. To conclude, some attention must be paid to this latter escape route from the dilemma.

Co-ordination by an agreed, reciprocal move to square 1 (both players to contribute) could take the form of the following:

1. *A spot contract.* A and B each make an instantaneous discrete contribution in exchange for the like by the other. This seems materially feasible in two-person (or two-coalition) games, but problematical in multi-person ones.

2. *A spot-and-forward contract.* This involves non-simultaneous moves. As first-degree default would *ex hypothesi* be the best move of the second player, this contract would not only not be self-enforcing, but not even some low stochastic degree of reliance could be placed on it.

3. *A forward contract.* The version of forward contract where

---

[17] Players face a known finite number of rounds. For either player it will be profitable to take the money and run in the last round. Therefore, it will also be profitable for any player to take it and run in the last-but-one round to beat the other player to it; and so on for each earlier round back to the present one.

continuous flows of contributions are made mutually contingent, excluding first-degree default and making the conditions to a substantial degree self-enforcing, seems well adapted to public-goods situations with few players. Self-enforcement becomes problematical in multi-person games because of the low visibility of each person's move in the crowd, just as in the case of the spot contract. In addition, second-degree default is also a possibility over a period.

Reliance on Enforcement

If contracts in many public goods dilemmas are not universally and reliably self-enforcing, can they be enforced in the state of nature? This is a question the standard social-contractarian approach does not ask. In the latter, it suffices to make the case that the public goods dilemma is a genuine one, admitting of no spontaneous solution. (It is fair to say that its negative stand on this point is, as a rule, too categoric, but let that pass for the moment.) Failing self-enforcement, the social contract becomes both necessary (the problem must be solved and has no other solution) and Pareto-superior (making no one worse off, hence allowing unanimous acceptance).

The standard approach is cavalier. It jumps at least one stage in the argument, the inquiry into the value of reliance on non-sovereign enforcement in the state of nature. Even if the final verdict were the same and sentencing the 'players' to the social contract an evident sequel, it seems to me that the proper procedure is to complete the case. It can be done expeditiously.

In the perfect state of nature, all are equally strong (or equally weak), coalitions leading to uneven distribution of force have not been formed, hence recourse to force has a higher opportunity-cost in attack than in defence. Consequently, the threat of first use of force is of relatively low credibility. Contract-enforcement by self-help is unpromising, likely to be met by defiance. Mutual aid and bought help are, strictly speaking, inadmissible because contrary to the 'equal force—no coalition' hypothesis.

In imperfect states of nature, by contrast, the threat of force is often credible because, if it is unequal, its first use may well be attractive to the wielder of the threat. Hence, non-sovereign contract-enforcement is possible in response to the right incentive structure. Variable-sum conflictual co-ordination games can find efficient solutions because it is possible, subject to appropriate distributional bargains, to incite the greater force to align itself in support of the higher sum of payoffs. In the public goods dilemma, two players both want to shift the solution of the game from the low payoff sum in square 4 to the higher payoff sum in square 1. Because of the temptation of the free-rider option, they need contract-enforcement to bind each other. They have a 'co-ordination surplus' (the difference between the payoff sums in squares 1 and 4) to dispose of; they can devote part of it to buying enforcement and achieve the co-ordinated solution of square 1.

However, there is still life left in the dilemma. With enforcement, it is possible to bar the low-payoff square 4 altogether, but other degrees of freedom remain. The enforcer has the choice between enforcing the contract leading to square 1—both contribute—and *contenancing default*[18] by one player, letting him free ride while forcing the others to contribute. The latter course leads to square 2 or 3, depending on which player strikes a bargain with the enforcer to the detriment of the other player.

Let the payoffs be cardinal and perfectly transferable values which undergo no change when passing from hand to hand. This does not by any means go without saying and is, in fact, improbable—transfers typically involve some 'leaky bucket effect'—but let us say it all the same to keep the argument simple. In terms of the numbers used in Figure 6, the payoff sum of square 1 is 8, while those of squares 2 or 3 are both 7. However, enforcing square 1 means a bargain to divide 8 three ways among the enforcer and two players, while countenancing default and allowing the solution to move to squares 2 or 3 supposes that a two-person coalition of the enforcer and one player have struck a bargain to divide 7 between them and force the remaining player to make an unrequited contribution. Hence, it can pay for a coalition of enforcer and one player to reject square 1 in favour of 2 or 3. Bought enforcement in the imperfect state of nature is perfectly consistent with this inequitable solution.

[18] The enforcer 'countenancing default' is, of course, nothing less than his defaulting on his 'meta-contract' to enforce the contract—it is 'meta-default'. It is worth reflecting that 'meta-contracts' are no more *sui generis* self-enforcing than contracts in general; strangely, there seems to be an automatic unstated assumption that they are. The question goes to the heart of constitutions, the 'rules of rule-making'.

Competition among potential enforcers could make it harder to reach; however, it is, so to speak, 'all a matter of the numbers'.

This conclusion is general, and retains whatever validity it has as the distribution of force is made progressively more uneven and the state of nature progressively more imperfect, reaching in the limit 'the monopoly of the use of force'. A solution of the public-goods dilemma allowing monopolistic enforcement, unrequited contribution by some, and free riding by others appears, in fact, to be as general a 'model' of the operation of the state as one can get with rational-choice assumptions alone. (Other modes of operation of the state need more and stronger assumptions to be explicable.) The social-contract response to the public goods dilemma is a special case of the general rational-choice 'model'; it confines the solution, as it were, to square 1, i.e. to a state of affairs where all contribute. No compelling reason is provided in any version of the social contract doctrine why squares 2 or 3 should not be chosen instead, if the incentive structure (the 'numbers') were to make them attractive.

Nevertheless, the internal evidence of contractarianism is unequivocal: there is something that stops the enforcement mechanism favouring some at the expense of others. Since agreement to the social contract is unanimous (or, in some versions, would be unanimous if transaction-costs among the parties were low enough), solutions where enforcement responds to payoff configurations among the players and enables free riders to take advantage must have been prevented by some trustworthy device. Pending further thought about the matter in the next chapter, let us merely label the device 'black box' or 'constitution' and take it for granted.

Given, then, that the partial or total disjunction of benefit from contribution creates a *dilemma* which makes spontaneous contribution to public provision both desirable and irrational, there is a solid enough contractarian case against the state of nature. It is not, properly speaking, that there would be war of all against all, and no public goods could be provided. There are certain contractual solutions, some self-enforcing and others with some chance of being enforced, for goods, including the protection of life and property, to be publicly provided by the voluntary co-ordinated actions of uncoerced individuals. However, these solutions appear as a whole unsatisfactory, incomplete, partial, or precarious. Some depend on the facts of the particular case, others carry too much default risk, yet other may be abused by free riders. There is an *a priori* presumption that coalition-forming would lead to some 'unfairly' forcing others to make unrequited contributions and create a vested interest in sub-optimal solutions. None of this makes the complete case *for* the social contract. It does, however, serve as the backcloth against which one can better see contractarian theory.

4

SOCIAL CONTRACT

If the parties to a social contract preserve their pre-contract identity and autonomy, their commitment is revocable. They can free themselves from it at some exit cost that bears some fairly close relation to the value of the contract to the other party and is well short of self-destruction.[1] Conversely, when a commitment is both indefinite in duration and literally irrevocable, their autonomy becomes incomplete and there is an albeit restricted sense in which their separate identities are merged into a new entity created on the basis of the contract, an entity which inherits and aggregates into a new whole the autonomies they have surrendered. It is this notion of irrevocability and the creation of a new entity that underlies the idea of the social contract as a 'contract of society'. By contrast, if pre-contract persons and groups revocably entrust a well-defined and limited part of their autonomy to a designated person or body, *keeping enough of it back* to suffice them *for reclaiming the rest* should the occasion arise, the resulting contract is a mere 'contract of government' between a pre-contract state-of-nature society and the pre-contract 'prince'.

These distinctions based on revocability are unrigorous and imprecise to a degree, but they have their root in traditional thought, and correspond to real functional differences. The idea of the revocable contract of government has, at least since Aquinas, served to justify claims of immunity from royal or imperial pretensions, limitations of lay authority, and the right of resistance.[2]

---

[1] 'Freeing oneself' may be effected either unilaterally by default or bilaterally by renegotiation. Default is a stochastic means of escape from a commitment; for with a given rigour of the climate of enforcement, there are nearly always non-zero probabilities of (a) the defaulter being forced to perform; (b) commuting his obligation to perform into a payment of damages; or (c) defaulting with impunity. Renegotiation, on the other hand, can be seen as agreed and certain release from a commitment in exchange for accepting a different one.

[2] Assertion of the right of resistance flickers on and off in medieval thought well before Aquinas. Without trying to impute some cause-and-effect relation, one might note that the idea prospers as serious conflict emerges between the Empire and the

The irrevocable contract was to convey the precise opposite, the justification and legitimacy of the sovereign's claim to obedience, by virtue of his commands providing the sole feasible solution to the problem of the public good.

When, according to Hobbes, the people of Israel 'voted' to make a covenant with God, making him their king *in exchange* for his promise to give them Canaan,[3] they made what was, at least in its form (if not altogether in its substance), a revocable contract of government between two parties who remained autonomous, performance by each remaining contingent on performance by the other.

Nothing could be further than this from Hobbes's own view of the post-biblical civil contract of society. For him, there are, strictly speaking, *no* pre-contract parties capable of proceeding to a contract. Pre-contract persons cannot promise future performance to each other. It would be but 'vain breath' if they pretended to. The social contract, by creating society and the sovereign out of the inchoate pre-contract, alone permits meaningful engagements to be made; it is its own enabling condition. The sovereign enforces obedience to itself. No possible standing is left to some supplementary contract *between* post-contract society and the sovereign, involving promises of mutual performance, failure by one party absolving the other from performing. It is true that the sovereign has an obligation to provide the sufficient conditions for its subjects' self-preservation, but it is contrary to its *nature* to fail in this; it is the bare *existence* of the sovereign and the concentration of force in its own hands that its existence entails that are the sufficient condition for civil peace. Default by the sovereign is logically impossible when its contracted-for performance consists in its *being*.

Rousseau spells out what is implicit in Hobbes, that the

Papacy. Interestingly, John of Salisbury in the 12th century alludes not to the right, but to the duty of resistance against royal abuse, cf. Hogue (1966; repr. 1985), 87. The history of the idea in Western Europe is inseparable from that of religious thought. Otto Hintze, one of the great authorities on European administrative history, considers that the right of resistance was the predecessor institution out of which gradually arose the system of representative government; cf. Hintze (1975), 302–53. This is consonant with the later lay enlightenment and contractarian theories, in which the right of resistance shrivels to insignificance since one need not resist oneself; where society is self-governing, there is no duality of purpose between governor and governed.

[3] Hobbes (1651; 1968 edn.), ch. 35, p. 442, quoted by Ryan (1983), 203.

irrevocable contract of society leaves no room for the revocable contract of government.

Since he who wields the power is always the master when its comes to applying it, one might just as well give the name of contract to the behaviour of a man who says to another, 'I give you all my property on condition that you render back to me as much of it as you please.' There is but one contract in the State, and that is the primitive contract of association. By reason of its existence it excludes all further contracts.[4]

The irrevocable, properly Hobbesian contract of society is a mechanical artefact, fashioned out of some large feasible set by the requirements of instrumental rationality. Law is an intellectual construct; it is what it is because society has the ends it does have. Admittedly, the terms of the social contract and the law that is constructed under them are conditioned by what man is, for the simple reason that what men want is not independent of what they are. But political society is *made*, not *found*. In the intellectual tradition that began with the nominalism of Franciscan theology and was carried on blandly enough by Grotius and Pufendorf on one side, the Spanish neo-scholastics on the other, till it reached its full merciless rigour in Hobbes, it is free will, human volition, preference, 'political hedonism', that explain the terms of the social contract. Yet paradoxically this tradition makes it irrevocable, allowing no release from it.

The revocable social contract, by contrast, is not artefactual and is not 'chosen'. In the tradition of Aristotle and Aquinas, its theory takes both pre-contract society and the pre-contract prince as 'organic' entities found in nature. Society can no more be constructed than a tree—at the most, it can be formed in accordance with its essential nature much as a tree can be cultivated and trimmed. The contract between society and the prince leaves two autonomous post-contract parties, both having the material capacity to cease performance, though the theory does not envisage society doing so unless given good cause by the prince.

Here lies the crux of the difference between the old Thomist and the new Hobbesian contract; the first deals with a society that has kept its arms, the second with one that has 'chosen' to disarm itself. In the first, resistance to the prince who transgresses natural law takes the form of resort to force or the threat of it. In the second,

[4] Rousseau (1762, 1960 edn.), 264.

resistance is unnecessary, but would be impossible if it were necessary. In Rousseau's intellectually weaker, in some ways decadent, quasi-Hegelian version of the irrevocable social contract, resistance to the general will would be tantamount to resisting one's own will, properly understood (the condition of proper understanding being the tautological one that one's own will conforms to the general will). What gives Locke's social contract its air of unreality, of toothlessness, and of placebo, is that it is a reversion to the old Thomist idea of revocability without the retention of armed force in civil society which would make performance by the contracting parties mutually contingent, and resistance to unlawful government meaningful.

It is a consequence of our definitions that the revocable social contract is a contract between a society of persons in the imperfect state of nature and an imperfect state which has not attained the monopoly of the use of force. Unusually for social theory, the 'model' fits quite well a real historical situation, that of Western Europe from the late tenth to the early fifteenth century. Starting with the disintegration of the precocious Carolingian state system and closing, albeit indistinctly and raggedly, with the successful reaffirmation of centralized power in a number of incipient nation-states, most of Europe knew an interval of brilliance and variety, an intellectual awakening, a rise of civility, for much of the time an economic upswing and a thorough polycentric dispersion across society of arms, money, and *savoir faire*—political, military, agricultural, and mercantile. It would be disingenuous to contend that 'this explains that'. Saxon and Staufer rulers had a lighter, less centralizing hand than Frankish ones. 'Countervailing' powers were generated by the renewal of tension between spiritual and temporal authorities as well as by internal tensions within each. There was a weakening of command-obedience and a great opening for individual emancipation and autonomy on two new 'frontiers'. One was pushed outward by the Crusades and the Reconquest of the Iberian Peninsula. The other, and almost certainly more important, one followed the axe and the fire as much of Western Europe, (essentially forest land) was swiftly transformed into arable, as villages gained some autonomy from towns while both grew richer, and as the balance of power between lord and serf shifted a bit at a time in favour of the latter. The newer ruling houses, the Capetians, Plantagenets, and Anjous, rose from the middle nobility and such authority as they managed to gain over other great lords was due more to their acquired wealth and force than to high birth and old legitimacy. All these circumstances helped, of course, but perhaps more as enabling causes, allowing rather than bringing about Europe's medieval flowering.

A dynamic, creative and improving state of affairs, which the high medieval period undoubtedly was, suffices to falsify the claim of the counter-reform and the enlightenment, which modern political thought repeats with parrot-like mindlessness, that civil disarmament in favour of the state and the submission of all to one rule have been indispensable for viable social coexistence and co-operation.

An imperfect, non-monopolistic state cohabiting with armed subjects, some of them disposing of power of nearly the same order, others capable of coalescing and forming comparable concentrations of force when sufficiently provoked, implies rival jurisdictions, parallel organs, and mechanisms of contract-enforcement; it admits at best of weak, *ad hoc* means for imposing uniform, 'collectively chosen' moves on individual 'players'. There is no sovereignty, or rather 'chaque seigneur est souverain dans sa seigneurie'. The very notion of 'collectively chosen', 'superior', 'preferred' solutions to social co-ordination problems is of limited significance in such a setting because where all know their natural place, distributional conflicts arise in more subdued form. Custom suppresses bargaining problems. Feudal patron–client relations, community loyalties, corporatisms, and parochialisms, involving as they do some degree of *de facto* exclusion of outsiders from locally produced public goods, tend to generate spontaneous solutions to co-ordination problems which might not work in more anonymous settings. These structures of exclusion correspond to Rousseau's 'particular General Wills'—'general only in respect of [their] own members, but partial in respect of the state'.[5] A more inclusive, amorphous and unstructured society might well have to aim at the general will, no less, to avoid grossly sub-optimal solutions in situations, notably in public-goods problems in a wide sense, where there are intrinsic distributional conflicts of the 'who gets what', 'who pays what' type.

Moreover, whether such solutions as are reached in the sort of

[5] Rousseau (1762; 1960 edn.), 194.

social environment which best fits the revocable social contract between imperfect state-of-nature society and imperfect state are 'preferred' or not is a question that might well not arise at all to the 'players'. If the motive of their choice is to reach the right, just, and proper arrangement, to conform to norms of what is a fit state of affairs, the natural order, talk of preference is either beside the point, or the term becomes a redundant empty verbalism, standing for any and every possible motive of action, not excluding humility, self-effacement, and the will to respect a certain 'natural' distribution *regardless of one's share under it.*

The social contract that, if kept, would stabilize such a state of affairs is an agreement between king and barons, king and the estates, state and society, as the case may be. It legitimizes the existing distribution of force between the parties. Neither is meant to encroach on the domain of the other; the prerogative of the ruler and the immunities ('liberties', 'rights') of the subjects are recognized as mutually contingent. If one pushes, the other is fully entitled *and equipped* to push back. The deterrent to encroachment is the existence of force on all sides; this social contract, for all the spiritual authority the church lends it, is essentially enforced by self-help. If there is no overwhelming superiority of force on one side or the other, a measure of civil peace and limited government are mutually compatible without, of course, being more than merely probable. In the nature of things, however, a situation of balanced forces is neither stable nor able to be made so by contractual means.

However, even in the face of unbalanced force, the right of resistance to tyrants is a real right, its exercise is materially possible even if risky. That non-performance by one party (e.g. disrespect of immunities) is sufficient warrant for non-performance by the other (e.g. disobedience), and that non-performance is feasible for both, prove that the contract is a genuine one. By contrast, under the irrevocable social contract, contingency of performances is entirely fictitious, and the very designation of 'contract' is a somewhat ironic misnomer.

For the sake of historical perspective, one might note that God was not a party to the medieval social contract. He was made a party to what was left of it in the sixteenth and seventeenth centuries, when the power of the sovereign had become preponderant. The balance between state and society, prerogative and liberties, was then no longer maintained by some contractual idea of reciprocal respect, backed by the sanction of force against comparable force, capable of resistance and refusal of taxation. It became a triangular relationship; the monarch was sovereign by divine right, he owed it to God to respect natural law and his subjects' rights under it; they, in turn, owed it to God to obey him. The right of resistance, still alive as late as the sixteenth and seventeenth centuries in Huguenot and Puritan thought, has faded away *pari passu* with its wherewithal, decentralized force, though it lingered on longer in England (where the standing army was small) than elsewhere.

Institutional Darwinism

As a matter of sequential fact, the revocable social contract has everywhere given way to the irrevocable one, and the imperfect state of nature has been obliterated by the emergence of perfect states, i.e. states possessing the monopoly of force. Henry VIII in England, Louis XI in France, Maximilian of Austria in the hereditary lands, Charles the Bold in Burgundy, the first Hohenzollerns in Brandenburg tamed the nobility and greatly reduced the powers intermediate between themselves and the smallest of their subjects. There is no significant exception in Western Europe to this sequence. Does it, then, lend support to some hypothesis about one rule or institution being predestined to prevail for being fitter, having greater survival value than another?

The obvious hypothesis, that of Institutional Darwinism, would explain the decline and disappearance of particular social arrangements and the survival or spread of others in terms of their relative efficiency, given the environment, or their capacities to adapt, given that it changes. Under this sort of hypothesis, there is a supply of subjects with diverse characteristics to choose from. The supply is generated by some random process; for living organisms it is genetic mutation, while for social institutions it may be cultural evolution subjected to historical accidents. Selection of subjects is exercised passively by the environment (including other competing subjects), which is kinder to some characteristics than to others. Subjects selected as fittest to survive propagate themselves, while those not selected are progressively obliterated.

Since the test of fitness to survive is survival, it is trivially true that the surviving subject (in our context, the surviving institution) was fitter. This simply results from defining the problem in the appropriate way. It does not make for a very interesting hypothesis. Institutional Darwinism, however, is really a different and more ambitious theory. In contrast to what I will, by way of shorthand, call plain Darwinism, it posits that an institution is selected by its environment, not for the characteristics that make *it* fit to survive, but for those that favour a symbiotic set of which it is a member. The set consists of complementary institutions and the host society they serve, that uses them, whose practices and civilization they jointly constitute. In the words of Hayek, the most distinguished institutional Darwinist, '. . . those people who *happened* to adopt suitable rules developed a complex civilisation which *prevailed* over others'.[6] However, nothing proves that there is an identifiable set of rules, practices, and institutions that is both suitable for the development of a host civilization and also the fittest to survive, or, *pace* Hayek,[7] that the civilizations that survive are those that rely on a particular set.

In order to see this clearly, let us backtrack and separate Institutional Darwinism from Institutional Gresham's Law. If institutions were selected for the characteristics favourable to *their own* survival, as in plain Darwinism, the surviving ones might well not be the ones most conducive to making the host civilization prosper and grow. A health service which healed some people and made most others dependent on doctors, hospitals, and drugs would certainly be fit to survive; it would create demand for itself and establish the pre-conditions of its own propagation. A prison system in which petty criminals became hardened and unreformable, or asylums that made the unhinged even madder, would likewise be self-perpetuating. A state security police meant to stamp out organized opposition to a government would thereby almost certainly ensure its own longevity. Each of these would be a non-survivor, self-liquidating institution if it were *suitable* in Hayek's sense, efficient in serving the purposes of the host civilization; before long there would be no more illness, no criminality, no opposition, hence nothing would be left for them to do. Their survival and growth, however, are fostered precisely by their inefficiency. Ill-conceived rules require additional rules to work at all, bad laws engender a need for more laws, bad teaching prolongs

---

[6] Hayek (1964), my italics.
[7] Hayek (1979), epilogue.

education, a pointless and fatuous bureaucracy inexorably breeds more of the same by tying things up in knots, while the workers' state in a classless society keeps getting stronger instead of withering away. 'Agency problems' are ineradicable from complexity; many if not all open societies have tawdry politics, bumbling policies and armies allergic to being shot at; and playing by the rules does not help to win games. For a variety of reasons, we should expect survival of the fittest to survive to produce a population of institutions with many monsters and with no bias towards the benign and the instrumentally efficient. When competing for survival, the latter may well be driven out by the former.

It is well in line with this expectation that there is no marked tendency in history for societies equipped with benign institutions to 'prevail'. The evidence goes both ways, if not the other way on balance. The liberal constitutional conception of Constant and Guizot; Röpke's, Eucken's and Hayek's *Rechtsstaat*; Buchanan's 'protective state'; self-limitation of government, stable property relations immune to political processes and indeed exempted from the domain of redistributive 'social choice'; a close correspondence between individual contributions and benefits; competitive equilibrium and sound money; practices and institutions contributing to the prosperity of the host civilization: not only did a state of affairs displaying these features never exist, but the nearest approach to it, that of mid-nineteenth-century Europe, is clearly proving to have been a singular event, 'a brilliant episode', a passing fluke.

Institutional Darwinism would work in the benign fashion ascribed to it, and 'nice' civilizations would spread, if the subject being selected by the environment for its characteristics that best help it to survive were the whole symbiotic set of host society with its complementary institutions. For this to be the case, single parasitic institutions in the set should have to lose more by weakening the host society that they gain by feeding upon it. Gresham's Law would then cease to operate, for 'non-nice' institutions would either not survive the adverse feedback they suffer from their own parasitic action which weakens their host society, or they would change their spots by a process of mutation-cum-selection.

There is no evidence whatever to bear out suppositions of this sort. Parasitic institutions survive everywhere and seem in no hurry to wilt or to mend their ways. Some look near enough immortal, or at any rate appear to have life-expectancies at least comparable to non-parasitic ones. Host societies continue to live with them, even if their performance is in many respects poorer than that of societies with a luckier history and better skills at institution-building. On the evidence of the past, however, there are few aspects of societal performance, apart perhaps from the ability to tighten belts and sustain wars, that are relevant to the ability to survive, to preserve one's identity and to subject other societies to it; initial endowments such as size and geography are probably more relevant than subsequent performance. Nor is there any solid, non-wishful reason to expect the contrary.

Genetic mutation may equip a subject with a competitive advantage over a multitude of others of its kind, all other things being equal between them. But a society that happens upon 'suitable' rules and institutions is one of a kind, no other thing is equal between it and its handful of competitors, and whether it prevails or not cannot be imputed to the set of institutions it is using.

When the overbearing ambition of Louis XIV set off the Second Hundred Years War that ended at Waterloo, France started off great and England small. It is tempting to ascribe the reversal of their relative places over the eighteenth century to institutional reasons. There is a case for saying that the stern nannying of Colbert and the other great administrators of the era left France over-governed and inordinately 'rent-seeking', its judiciary parasitic, its economy overtaxed and unenterprising. Perhaps England, more lightly governed, was in fact better served by its institutions. But it would be gratuitous to assert that this was more than one of the multitude of reasons why England prevailed. One might as well say that the relentless expansion of Russia that has been continuing with hardly a break for the last half-millenium was due to the benignness, suitability, and efficiency of her institutions—a claim that would be as startling as it is untestable.

If Institutional Darwinism, predicting the spread of institutions that help the survival of the fittest host civilization (rather than simply of the institutions that are themselves fittest to survive while being parasitic upon the host civilization), is not very good theory, it can hardly explain why the perfect state supersedes the imperfect one. The demonstrable capacity of the state to acquire the monopoly of the use of force bears no necessary relation to its ability to serve the host society. What it does 'prove' is its own fitness to survive as an institution, without prejudging whether it is predatory, parasitic, or benignly instrumental.

Plain non-normative Darwinism, under which it is trivially true that the perfect state was fitter because it has in fact obliterated the imperfect one and put an end to the state of nature, can of course be filled with content to make it non-trivial. Applied to the state, such a theory would give reasons why we should expect force in variable, geographically, ethnically, and culturally defined spaces to tend towards monopoly rather than, say, some competitive or oligopolistic equilibrium. The greater survival value of force-monopoly would have to be the analytic corollary of some acceptable and testable hypothesis about the world. The 'technology' of force might be such that 'increasing returns' accrue to a unit of force as the size of the force employed gets larger; if this were true over some definable space, there would be no equilibrium short of monopoly and no competing force could long survive. Alternatively, history composed of a series of random shocks (feuds, wars, marriages, calamities, great men, discoveries, inventions, etc.) might add up to some systematic, non-random effect which is biased in favour of centralized force. Other, less mechanistic, hypotheses could be constructed.

None of this, however, lends any particular comfort and support to the idea of an irrevocable social contract—an idea for which the emergence of the (perfect) state has to be an outcome that all persons in the state of nature would have willingly chosen had they been placed before such choice.

Reconciliation

The point of social contract theory is, of course, not why the state has emerged, but why rational men would unanimously consider it the best feasible instrumental solution to problems of social coexistence. There is built into the very foundation of the theory some more or less well argued proposition about coexistence being problematical, either quite insoluable in the state of nature (e.g. the war of all against all) or admitting only poor solutions (e.g. only self-enforcing agreements can count).

We have already noted the parallel course of a historical

development—the more or less gradual disarmament of individuals and groups and the concentration of force in the hands of states as Europe was emerging from the Middle Ages—and of the evolution of the contractarian ideology from its Thomist towards its Hobbesian form, which it has kept, unchanged in its essentials, despite its dilution by Locke and its mystifications by Rousseau, to the present day.

I use the word ideology advisedly; it is not generally pejorative, or if it is, it ought not to be. It has several functions and is composed of several phenomena. The ideology I propose to look at here is a bundle of related propositions about man's condition in society, whose function is to reconcile what is the case with what it ought to be in order for a given audience better to understand its own condition. 'Reconcile' is used as accountants use it when balancing two sets of figures, 'ideology' functioning as the 'balancing item'. One element in it is 'telling people what they want to hear' (confirmation of their beliefs), another 'telling some people what others want them to hear' (proselytizing, spreading a creed); an efficient, live ideology requires both. But to gain a significant audience and to endure (two tests which contractarianism has certainly met) an ideology must amount to more. For one, it can be a rationalization of a given state of affairs, showing why it fits our condition, why it is compatible with the interests or preferences of a given audience. It will be an argument for acceptance, given the costs of striving for something better. The ideology will then be legitimizing, it will protect a state of affairs. Its efficiency, however, will depend on keeping good measure and not doing outrage to the sense of reality of its audience. Whether a too Panglossian doctrine, such as the end-of-ideology view of interest-group democracy where political bargaining ensures that they all get a look-in and a fair share, or the jam-tomorrow theory of building socialism with its ever-receding goal staying permanently almost within reach, can legitimize and help conserve a state of affairs for long is uncertain.

Ideologies of the opposite intent, meant to rock the boat, also act as a balancing item between is and ought, reconciling the two by critical analysis and affirmation of the feasibility of a better goal. Thus, alienation, the deformation of man, can be deduced from the capitalist 'relations of production'; man must be restored to himself; socialist 'relations or production' are predestined to emerge and prevail. The audience of such an ideology finds its dissatisfaction with a given state of affairs founded and clarified, and is shown the bridge connecting it to a better one. Analysis and prescription, fact and faith, are, of course, inextricably mixed in both legitimizing and revolutionary ideologies.[8] The best statement of what they are and do is Schumpeter's:

> *For ideologies are not simply lies*; they are truthful statements about what a man thinks he sees . . . Though we proceed slowly because of our ideologies, we might not proceed at all without them.[9]

The *modus operandi* of contractarianism, which legitimizes the state by an argument ultimately rooted in individual preference (rather than in divine right, natural law, the order inherent in the essence of things, national interest, or positive law), needs to be made quite explicit. It seems to me that it can be broken down into logically distinct stages.

1. The perfect state puts an end to the state of nature. How does anyone know whether this is good or bad for him? The use of force is now reserved to the sovereign, its private use is ruled out by the disarmament of all; self-help, mutual aid, and bought help, largely dependent on threats versus counter-threats of force or the chances thereof, become weak if not altogether ineffective. Defence of one's interests is therefore ultimately contingent on the support of the state, as are threats or encroachments upon them. With the state's support on one's side, gains (including, of course, avoided losses) must be larger than in the state of nature. With the state supporting one's adversary, probable losses (including forgone gains) are also larger. The pair of alternative social-contract 'payoffs', as far as one can predict them, seems to straddle the pair of state-or-nature payoffs. In game-theory language, there is consequently no dominant strategy. One cannot tell whether the outside pair is worth more or less than the inside pair. If one could choose, one would have no compelling reason to choose one or the other prospect. Under some mechanistic rule of thumb (e.g. 'choose the prospect of the smaller loss even if it means accepting the associated prospect of a smaller gain'), however, it would seem actually more 'prudent' to choose the state of nature.

2. The argument now proceeds to show why the state will not

---

[8] Boudon (1987) nevertheless considers that categories of truth and falsity are largely applicable to ideological propositions.
[9] Schumpeter (1949), his italics.

blindly throw its weight one way or the other, for or against one's interest. If the probability of its supporting one interest rather than another can be assessed by reasoned judgement, one's preference for the state versus the state of nature can also be so assessed. This is *a fortiori* true if the probability is controlled, influenced by some known mechanism operated by the subject. We have here a crucial postulate in the contractarian ideology: unlike the old, pre-Hobbesian sovereign who was a *person* (no matter whether literally, or in the holistic sense of a composite body, a sum of parts, a collective entity) capable of having ends which may well have conflicted with the interests of the subject, the new sovereign is a mechanical *instrument*. It is subject to its subjects, it represents and responds to their interests or preferences, and has none of its own to pursue. Granted the postulate of the instrumental, non-autonomous state, there is no logical obstacle to the idea of some mechanism (constitution, 'social choice rule') totally controlling the way the state exerts its force. Installation of the mechanism does not entitle a person to expect the state to support his interests on balance, but helps him assess and sometimes even to influence the likelihood of its doing so.

3. It is alleged to be:

idiotic to say—'You and I have made a compact which represents nothing but loss to you and gain to me. I shall observe it so long as it pleases me to do so—and so shall you, until I cease to find it convenient.'[10]

While it is not particularly idiotic to seek such an agreement, it would be idiotic for another party to enter into it unless we both expected to be on the gaining side by virtue of our control over the operation of the state. However, if there is a losing side at all, some must be on it, even if it is not you and me. If the state's supporting some against others were a zero-sum game, entering into the social contract would involve collectively inconsistent expectations: all could not expect to gain and be right.

Unanimous preference for the state, in order not to be disappointed, presupposes some kind of positive sum, a two-edged concept at the best of times because of distributional considerations (who gets what?) and arguably meaningless if there are losers as well as gainers (who is to say that the gainers' gain outweighs the losers' loss?).

[10] Rousseau (1762), 178.

4. All renouncing the use of force must consequently not create any losers. It is true of every person who disarms himself when all others do, that

Instead of giving anything away, he makes a profitable bargain, exchanging peril and uncertainty for security, natural independence for true liberty, the power of injuring others for his own safety.[11]

5. However, the claim that in disarming nobody is giving *anything* away provided all others disarm is manifestly false. There is a visible trade-off; some might find it profitable and others not. Unanimous preference cannot be deduced from it. A stronger argument is needed which overrides the indeterminacy of trade-offs, the balancing of conflicting interests and competing ends, with some putting 'natural independence' above 'true liberty', others below it. The social contract must yield a good (or goods) that none put below natural independence *and* that only the social contract can yield.

6. Hence, the twin propositions that man-made public goods must be aborted in an inherent dilemma, and that the social contract can, and only it can, resolve the dilemma, are necessary to make whole the structure of the contractarian argument. They are the 'scientific' core any ideology must have in order to endure.

The propositions are supported by the common insight that if a benefit can be enjoyed without a contribution, there will be no contribution, hence there will be no benefit. However, a state executing the directions of a 'social choice' mechanism can suppress free riding and provide publicly whatever[12] goods and services,

---

[11] Rousseau (1762; 1960 edn.), 198. In our current jargon, he asserts that (a) the social contract has a positive sum; and (b) it is strongly Pareto-superior to the state of nature, i.e. all are gainers.

[12] Given the capacity to suppress free riding and force all to contribute resources, efforts, self-restraint, and conformity to rules and laws, a public good is whatever is *de facto* provided in this manner. The category goes obviously beyond the narrow schoolbook definition of public goods in terms of 'non-excludability' and 'joint supply'. A fuller treatment of these questions must await Part Two. It should already be clear, however, that since the state is an instrument for overcoming the need for a close nexus between contribution and benefit, it will uncouple them wherever and whenever the parties to the social contract signal by an agreed code that they would prefer to have no nexus, or only a weak one. It seems to me inconsistent with contractarianism to confine publicness to some category (e.g. the category of schoolbook public goods) other than the one defined by the preferences of the parties. To paraphrase Goering: it is the public that decides what is a public good.

social virtues, and co-operative behaviour norms would otherwise get caught up in the public goods dilemma.

7. The state is the necessary and sufficient instrument for solving the positive-sum, no-losers game of the public-goods dilemma. No matter how it came about in real time,[13] it would have been created by social contract, for it can be deduced from almost any widely accepted conception of human rationality that everybody would prefer such an instrument to be available. One need not seek the *cause* of the state if all approve of its *reason*: that suffices for its legitimacy.

Restricted Domain: The Hobbesian Asymmetry

Hobbes establishes the existence of a public-goods dilemma in one restricted domain, that of self-preservation. In that domain the dilemma is ubiquitous; as he defines civil peace (i.e. not *de facto* peace, but its certainty), it is impossible ever to attain it anywhere in the state of nature.

First, he sets up the right structure of 'payoffs'. Men want 'felicity' and the 'commodious life' as their real ends in this world, but need power instrumentally to reach them. Since 'the power of one restricteth and hindereth the effects of the power of another', the good they maximize is a difference, 'the excess of the power of one above that of another',[14]—hence his recurring references to 'eminence' and the competition among men for *relative* position, instead of the striving for absolute levels. That a person's purposes are served just as well by the lowering of others as by his own elevation is hardly indisputable, but it is deeply rooted in Hobbes's view of the world and I have no particular comment to offer beyond noting it. It is obviously relevant to the attractiveness of breaking the peace when both will lose, but the attacker expects to lose less than the defender.

Hobbes then makes sure that first use of force becomes a generally favourable strategy: 'where an Invader hath no more to

---

[13] The 'original establishment', as contractarians can safely admit, springs from 'usurpation or conquest or both', (Hume, 1748; 1960 edn., 151), 'formed by violence and submitted to by necessity' (p. 154).
[14] Hobbes (1640, 1650), ch. 8, sect. 4, quoted by Macpherson in the Introduction to Hobbes (1651; 1968 edn.), 35.

fear, than another man's *single power*' and the latter has planted, sown, or built, '*others* may probably be expected to come with *forces united* to dispossesse' him of his property, life or liberty; and 'the Invader again is in the like danger'—hence there is a 'diffidence of one another' and 'no way for any man to secure himself . . .'.[15] The twist in the argument by which the required conclusion is reached is that inequality of force in favour of its first user is built in by an opportune shift from the singular to the plural: the invader faces only the 'single power' of another, whereupon 'others come with forces united' to invade; the invader has become a band, a coalition of *invaders*, while the invaded still has only his 'single power'. Coalitions will form for attack, but not for defence. The invader, when it is his turn to be attacked, will be back in the singular mode and suffer from the same built-in disadvantage. Hobbes, of course, is perfectly entitled implicitly to assume that reactions are lop-sided and force will coalesce with force for attack only—but so are we to spell this out. The effect is to load the incentive and lighten the opportunity-cost of attacking: the payoff going to first use of force becomes generally positive. The Hobbesian Assymmetry between attack in a pack and defence in isolation makes it impossible to be confident in a react-only strategy. Deterrence cannot work.

The first fundamental law of nature is 'to seek Peace . . . as farre as he has hope of obtaining it', but since diffidence obliterates hope, 'he may seek . . . the advantages of Warre'.[16] Lest Hobbes's subtlety on this point be overlooked, let us make very clear that there need be no war for his reasoning to hold, and the prevalence of civil peace would not falsify it; for 'warre' is not actual war, but 'the time there is no assurance to the contrary',[17]—that is, in the state of nature, by its definition, war is always.

Civil peace is the instrumental good leading to the preservation of self and property. It is a public good which, given the 'strategies' of all other 'players', any particular player can enjoy without contributing to it by seeking peace. Hobbes has constructed a public good dilemma with respect to civil peace, as is readily apparent from the matrix in Figure 8, for two strategies and two players A and B. Let the preference-ranking for both players be,

[15] Hobbes (1651; 1968 edn.), 184, my italics.
[16] Hobbes (1651; 1968 edn.), 190.
[17] Hobbes (1651; 1968 edn.), 186.

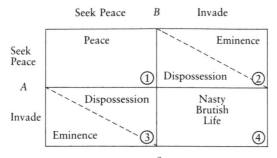

FIGURE 8.

in descending order: Eminence, Peace, Nasty brustish life; and Dispossession. Were *A* to seek peace, his payoff would be either peace or dispossession (of property, perhaps of life). If he invaded, he might get either eminence or the nasty brutish life that Hobbes regards as our common state-of-nature lot. Since they think and are placed alike, the same is true of *B* as of *A*. The pair of payoffs to 'invade' are superior to the pair of payoffs to 'seek peace' for either strategy adopted by the other player. Since 'invade' thus dominates 'seek peace', the game has a stable equilibrium solution in square 4. Both players prefer square 1, but it is inaccessible, for given the payoff rankings, no player could seek peace without the other invading him.

Hobbes's next and final step to prove that Leviathan is the unanimously preferred solution is to rule out overcoming the dilemma by private contract as 'vain breath'. It is evidently irrelevant to his main thesis whether Leviathan is a pre-contract entity, already formed by history, that the social contract endows with consentual legitimacy, or an entity that had first to be created by a social contract. Moreover, if civil peace could be secured both by private contract and by Leviathan, the social contract choosing the latter would require some additional explanation.

Chapter XIV of Leviathan lays out the alternative structures contracts can have. There is the transfer of 'Right together with that of the thing . . . as in buying and selling with ready money; or exchange of goods'.[18] We recognize this as the spot contract with promises being immediately and simultaneously performed, goods against ready money or other goods; it is, as we know, self-

[18] Hobbes (1651; 1968 edn.), 193.

enforcing and Hobbes is rightly unworried about it. There is next the contract where 'one of the Contractors, may deliver the thing . . . the other to perform his part at some determinate time after'.[19] We call this a half-spot and half-forward, or part-executed, contract. It is typically not self-enforcing and involves first-degree default risk. Hobbes calls it simply Pact or Covenant and continues to be unworried about unenforceability. On the other hand, he despairs of the third type of contract' wherein neither of the parties perform presently'.[20] He calls such contracts 'Covenants of Mutual trust'; our own term is 'forward' and that of the lawyers 'wholly executory'. We have noted earlier (Chapters 1 and 3) that such contracts are self-enforcing to some extent, depending on the particular variant (once-for-all or repeated, discrete, or continuous performances), while the default risk that attaches to them is only of second degree. Hobbes, however, implicitly treats a forward contract as the least self-enforcing, most default-prone type of the three, so much so that he declares it to be void, except that 'if there be a common Power set over them both . . . to compell performance; it is not Voyd'.[21]

A 'covenant of mutual trust' must break down if the parties to it rank the possible 'payoffs' in the order seen by Hobbes, act consistently with the preference-ranking *and* perform non-simultaneously, sequentially, in discrete terms. There is in that case a first and a second performer. If the first performer, true to the covenant, seeks peace, the second (if rational) must invade him. If, on the contrary, there is no first and second performer, i.e. if nature or the rules allow simultaneous play, there is no intrinsic difficulty about making performances mutually contingent (each keeping the peace only as long as the other does). A 'covenant of mutual trust' is then self-enforcing and does not *need* a common power above the parties to escape being 'void'; the mutually preferred outcome (square 1 in Figure 8) becomes accessible to the players, though it is arguably unstable under Hobbesian motivation without a third-party enforcer. The risk of second-degree default is rather like receiving a declaration of war, both parties resorting to arms at the same time; first-degree default, by contrast, is an attack by one party upon the other, who had first disarmed.

[19] Hobbes (1651; 1968 edn.), 193.
[20] Hobbes (1651; 1968 edn.), 196.
[21] Hobbes (1651; 1968 edn.), 196; cf. also p. 202.

One can further shore up Hobbes's construction and make the dilemma he posits hopelessly insoluble by excluding mutual contingency of performance. If neither party can see what the other is about to do, neither can regulate his move accordingly; hence A cannot induce B to go on performing as agreed by the threat of A's non-performance should B show signs of stopping to perform. B's lack of visibility, anonymity, his hiding in a crowd come close to satisfying this condition, making it impossible for A to rely on the covenant; and the same is true for B if A is hidden in a crowd.

This is arguably implicit in Hobbes, though it is as well to try and make it explicit. The other great implicit postulate of Leviathan is domain-restriction. Hobbes leaves it partly unexplained. In his scheme of things, people form a society and surrender their autonomy to the sovereign they create by contract, because they cannot otherwise solve the dilemma they run into in providing *one* public good, civil peace. Felicity and commodious living in the commonwealth happen as a matter of course. Once civil peace is provided publicly, commodious living is obtained privately by minding one's own business. No other public good is required. For felicity, the domain of the sovereign need not extend beyond that needed for preserving everyone's life and property.

In surrendering his arms and subjecting himself to the sovereign, man has done his bit for the commonwealth and has earned the right to attend to his private interests. Unlike the classical Greek or the modern democratic citizen, the subject in Leviathan neither needs nor is encouraged to meddle with public affairs, principally because there is little to meddle with in such a narrow, restricted domain. He concedes absolute, unchallengeable authority to the sovereign; for reasons that nowhere really become clear, the sovereign never uses his unchallengeable authority for extending the public domain and encroaching upon the affairs of the subject. It must be supposed (though the supposition does not sit well with the Hobbesian view of the monarch) that this is because the sovereign has no personality, hence no reason or desire to do anything of the sort; his will is merely a vector, a composite will of the subjects. His is a minimal state simply because his subjects need him for a minimal purpose only.

Restricted Domain: The Minimal State

This seems to me the proper juncture for inserting into the contractarian perspective the minimal-state argument of Nozick, an argument that he considers non-contractarian. Like Hobbes, he derives from individual preferences a rational motive for unanimous acceptance of a state-like arrangement involving the monopoly of the use of force. Unlike Hobbes, he explicitly seeks to fence off the domain over which the arrangement is to have effect. For 'social contract', we must substitute the vaguer 'arrangement' both because the underlying promises and performances are of a private, bilateral rather than 'social' character and because Nozick seeks to have the social result *emerge* from unco-ordinated individual choices, rather than being deliberately contracted for. His insistence on the formation of the state being an 'invisible hand process', if valid, would exclude viewing it as if it could have resulted from considered design and unanimous agreement.[22] However, despite his representation of the process as unintended—'How to Back into the Minimal State without Really Trying' is one of his chapter-titles—there is a strong element of 'closet contractarianism' in Nozick's construction, and it seems to me worth while trying to show how, despite the author's intention, it remains within the tradition of social-contract theory.

In what amounts to the pure state of nature, Nozick has invisible-hand causation call forth 'for profit' protective associations; help in deterring and redressing torts and in contract-enforcement, bought from them, is superior to self-help. One protective association becomes dominant. It is the incipient imperfect state in an imperfect state of nature. Those joining it find that they are better off if no one stays outside it. At this point, the argument moves over an awkward hurdle. The joiners want to have no stayers-out. Staying out causes some danger to the joiners. While this is insufficient ground for forbidding all staying out, the risk to the joiners nevertheless impairs the right of the stayers-out to stay out altogether at their discretion. If their right were intact, the joiners

---

[22] 'I . . . see little point to stretching the notion of [the Lockean] "compact" so that each pattern or state of affairs that arises from the disparate voluntary actions of separately acting individuals is viewed as arising from a *social compact*, even though no one . . . was acting to achieve it.' Nozick (1974) 132.

would have to offer them sufficiently attractive terms to use their discretion for joining. Two situations may now be encountered. In one, which Nozick does not consider, the stayers-out have such strong reasons for doing so that their opportunity cost of joining is 'too high'. The surplus gain available to all if all join is insufficient to offset the opportunity cost of the original stayers-out, and they would lose even if the entire potential gain were offered to them alone. In the other possible situation, envisaged by Nozick, universal joining is Pareto-superior. It is a non-pure, conflictual co-ordination game where joining by all produces a surplus payoff potentially sufficient to make at least some better off without making anybody worse off; the distribution of the surplus payoff, however, is a matter of extra-game bargaining. Co-ordination is aborted if bargaining over the distribution of its fruits fails.

Nozick rules out failure by introducing the category of 'unproductive exchange', to the effect that the joiners are entitled to expropriate the right of the stayers-out not to join, compensating them only for the actual disadvantage, if any, that they suffer if they join. Compulsory sale on terms fixed in this way means that the parties deal on the point of the contract-curve most favourable to the buyer-joiners rather than on the point most favourable to the seller-stayers-out, or somewhere in between.[23][24] We are unconcerned with the coherence of the ethics of the matter; whether axiomatic, undemonstrable, non-derived property rights are compatible with compulsory purchase is neither here nor there for our argument. What does concern us is the suspiciously circular manner in which the dominant protective agency takes and exercises the powers of a state-like entity to help along, by compulsory expropriation of opposing rights, the process of its own becoming state-like.

For it seems to be the case that co-ordination takes place, all join and the dominant protective agency becomes the monopolistic (minimal) state, because some have seen the advantage and preferred to join, while others have been forced to give up, against compensation we know to be sufficient but they were not asked to agree to, their preferred option not to join. However spontaneous

[23] Nozick (1974, ch. 4, especially pp. 84–6. For a painstaking unravelling of the tangle Nozick creates in arguing for his 'principle of compensation', cf. Mack (1981).

[24] It seems that with a bit of bad luck the sellers may even be forced to sell on terms that actually put them on to a lower indifference curve, i.e. make them worse off than they were to begin with. Cf. Nozick (1974), 145–6.

the action of the former, the exercise of expropriating the latter and forcing them to join is hardly conceivable without somebody, presumably the dominant protective agency, carrying it out and backing it with the threat of centralized force. Why the resulting state of affairs is said to 'arise from the disparate voluntary actions of separately acting individuals' is unfathomable; is this how we are to conceive a non-contractarian, spontaneous invisible-hand process?

By way of a control experiment to decide between unintended emergent effect and intentional social contract, Nozick confronts individuals with the explicit choice of staying out in the imperfect state of nature or creating the monopoly-of-force Minimal State; would their conscious choices reproduce the non-intended, emergent outcome of the invisible-hand process?[25] If in a two-by-two game A and B both join the sole available protective association, they both enjoy Protection as their payoff. If they both stay out, they preserve Autonomy. If A joins and B stays out, A enjoys Impunity (he is protected against B's acts, and his own acts can be sanctioned only by his association and then only if he transgresses the rights of its other clients, but not those of B), while B suffers Subjection, and vice versa if A stays out and B joins. The game matrix is as in Figure 9.

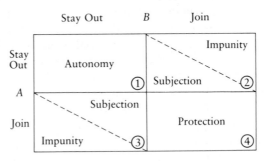

FIGURE 9.

The solution depends on the preference-ranking of the four payoffs: Impunity, Protection, Autonomy, Subjection. Impunity is evidently best and Subjection worst. But the ordering of Protection

---

[25] Nozick (1974), 122 ff. Nozick sets up a game matrix with no less than 16 pairs of outcomes, though only 4 are needed to obtain his result. In the text, I am taking modest liberties further to simplify the 'game'.

and Autonomy is an open question; a person may prefer either one or the other and yet be sane and reasonable. If both A and B prefer Protection, they both have 'join' as their dominant strategy; the solution is square 4, a stable, self-enforcing equilibrium-point, which they both prefer to square 1. Nozick, rightly, is not very interested in this case. The test of emergent effect versus intentional contract is provided by its opposite, when both players prefer Autonomy (or, as Nozick formulates it, when $x > 5$). Despite reversing the preference-ranking, the dominant strategy remains the same for each player, i.e. 'join'; each payoff in the pair associated with 'join' ranks higher than the corresponding payoffs in the pair associated with 'stay out'. Yet the resulting solution in square 4 is now sub-optimal, inferior to square 1. The players get Protection though they prefer Autonomy.

Due to the familiar public goods dilemma, if some players opted for Autonomy, others would free ride on it, resulting in Impunity for themselves, Subjection rather than Autonomy for the stayers-out. Co-ordination of every player's move on 'stay out' is therefore impossible without third-party enforcement, which Nozick, perhaps fairly enough, identifies with the state. He finds that it would be nonsensical to suppose that the players would conclude a social contract and create a state in order to achieve their preferred outcome of Autonomy, which in this context means not to have a state. Instead of being absurd and agreeing to abandon anarchy in order to be able to have anarchy, he concludes that they will let matters be, allow the non-co-operative dominant strategy to take its course and join the protective association. Once the awkwardness about obstinate stayers-out is resolved by their compulsory incorporation against compensation, the protective association becomes the Minimal State. Abstracting from this last, somewhat dissonant, phase, the outcome is unplanned and unintended. Its contractarian test ('would it have been unanimously agreed to if it had not come about for other causes?') is said to be negative, for such agreement—to have a state in order not to have one—would have been perversely self-contradictory. The product of the invisible-hand process cannot possibly be construed as if it had been, or could have been, produced by the social contract.

Since the hapless players are really in a cleft stick, it is as easy to read their conduct Nozick's way as the opposite way. Whatever they do, their action misfires. The means to their end negates it.

Their strategy is no more and no less absurd if interpreted as a social contract than as tacit acquiescence in the work of the invisible hand. Both interpretations offend against good sense. In one, we say that people can only have the autonomy they prefer if there is a state to enforce the co-ordinated 'stay out' strategy, repressing the dominant 'join'; yet they cannot have the state repress 'join' without joining it first. In the other, we claim that when people find themselves endowed with a state, they give up the aim of autonomy in anarchy, deterred as they are by the recognition that only the state could help them get there. Yet this is wrong-headed too; given that they are already endowed with a state, having to employ it in the pursuit of anarchy is no deterrent. Only avoidable costs deter.

Both ways of reasoning to justify 'joining' when one prefers to 'stay out' are incoherent if people are assumed correctly to foresee the consequences of each alternative strategy. Coherence can be restored by not making this ambitious assumption. In trying to transform the unstable Autonomy into a stable equilibrium by a social contract, the contracting parties need enforcement to repress the anti-social but individually compelling choice of 'join' which would menace the stayers-out. In accepting the state as enforcer, they admittedly defeat their purpose. But it would not be the first time, and assuredly not the last, that they sought one thing and got another. Arranging for repression of an anti-social option can perfectly well be intended to secure 'more freedom' yet result in less.

The mistake is a matter of wrong empirical *judgement*, naïvety, poor foresight or whatever, but not of faulty *reasoning*. Poor foresight restores the coherence between a preference for autonomy (or, in Nozick's terms, anarchy) and the acceptance of the state. Without such coherence, it is difficult to credit the emergence of the state, however minimal, to the invisible hand. With such coherence, unanimous individual preferences would ratify the emergence of the state: Nozick's theory would be swallowed up in the contractarian mainstream.

The reason I have inflicted upon the reader this wearying argument about the number of angels dancing on a pinhead was not to let him see the right answer at last, for after all this time its intrinsic interest is greatly diminished. However, it has some instrumental use for the argument about 'domain' that we will presently test. I expect to put the thesis that restricting the domain over which the state is to be used to bring about the best feasible state of affairs is inconsistent with the basic rationale of the social contract. Hence, consent-based, socio-contractual states are by their nature 'non-minimal'. It seemed to me worth the tedium to establish as a preliminary that it does not suffice to disavow the socio-contractual character of a state, to set up 'rights-based' constraints to limit its domain and to call it minimal, if its *raison d'être* is to be the instrument of individual preferences.

5

SOCIAL CHOICE

Various reasons have been put forward in political philosophy as sufficient to make man a consenting citizen. Provided they deduce his willingness to obey sovereign commands from a postulate of some form of individual rationality—man's attempt to find his best means–ends correspondence to maximize whatever he wants for himself or others—the reason proposed is always related to the effects he hopes or fears that *other* individual's actions may have upon *his* ends.

More narrowly, becoming party to an irrevocable social contract is justified by the object of ensuring uniformity of everyone's choice for the best in all cases where there is some presumption that, but for the social contract, they would either not be uniform or would not be for the best. Both of the latter alternatives would produce inferior outcomes—the first typically in the shape of some persons free riding on the contributions of others,[1] the second in the shape of there being no contributions. Such cases present conflictual co-ordination problems with an inferior and a superior solution. Uniform choice for the best, leading to the superior solution, is not necessarily ensured by individually rational free choices.

Uniform choice must be understood broadly. In its simplest form, it results from obeying such rules, or the detailed commands that implement them, as 'all shall drive on the left'; 'none must litter in the park'; 'all but the poor shall give to the poor'; 'all who benefit from a good shall contribute to it'. More complex uniform choices would ensue from obeying some such rule as 'all shall contribute as they benefit', the resulting conduct being non-uniform from one

---

[1] To say that an outcome where free riders benefit from the contributions of others is inferior is open to challenge. One could defend it by arguing either that unfairness is sufficiently bad in itself to outweigh the cost of reaching a different outcome, or that in the presence of free riding contributions will be inadequate, less than some optimum. Neither argument is very strong; one of the flaws of contractarianism is to treat them as self-evident propositions.

point of view (some contributing more than others) and uniform from another (all contributing their due).

Outcomes are inferior or superior with reference only to their rank in the preference-orderings of the contracting parties; having these orderings prevail when arranging for outcomes was in fact their ultimate reason for concluding the contract. One consequence of this is to exclude from the determinants of how highly an outcome is ranked all preference–independent standards.[2] God's will, virtue, natural right, taboo, duty, and precedent are not, of course, banned from the contractarian field of vision—in some versions of the theory, certain preference–independent standards, such as social solidarity or cultural homogeneity, must be widely adopted before a social contract can work at all—but they must operate by being 'internalized', by *entering into* individual preference-orderings. They must not be allowed to constrain or to override them, so to speak, from the outside.

For general purposes, it seems to me convenient to divide present-day contractarian thought into three branches, by and large associated with the names of Buchanan, Rawls, and Habermas. They share an insistence on unanimity as the necessary and *achievable* condition of the social contract. They all derive it from a rationality postulate, but in very different ways. Buchanan confines the unanimity requirement to agreement on rules of a high level of abstraction, where people no longer have identifiable interests capable of giving rise to conflicting preferences for rules. Rawls sets up a contract-concluding ('original') position, where persons are supposed to behave as if they had no distinct identities—hence anything some agree on is *ex hypothesi* agreed by all. Habermas, perhaps less conclusively, puts people in an 'ideal speech situation', where they teach each other jointly to define a set of generalizable interests none has reason to disagree with. Each of the three types of approach offers a solution of the co-ordination problem by getting round its conflictual aspect in the distribution of the 'payoff'.

Whatever degree of freedom may subsist about the form and content of the social contract, it is poorly drafted and cannot serve its purpose unless it includes three core clauses.

---

[2] For contractarians, the ranking of outcomes must not be influenced by 'some transcendental notion derived from God or Karl Marx'. Brennan and Buchanan (1985), 147.

1. The first is the Social Choice clause. It stipulates acceptance by all of a set of rules, or constitution, such that its proper application to any pair of feasible states of affairs always identifies one of the pair as the socially chosen one. One of the pair is necessarily the status quo, the other is a 'bill', a feasible alternative involving changes over some 'domain'. It may be desirable but not necessarily possible to have a rule that can identify the chosen one out of more than two feasible alternatives. There may be a subset in the set of domains, such that the social choice over the subset is always the status quo (e.g. a domain of 'inviolable rights'). We may call such a subset the 'exempt domain'. If the exempt domain is empty of content or, what comes to the same in practice, is filled with pious vacuities only, its complement extends over all feasible states of affairs and social choice has 'unrestricted domain'; it can decide anything.

2. The second core clause is the Enforcement clause. It provides for an agency, the state, and mandates it to identify and repress all individual actions that are contrary to the intent of social choices. This clause involves agreement by all to vest in the state the exclusivity ('monopoly') of all the functions that must be performed to carry out this mandate.

3. The indispensable core of the contract is completed by the third, or Disarmament, clause, which establishes the monopoly of force and ensures the effectiveness of the monopoly of functions agreed in the second clause. It acts as if all armed force which persons and their coalitions disposed of in the (imperfect) state of nature had voluntarily been transferred to the state, and civil rearmament agreed to be forever contrary to the intent of social choice. While the Enforcement clause expresses consent by the parties to have state force used against them under certain conditions, the Disarmament clause is irrevocable consent not to resist it, by making resistance or revocation of the contract impossible within its terms. (This clause may fail to achieve its purpose, and armed rebellion break out, in much the same sense as a marriage may break down under a matrimonial regime that does not provide for divorce.)

The core of the contract is necessary but not sufficient to define the operation of the state and the command–obedience relations between it and persons in society. More must be contractually stipulated, or left by the contract to be settled by delegation to an agreed procedure or to designated persons, e.g. a constitutional convention. In addition to the agreement on having a social choice rule at all, its substantive content (when do we say that an alternative is the chosen one?) must be specified, and the domain, restricted or unrestricted, within which it may select among alternatives must be stated. These two questions are considered as one in the standard axiomatic treatments of social-choice theory, but it seems to me clearer to separate them.

Unrestricted Domain

Would the contracting parties unanimously agree to create a domain exempt from social choice? Would the restriction be at least weakly 'Pareto-superior'? In more traditional language, if there were no constitutional limitation of sovereignty, would there be opposition to introducing any? Since the three core clauses are silent on the matter, there is some presumption, but no explicit assurance, that social choice is absolutely sovereign, that it can do anything feasible. However, the implicit intent of the social contract in the matter of domain needs to be discovered by analysis.[3]

Unrestricted domain implies that the social-choice rule is able to take some account of all individual preferences, ranging over any and all domains in taking stock of all alternatives. If it is never able to select a feasible state of affairs proposed by a certain bill, no matter how it ranks in individual preference orderings, we will say that the status quo the bill aims to change is exempt; the set of such protected status quos is the exempt domain. A clause establishing some such domain, to the effect that the social choice rule must never alter it, has to involve a genuine restriction. There may be bills stipulating feasible changes in the status quo which could, but never would, be adopted; individual preferences for such states of

---

[3] 'Totalitarian democrats' (to use Talmon's term) would not admit that any limitation of sovereignty could be implicit in the social contract. Nor would they consider it desirable, provided sovereignty was popular, i.e. the social-choice rule was democratic. In perspective, let us remember that for Rousseau *limiting* sovereignty is *denying* it: '. . . the right exercised by each individual over his particular share must always be subordinate to the overriding claim of the Community as such. Otherwise there would be no . . . real power in the exercise of sovereignty'. Rousseau (1762; 1960 edn.), 188.

affairs would be possible but utterly improbable. 'All our newborn children are to be killed' is a change in the status quo that no sane individual would prefer to letting them live. Banning such a bill is a pious superfluity, for the contingency that the social choice rule might operate in such a way as to adopt it is not one against which sensible contracting parties would want to be constitutionally protected. Nor could they—for if by mischance Herod became their king, the only practical domain-restriction would be to have no children. On the other hand, 'all incurably ill children shall be killed', while repugnant to many, may seem the charitable lesser evil to some. Should their preference be left out of account by putting innocent lives (and other 'inviolable rights') in the exempt domain? Or should the choice-rule let preferences have their way and the chips fall where they may?

In order to serve the fundamental purpose of the parties, the social contract must in some manner give rise to a choice-rule which is preference-dependent and standard-independent. It must select a state of affairs not for what it intrinsically *is* compared to some standard or norm, but for its superior ranking compared to the ranking of its alternatives in the preference-orderings of the parties.[4] In whatever manner the rule produces the choice *from the orderings*, it must not produce it from anything *else*.

Domain restriction contradicts this principle: it excludes certain states of affairs from selection for reasons that have to do with what they *are*, not with how well they are *liked*.

Over the exempt domain, preference does not prevail; some standard does. But this cannot correspond to the intent of the contracting parties. For if a standard is decisive, it either produces the same social choice as preference would have done, in which case it is redundant, or overrides preference and produces a standard-bound social choice. In the latter case, it acts as a genuine domain-restriction. If the social contract is an agreement to co-ordinate

---

[4] Connoisseurs of Arrovian social choice theory will recognize this as the Neutrality condition, or property, of the choice rule. It requires that if, under some distribution of individual preferences between two states of affairs, the rule chose one, upon a reversal of the preference-distribution it must choose the other, i.e. that it should pay no heed to states of affairs, but only to the sets of preferences they engender. For the rule, what counts is how well a state of affairs is *liked*, not what it *is*. Cf. Sen (1985), 1768–9, for an authoritative statement of the key role of Neutrality in the Arrovian (and, I would add, in all contractarian, standard-independent) theory.

choices in order that whatever can be bettered shall be, domain-restriction contradicts its object. Putting it differently, if it is agreed that the social-choice rule operates to maximize the just sum of preference-rankings—and in so doing it takes society as near as it can get to its most preferred composite goal, however defined—accepting an exempt domain is inconsistent with maximization. This latter argument, of course, depends on the social-choice rule in force being recognized as one that can both better identify the composite-goal (add up individual preferences to arrive at their correct, just sum) and take the contracting parties nearer to it than any other. If it were not, it might be rational to frustrate its operation by putting an exempt domain in its way, but it would be 'more rational' to replace the inadequate rule by a more adequate one.

Evidently, the social-choice principle that whatever can be bettered shall be, and that the elimination of an obstacle to this principle is itself a betterment, does not *dissolve* conflicts; it *resolves* them against the will of one or another party. This means that some contracting parties might, in certain cases, expect to be better off if the conflicting preferences of others did *not* prevail, thanks to *their own* interests being protected against potentially adverse social choice by a domain-restriction. This is a perfectly valid motive for restricting the domain; but since everybody cannot want to erect the *same* domain-restriction to protect his interest against everybody else's conflicting preference, agreement on any given exempt domain could not be unanimous *unless it were redundant*. Hence, no meaningful, non-pious domain-restriction can be implicit in the unanimous social contract itself.

Enforcement of Domain-Restriction

There is arguably no such intent-negating obstacle to post-contract constitutional limitation of sovereignty by *non-unanimous* decision. Some may manage to impose it over the opposition of others, delineating an exempt domain which they expect will protect their preferences against the risk that contrary preferences might otherwise prevail in social choice. Putting property relations in the exempt domain would be the most obvious example, the propertied having a sound reason for having property rights declared inviolable rather than subject to social choice, if the latter takes account of the preferences of the propertyless.

More sophisticated (if less robust) constitutional arguments have been marshalled around a different sort of non-unanimity, the discord between preferences and meta-preferences. The former are what the social choice rule is 'programmed' to translate into actual choices. The latter may inspire a wish that the former were different, or a fear that they might be.[5]

Everybody might be covetous, inconsiderate, disrespectful of the interests and preferences of others, and unwilling to put tomorrow's concerns above instant gratification. Yet everybody might wish (have a meta-preference) that his preferences were different and might like to prevent social choice from reflecting the ugly ones he does have.

One could exclude certain tempting but reprehensible alternatives by suitably extending the exempt domain. Alternatively, it may be that the ugly or merely imprudent preferences that we seek to frustrate by domain-restriction are those we fear today that we or our children might have tomorrow. Our meta-preference tells us to erect barriers today against the social-choice rule giving effect to these preferences in the future. The wish for other preferences than the ones we have is rationalized by the 'weakness of will' argument; the fear that future preferences might be other than present ones, by distrust of our future selves or of future generations. Without weakness of will or distrust or both, preferring that one's preference be overridden would be insane.

Where, however, do meta-preferences come from? And what makes the two halves of a split personality disagree with each other? Meta-preferences for plain preferences can always be explained by meta-meta-preferences and so on in an infinite regress, 'ends' at one level being judged and ranked as if they were the 'means' to ends at the next higher level. At some stage, however, the problem of a 'stopping-point' in the regress must be faced. The introduction of a multi-layered structure of preference-orderings in order to explain self-limitation and self-denial on preferential grounds inevitably pulls the argument beyond preference. Ultimately it is impossible to account for 'preferred barriers to preference' by going from layer to layer, without an ultimate stopping-point

[5] For the fundamental formulation of the thesis as regards persons, cf. Frankfurt (1971).

outside preference, anchored in some exogenous standard such as duty, virtue, faith, or precedent. Contractarian theories which claim to find an endogenous explanation of limited government and secure 'rights' liberties and immunities in rational choices that reflect preference-orderings only seem to me to delude themselves (or else to use a tautological concept of preference in terms of which any actual outcome is a preferred outcome).

Layered preferences are believed to supply the enforcement of domain-restrictions. A promise to oneself not to transgress a self-limiting rule is not a contract and involves no give and take, no contingency of one performance upon another. It is prima facie unenforceable. However, breaking the promise by letting one's preference prevail is said to involve a 'cost' because it is humiliating, shameful, dishonourable, damaging to self-respect. There must then be presumed to be an upper-layer ordering that places the preferences that would lead me to break my promise to myself, and the preferences that would cause me to feel shame for doing it, in some relation, one above the other; if shame prevails, my promise is safe. But this upper-layer preference, or the layer above it or the one above that, is a matter of standards, not of preferences in the ordinary meaning of the word.

Constitutional limitation is a promise by society to itself not to seek certain outcomes that it might be tempted to seek, not to 'violate rights', not to let preference-aggregating social choice prevail in some exempt domain. The idea of enforcement of this promise by the state against a society that wants to break it is absurd and self-contradictory if the state is society's instrument, programmed to execute its instructions. The absurdity is formally declared to be overcome by a particular device that helps divide the instrument into separate 'branches'; if the executive branch were to receive an unconstitutional instruction, the judiciary branch (e.g. the constitutional court) would tell it not to execute it. The real solution, if there is one, resides in no formal device such as the separation of state *functions* (which has come misleadingly to be called 'separation of *powers*'), but in the right balance between temptation and shame, between the charms and attractions of a certain social alternative and the embarrassment of ignoring the constitution or the moral and material awkwardness of getting round it. Once more, we find the enforcement of domain-restriction, such as it is, either anchored in standards of national or personal honour and respect for precedent, or not at all. The constitution is safe if the temptation to transgress it is not very strong, and the safest constitution is undoubtedly one that restricts social choice least.[6]

Non-Fatuousness

We must briefly revert to unanimity, mainly in order to guard against a misunderstanding. It is inherent in the concept of a valid contract that the parties had agreed to it; the social contract is unanimous, uncoerced. It is an agreement to exert and to accept coercion or the threat of it in imposing social choices. The social-choice rule is inherently an anti-veto rule, designed to produce non-unanimous decisions. It would be fatuous unanimously to agree to obey a social-decision rule that required unanimity, for no previous agreement is needed always to accept one's own decisions.

Non-fatuousness, then, is that property of the decision rule which enables it to impose the choice of a state of affairs upon those contracting parties who would prefer another. It may be that living under a fatuous rule, requiring unanimity, would itself be conducive to unanimity, for people would make greater efforts to reach compromises. This is as it may be: the history of the *liberum veto* (in seventeenth- and eighteenth-century Poland, in the United Nations Security Council) is not encouraging. It may even be the case that a unanimity rule is a perverse incentive to preference-concealment, sham opposition with a view to be bought off dearly, given the value to a group of obtaining the agreement of its last hold-out member who alone obstructs a decision. These speculations point both ways and can hardly be conclusive in favour of unanimity.

In an argument that seems to me to treat the social choice rule as if it were the prior and more fundamental social contract itself,

[6] In the nationwide debate culminating in the refusal of the US Senate to confirm the nomination of Judge R. Bork as Associate Justice of the Supreme Court in October 1987, a columnist in the *New York Times* attributed Judge Bork's unpopularity to his 'grudging and ungenerous interpretation of the Constitution': precisely. It is the nomination as guardians of the Constitution, of ungrudging and generous interpreters, that makes for what has come to be called a 'living constitution'. A 'living constitution, attuned to mainstream opinion', will, if anything, anticipate popular desires rather than barring the way to them.

Elster seeks to establish a distinction between motives fit for the market-place and for the forum,[7] arguing that social-choice theory deals with motivation that belongs to the market-place, creating 'citizens' sovereignty' by analogy with 'consumer sovereignty'. This can hardly be right: social-choice theory does not deal with a particular class of motives ('fit for the market-place'). It is perfectly general in letting motives be what they will; it is designed to respond to 'other-regarding' and 'self-censoring' ones no less than to any others; nor does it shut out politics as seen in the Habermas imagery, as a process of reconciling motivations. (For what social-choice theory does do in this respect, cf. Sen,[8] whose account could probably not be bettered.) One might simply like to add, benefiting from Elster's point as a foil, that non-fatuous social-choice theory *begins* where both 'consumer sovereignty' and 'citizens' sovereignty' *end*. It is a theory of individual *non-sovereignty*, where the set of persons for whom a state of affairs is chosen can be larger than or different from the set that chooses it. Since the overlap of the two sets is allowed to be incomplete (it would be complete if each citizen could 'decide for himself', for then both sets would contain only the one citizen and there would be no social choice), at least some individuals can be overridden by others, which contradicts their sovereignty, whether consumer, citizen, or anything else.

Predisposed Rules

I have attempted to show that while people are unanimous in agreeing to the social contract, they cannot be unanimous in agreeing to a non-redundant *restriction of the domains* over which social choice is to operate, for, if some have reasons for exempting one domain, this is precisely because others have reasons for wishing social choice to prevail there. The rule by which social choice proceeds to select alternative states of affairs *within* the domain, restricted or not, is similarly inconsistent with unanimity, and for basically the same reasons. In fact, the self-begotten choice rule and its legitimacy are a particularly fragile aspect of contractarianism, where a social-choice rule is itself 'socially chosen'. For if its operation is meant to resolve conflict, it is liable to favour some

[7] Elster (1986a), 111.
[8] A. Sen (1986), 233–6.

over others and is consequently inconsistent with unanimity. Therefore its choice requires a prior choice rule which is itself both non-fatuous and legitimate. Choosing this prior rule, in turn, requires a rule that is prior to *it*, and so forth.

The main contractarian thesis is that as we proceed in justification from a rule to a meta-rule and then perhaps to a meta-meta-rule, we finally reach heights of constitutional generality, publicness, and longevity such that a 'veil of uncertainty' will shroud the way these rules may affect our particular interests.[9] We just would not be able to judge whether they would be more likely to promote or to hinder them, both because they are general and because we cannot predict our long-run interests except for knowing that we will want *some* social-choice rule. (This 'veil of uncertainty' is meant to be a *description* of facts—it asserts that people actually cannot guess which constitutional rules will favour or penalize them—and not a *prescription*, as the 'veil of ignorance' in Rawls's *A Theory of Justice* (1972), of what people must not know about themselves in order to choose just rules.)

Let us revert to co-ordination. In pure co-ordination, the efficient solution produces a surplus 'payoff' which distributes itself among the participants. The distribution is inherent in the solution and is not separately agreed or imposed. In non-pure co-ordination, however, the distribution is not determined by the efficient solution itself. Hence, it becomes the subject of latent or overt conflict. It is, for instance, impossible to apply the social-choice rule for overcoming some public-goods dilemma without, by the same token, deciding the incidence of the required contributions upon different persons (categories, groups, classes) and, by implication, eventual free-rider benefits as well. Whatever else social choice is about, it is about the public provision of goods and services, and about taxation, both in the very widest sense; fundamentally, it is about taking and giving, about relaxing or severing altogether the nexus between contribution and benefit.

The 'veil of uncertainty' argument is right in either of the two following instances:

1. it is possible to devise a set of constitutional rules that is decisive, i.e. capable of identifying the 'socially chosen'

---

[9] Buchanan and Tullock (1962); Buchanan (1986) 171.

alternative from any pair of feasible states of affairs, without being *predisposed* to favour particular subsets of society;

2. if it is possible to choose a set of predisposed constitutional rules such that individuals cannot judge the likelihood of finding themselves in favoured social subsets.

Under Non-Fatuousness, the constitution generates social choices that deal with co-ordination involving both efficiency and distribution. These choices could be *random*—for example, within a bargaining range the distribution of benefits from co-ordination, or the burden of contributions thereto, could be decided by rolling dice. Although *impartial*, the method would not be a choice *rule* in the accepted meaning of a social-choice rule, a meaning whcih implies *non-randomness* in that it must respond to preferences.

A rule capable of generating distributional choices is necessarily predisposed towards the distributional preferences of those entitled under the rule to make the social choice. One rule (to take the elementary example of choosing the incidence of contributions to public goods) will quite obviously be predisposed to select a poll tax, another a proportional, and a third a progressive tax. If it is a 'meta-rule' intended to generate the rule (as Hayek might wish to put it, if it is 'law' rather than 'legislation'), it will be likewise predisposed to generate the particular rule that is predisposed to make the particular selection—for otherwise it would be fatuous, irrelevant to and incapable of resolving given types of conflict. Consequently, it is immaterial whether the 'original' constitutional choice is among kinds of outcomes, or among rules that are predisposed to generate given kinds of outcomes, or among 'meta-rules' that are predisposed to generate given rules. There is, contrary to the orthodox view of the matter, no breach of continuity between choosing within rules and choosing rules. At whichever level the choice is made, the chosen alternative must be logically capable of giving rise to a probability judgement p, that it will be favourable, and a residual judgement $1 - p$ that it will be unfavourable, to the interests, preferences, etc. of any given social subset, without the least prejudice to the insight, quality of information, or political understanding that goes into that judgement.

Condition 1, then, looks very much like looking for the black albino: a rule in whatever layer is either *impartial* and irrelevant to the resolution of distributional conflicts, or *predisposed* to resolve them in some particular way, *no* predisposition ($p = 1 - p$) being a special limiting case which there is no particular reason to expect to find.

Condition 2 is only superficially less forbidding. Let there be a conservative meta-rule which is more likely than its radical rival to generate rules favouring the distributional status quo, while its predispositions in other domains are either similar to those of the radical rule or do not matter to a person called upon to make a constitutional choice. If condition 2 held, this person would be equally disposed to accept either the conservative or the radical meta-rule, whichever looked easier to get agreed, for he would not know whether he had an interest in maintaining the distributional status quo or in changing it.

For reasons that are discussed more fully in the Appendix to this chapter, under 'standard-independent', preference-governed choice-rule changes in the status quo favouring the poor generally prevail over those favouring the rich. (The precise borderline between poor and rich depends on the specifics of the choice rule—it runs through the median person under bare majority rule.) The person we are considering may be rich in this sense and prefer the conservative rule (or vice versa if he is poor). However, the 'veil of uncertainty' is supposed to deny him such knowledge mainly on the grounds that his being rich or poor, and the side he is on in conflicts over distribution, are transient matters. Yet if they are (which is by no means evident if there is a time-discount that leaves little weight to his position and interests in those distant future periods in which his place in society is most likely to differ from his place today, since they are the most thickly 'veiled by uncertainty'), he has a second, more fundamental level of real or putative self-knowledge to guide him. He has, or thinks he has, a certain character, background, and other moral endowments, and confidence or mistrust in his innate luck. It is impossible for a rational person to reconcile this sort of self-knowledge with an indifference to the pre-disposedness of social-choice rules. When fixing the rules of basketball, tall and short persons cannot unanimously prefer to place the basket at the same height, nor should sensible players with long and short purses advocate the same table-limits at poker. On the contrary, prudence alone might dictate that if we are differently placed in life, among rules liable to affect our places in life, you should reject the ones I propose.

In sum, the conditions under which a social-decision rule would be unanimously preferred or judged indifferent to another require that, one way or another, those called upon to choose the rule should ignore their particular preferences and interests, becoming either superhuman Founding Fathers or subhuman zombie clones of each other. Failing this, the social-choice rule must itself be selected by non-unanimous 'social choice'; the logical and moral circularity involved gets no less unsatisfying for being disguised.

Agility and Sluggishness

The predispositions of collective-decision rules to produce kinds of outcomes can be considered in an even more general perspective. Let us first sort out two main types, 'mandates' and 'aggregations'.

1. We mandate a person or subset of persons A to make all social choices for our set. The mandate is either for a definite period, non-revocable and non-renewable, or else it is perpetual.[10] The priesthood, or a dynasty with precise rules of succession (such as the alleged Salic law), an aristocracy or an oligarchy, a council of elders, the three wise men, or the self-perpetuating Central Committee of a totalitarian party have historically filled such a role. The choice made can still be said to be preference-based if our agreement to it can be construed to mean that

(a) we have a meta-preference for A's preferences; or

(b) we think A can best divine our own preferences.

If A is a holistic entity with a single mind—as would be the case, for instance, if the ideal image of the Leninist party, its ends and ends–means calculations, constantly unified by the process of 'democratic centralism', were accepted—all is well with the rule. Likewise, no problem arises if A is a single person, the prince or the dictator. However, if A lacks internal homogeneity, the preferences (or the judgements about our own preferences) of its several minds must themselves be aggregated to produce a decisive choice. Let us tag

[10] If the mandate is indefinite but revocable, or renewable, its maintenance becomes subject to the continuing responsiveness of the mandated subset to the wishes (aggregated preferences) of the mandating set. The arrangement is too precarious to be a genuine mandate. It is designed to produce the sort of results indirectly that the rule used for revoking or renewing the mandate would produce directly. I would subsume such a precarious 'mandate' under 'aggregation'.

this a 'second-order aggregation problem', to distinguish from the first-order one, to which we now turn.

2. We want the rule to produce choices binding for our whole set by taking some account of the preferences of every one of us; choice is then the produce of some sort of first-order aggregation. Tacitly, or explicitly, we must have agreed on a convention of integrability; we do not hold it to be meaningless to compose a homogeneous sum out of our heterogeneous preferences ('adding apples to oranges'). The convention looks more acceptable if instead of preferences (which can at best be inferred), we claim to aggregate preference-expressions *and* allow only one mode of expression, voting. Two main options become available.

(*a*) Each of us gets one 'yes' or 'no' vote to cast on any pair of alternatives, e.g. 'yes' for a bill, 'no' for the status quo, and our votes are simply counted to yield a single (positive or negative) algebraic sum[11] (as under simple majority rule), or some other relation between the two sums of positive and negative votes (as under qualified majority rules). Under this option ('Anonymity'), the response of the social-choice rule to every preference-expression is the same no matter *whose* expression it was. Translated into the language of 'social' or 'collective' utility-maximization (which can be done for heuristic purposes, without calling for a dead language to be resuscitated for ordinary speech), using this option means that the rule maximizes successfully if all the preferences the votes have expressed are *both* interpersonally comparable *and*, on comparison, have been found to have equal weight. Each of these conditions is hard enough to take singly, and harder together.

(*b*) The weighting of votes is accorded some intrinsic merit, because a social-choice rule which can take some account of the intensity of a *preference*, the importance of an *interest*,

---

[11] '. . . take from the expressions of these separate wills the pluses and minuses—which cancel out, the sum of the difference is left, and that is the general will'. Rousseau (1762; 1960 edn.), 193–4. The French original is even more hair-raising: literally, the pluses and minuses 'mutually destroy each other' ('*s'entre-détruisent*'). Those unfamiliar with the *Social Contract* must bear in mind that despite the amazing ease of the operation he describes above, for Rousseau the algebraic sum of the yeses and noes only expresses the general will if the voters ('a blind multitude') are *not mistaken* about it. Rousseau (1762; 1960 edn.), 204.

the value of *knowledge*, and the degree of a *concern* has
some claim to generating better results than one that is
designed not to do so. For such a claim, however, one needs
an independent standard for gauging the goodness of results,
the search for which would take us into deep waters.[12]
Rather than making the ambitious claim that weighted voting
generates better results, it may more modestly be said that it
generates more coherent ones, for if weights approximate
preference-intensities, weighted votes can be aggregated
without risking intransitive (irrational) rankings of more than
two alternatives.[13] The decisive argument about weighted
voting, however, seems to be the quite down-to-earth one,
that there are simply too many competing criteria for
distributing weights to voters. Once the more outlandish
ones are discarded, a large number are left, each of which is
of comparable merit to every other. None stands out as
salient, conspicuously easier to agree on than the others.[14]
Hence, it is hard to conceive of an influential social-choice
ideology in favour of a particular system of vote-weighting
('one extra vote for every three years of school, one extra
vote for every three years by which the voter's age exceeds
fifty years'), in the place of the powerfully simple ideology of
no weights ('one man, one vote').

The aggregation of everybody's unweighted vote can, nevertheless,
involve weighting between 'yes' and 'no' votes if the decisive subset,
needed to declare an alternative the 'social choice' for the whole set

[12] The result r chosen by social choice rule x has to be better than the result s
chosen by rule y, in some sense other than that it would be 'socially chosen' by some
third rule z. The relative goodness of two non-unanimous choices cannot merely
mean their relative ranking by a third non-unanimous choice.

[13] Bernholz (1986) has shown that the same result, as well as certain other
advantages, can be obtained by decentralizing decision-rights, so that instead of all
voters pronouncing on all questions, rights to choose between different pairs of
states of affairs are assigned to different subsets of voters; in the limit, each voter
decides over one pair. If there are enough (genuinely different) states of affairs to
choose from, no stable subset of society will be able to act as a potential blocking
minority on all of them (non-oligarchy). A link between Bernholz's decentralized
solution and the 'intensities of preferences' solution can be established by making the
assignment of decision-rights over designated pairs of alternatives negotiable. People
would trade decision-rights according to the intensity of the concern or preference
they felt about each issue. Evidently, the more decentralized the choice, the less
'social' it is; in the limit, every citizen is sovereign and every choice is individual.

[14] The concept of 'easier to agree on than less salient alternatives' is due to
Schelling (1963), esp. pp. 111–15, who calls it a 'focal point'.

concerned, is not symmetrical as between the status quo and a bill seeking to change it. 'One man, one vote' is in such cases split into two rules, 'one man, one yes' and 'one man, one no', but yeses and noes count differently. In Figure 10 we can see the most fundamental predisposition of choice rules, that to agility or sluggishness, being generated by the relative weighting of yeses and noes.

Social Choice				
Veto	Aggregation Rules			No Veto
'NO' is Overweighted		Unweighted	'YES' is Overweighted	
Unanimity	Super Majority Rule	Tiebreaker is decisive	Minority Rule	One 'Yes' suffices
Sluggish			Agile	

FIGURE 10.

Let a person consider his post-social contract constitutional choice. The basic function of the constitution will be to fix how we may accept or reject 'bills' proposing to alter the status quo. The agenda, or 'menu of bills', is generated by some process I will leave unspecified. In a period n bills are proposed together on the menu, or in a random sequence; each is voted upon separately. Let the person expect to rather like m bills and rather dislike the rest; the probability of his preferring any bill on the unknown menu to the known status quo is m/n. Evidently, if $m > n - m$, he expects things to go better for him and for those he loves, under 'agile' rules. They overweight 'yes' votes, making it easier for bills to pass than to fail. The converse is the case of $m < n - m$; he would then want a 'sluggish' rule, predisposed towards the status quo. (Note that under a very agile rule, where a handful of votes suffices to pass a bill, another handful is easily found to pass one that cancels its effect upon the status quo. Under such a rule, groups of voters would keep 'rocking the boat', in turn making and unmaking contrary states of affairs, unless some stabilizer rule were added to prevent this or to slow it down.)

If he has insufficient reason to expect more bills to be good than bad (and vice versa), or to suppose that the good done to him and those he cares for by a good bill will be greater than the bad done by a bad bill, the person concerned cannot have a reasoned preference for the agenda of bills as a whole or the status quo as a whole. He would then be indifferent between sluggish and agile rules.

Since he can vote under any rule considered, he can improve the odds of a good bill winning over the status quo and the status quo winning over a bad bill by casting his own vote purposefully. However, the improvement (whether perceptible or negligibly small) is the same under agile as under sluggish social-choice rules, and fails to provide a reason for opting for one rather than the other any more than for going for the golden mean.

Equiprobability I[15]

How does one account for the prominence of bare majority rule in social-choice rules both at the level of society as a whole and of other collective entities which accept decisions taken non-unanimously as binding? Is there a basis for the implicit belief that majority rule is prominent and widespread for the very good reason that it is *best* in some sense, giving more satisfaction than either more sluggish or more agile rules?

We have argued earlier that it is inconsistent with the *raison d'être* of the Hobbesian, irrevocable social contract to have social choices made under a rule which selects states of affairs for what they *are* (standard-bound rule) instead of for how well they are *liked* (preference-based rule). If this characterization of the social contract is valid, sluggish rules which discriminate in favour, and agile ones which discriminate against, a state of affairs because it happens to be the status quo should be ruled out *on this ground alone*. (Discriminating in favour of a state of affairs because of what it *is* violates the Neutrality axiom of social-choice theory— though this fact alone need not particularly impress a person searching for the rule that would best suit his purpose.) However, there are other, more positive arguments to the effect that simple

---

[15] Equiprobability I plays a role in the acceptance of simple majority rule, Equiprobability II (ch. 6) in accepting to be a 'sucker' rather than a free rider. The resulting parallel between majority rule and being a sucker is purely fortuitous.

majority rule will have to be the social-choice rule if a number of sensible conditions are to be met.[16]

If everybody else is allowed one vote, given the menu of bills and given some rule of vote-aggregation, the probability of the social choice being what a given person wanted depends directly on the probability of everybody else voting the way he did. No matter how ill-disposed the menu of bills is towards him and no matter how agile the choice rule, if the probability of others voting 'yes' only when he votes 'yes' is very high, very few bills will pass that he dislikes. Conversely, if there is a high probability of others voting contrarily to him, the bills that pass will tend to be bad for him, even though the legislative damage to his interests and preferences may be limited by a sluggish choice rule and a largely innocuous menu of bills. There is a central case where, for a given person, other people's interests and preferences and the menu of forthcoming bills are expected to be such that the probability of *anybody voting the same as anybody else* is ½, hence the probability of x voters being unanimous is

$$\frac{1}{2^{(x) - 1)}}.$$

Let us call this Equiprobability I for short.

Under Equiprobability I, given that everyone else is as likely as not to vote with him, everyone would expect to do best under the barest of bare majority rules, where the probability of the bills he likes passing and those he dislikes failing is at its maximum.

As a corollary, the sluggish super-majority rule would maximize a person's chances of social choice favouring him if he were more likely than the average to vote *against* a random bill. The agile minority rule would, on the contrary, favour him if he was more likely than the average to wish to change the status quo and vote *for* any random bill.

The plot thickens somewhat if a random bill is as likely as not to be beneficial, but the distribution of expected benefit and harm over the menu of bills is so unequal in extent and intensity that simple averaging of good and bad bills will not do. If some extremely menacing or highly beneficial bills, or both, have to be envisaged, constitutional rules ought to be evaluated as if account were taken of the (cardinal) utilities and (numerical) probabilities of each bill.

[16] Cf. May (1952); Taylor (1969).

This is the prudential way to go, but it is obviously a very poor likeness of any conceivable kind of *de facto* search for favourable constitutional rules.

Finally, the post-contract individual, on the point of deciding where he should stand in an imaginary constitutional convention which will somehow choose the rules of social choice, must face the prospect that the menu of bills that will be fed into the mill of social choice, once the latter is duly constructed, is neither exogenous nor random. If individuals can not only express preferences for given bills, but initiate some (or have 'political entrepeneurs' do it for them), the proposals that will appear on the 'menu' for resolving distributional conflicts, primarily in the domains of resource-allocation for alternative public goods and of taxation, will themselves be the emergent result of alternative winning coalitions under the prevailing choice rule.

This is perhaps best grasped through a specific example. A super-majority rule of three-quarters will give rise to a preponderance of distribution bills favouring the poorest three-quarters of the voters. They will always constitute the dominant winning coalition in matters of distribution, the total 'payoff' available to them by discriminating against the richest one-quarter being superior to the payoff available to any three-quarters from any other less rich quarter, or from any lesser fraction than one-quarter. Analogous predictions can be made for the redistributive implications of any other preference-based social-choice rule. Under one-tenth minority rule, the dominant winning coalition will be the poorest one-tenth.

Equiprobability I, then, must rest on one of two conditions. One would be a person's failure to comprehend the intrinsic distributional consequences of social-choice rules. This is the sort of failure that is reflected in bedtime tales about government limited to the preservation of life, liberty and property, government that is democratic and minimal at the same time.[17] The other condition, to which so many arguments lead as do roads to Rome, is lack of self-knowledge, hence lack of any realization on the part of a person that he belongs, or is likely to belong in the future, to one part of

---

[17] On this point, it is hard to improve on Burke: 'In vain you tell me that Artificial Government is good, but that I fall out only with the Abuse. The Thing! The Thing itself is the Abuse!' Burke (1757; 1982 edn.), 67. For Burke's 'abuse', modern political science tends to substitute 'agency problem', while political oratory mostly uses 'bureaucracy', 'electioneering', 'pork barrel', or 'personality cult', as the case may be. Seemingly disparate, these terms are all on the same level of argument.

society rather than another and consequently has a vested interest in an agile or a sluggish constitution. Why such lack should be deemed morally meritorious, and why the logical consequence of Equiprobability, the preference for the most democratic of rules, should be invested with solemn normative significance, is a question I am unable to answer without resorting to circular reasoning.

Accepting Command where Contract Fails

This seems to me to wind up our review of the contractarian case. In a 'paradigm shift' that has run most of its course from Aquinas to Hobbes, the 'sovereign' has become the 'aggregate of preferences'. The social contract now has, as its essential rationale, the unanimous refusal of all to live with the public-goods dilemma of the state of nature. Overcoming it is a superior outcome for all. Willing the end, they will the means, the submission to a social-choice rule, accepting command where contract fails. The legitimacy of the entire construction is proved by its deduction from a postulate of individual rationality; if it had not emerged from multiple historical causes, rational men would have chosen to erect it.

It is ironical or confusing, or both, that the logical core of the social contract, and of the contractarian ideology reconciling it with the facts of social life, is precisely the purported failure of contract. The core thesis (formally a 'prisoners' dilemma') is that where reciprocal performances are not mutually contingent and where benefits do not depend on contributions there are no contractual contributions and hence no benefits. This dilemma holds for civil peace and the rule of law no less than for any other good that society decides shall be provided publicly.

Part Two of this book is mainly an argument intended to show the spurious nature of the dilemma and the possibility of non-commanded solutions. Common sense suffices to find conditions, which are not unduly demanding, under which even single-mindedly motivated persons would voluntarily contribute resources, self-restraint and decent conduct to the provision of public goods. It turns out, however, that much the same institutions whose claim to legitimacy was socio-contractual and whose acceptance was predicated on the public-goods dilemma would tend to emerge almost by inadvertence, in largely unintended ways, even in a society that has taught itself to produce public goods by contract. The burden of the concluding chapter of Part Two is that, contrary to social-contract theory, there is no valid reason for calling these institutions legitimate and regarding the results of their interactions as something we have willingly accepted and should hold in respect.

APPENDIX: REDISTRIBUTION

I

For every pie, there is a pastry-cook who must have baked it for a reason. He did it under conditions which may or may not continue and bring about the baking of another pie. For these production-bound causes, the pie already belongs to someone and does not pose a distribution problem. Manna from heaven, on the contrary, is an example of a non-produced good waiting to be distributed.

If we abstract from the pastry-cook, we can conceive of a pure, once-and-for-all pie-distribution problem. *A priori*, anybody may get any share, from getting the whole to getting none of it. How much will anybody get? It is a well-known result in social-choice theory that a pure distribution problem among three or more people has no stable solution under majority rule. For any given division of a pie, adopted by a majority vote, another can always be found which will be chosen in preference to it.[18] Though composed of coherent, hence transitive, individual preferences, majority-determined 'social' preference for distributions will be intransitive, i.e. seemingly incoherent.

This is illustrated by showing the individual rankings of *given* distributions; the incoherent social ranking results from coherent individual ones. With three voters, Tom, Dick and Harry (who may be individuals, groups, classes), the rankings by each voter of three proposed distributions, D_1, D_2, and D_3, are:

Tom $D_1 > D_2 > D_3$
Dick $D_3 > D_1 > D_2$
Harry $D_2 > D_3 > D_1$

[18] Ward (1961).

Two votes out of three decide the social ranking. Tom and Dick vote for D_1 rather than D_2, Tom and Harry for D_2 rather than D_3, and Dick and Harry for D_3 rather than D_1. An endless cycle of majority choices will follow the self-sustaining sequence D_1, D_3, D_2, etc. However, a different set of individual rankings could very well give rise to a coherent, transitive 'social' ranking and no cyclicality. For instance:

Tom $D_1 > D_2 > D_3$
Dick $D_3 > D_2 > D_1$
Harry $D_1 > D_2 > D_3$

Expressed as three ways of dividing £100, it is immediately obvious why the 'social' choice of D_1 is now stable if D_2 and D_3 are its only alternatives:

	D_1	D_2	D_3
Tom	£40	£30	£20
Dick	£30	£50	£70
Harry	£30	£20	£10

So far, then, we have merely demonstrated the not very novel proposition that three (or more) distributions, no less than three (or more) alternatives of anything else, may or may not be the object of voting paradoxes. As long as we are dealing with choices among given distributions, we cannot say anything more exciting than this, for it is clearly possible to find three distributions D_1, D_2, D_3, such that their 'social' ranking is transitive and the voting for them non-paradoxical.

II

What makes the pure distribution problem interesting, however, is that when the alternatives are not exogenously given, but can be influenced by the social-choice mechanism itself, the only distributions which become available for choice are such that 'social' choices among them are unstable.

Let us envisage the problem as a three-person majority game with unrestricted domain (i.e. anything goes provided at least two out of three want it), and a constant sum to be divided. Let there be an initial distribution where Tom has £50, Dick £30, and Harry £20. There are three possible two-player coalitions. The maximum payoff sum available to each majority coalition is the initial share of the third or minority player.

Coalition:	Tom and Dick	Tom and Harry	Dick and Harry
Payoff:	£20	£30	£50

Each player seeks to be part of the winning coalition. To succeed, he must induce one other player to join him. Under a first, tentative distrubution rule, his sole means to this is to offer the other player a division of the payoff which leaves the latter just better off than the best possible rival offer, without being so generous as to leave the successful offerer no better off. Coalition-forming involves solving this bargaining problem. Let there be a threshold difference of £1 before one payoff is better than another. Tom can profitably offer up to £19 (Harry's £20 less £1) to Dick, or £29 (Dick's £30 less £1) to Harry. Dick could offer up to £19 to Tom, or up to £49 to Harry. Harry could offer up to £29 to Tom, or up to £49 to Dick. Both Dick and Harry can outbid Tom for each other's support. Dick needs to bid no more than Tom's best offer to Harry, i.e. £29 plus £1. On the same principle, Harry needs to bid no more than £19 plus £1. Consequently, the new distribution will probably, though not certainly, be:

Tom	Dick	Harry
£0	£50	£50

It is immediately clear that under this distribution the players have incentives to negotiate a different one. Tom can offer up to £49 of Dick's money to Harry, or up to £49 of Harry's money to Dick, and still be better off. The resulting distribution may then be:

Tom	Dick	Harry
£1	£0	£99

In the next round, Tom and Dick can offer each other a division of Harry's £99. Harry in self-defence can offer up to £98 of his own share to Tom, or £98 and Tom's £1 to Dick. The next distribution will hence be either a bargaining range:

Tom	Dick	Harry
£99–£1	£0–£99	£1

or a 'corner solution':

Tom	Dick	Harry
£99	£0	£1

or:

Tom	Dick	Harry
£0	£99	£1

The tentative rule can now harmlessly be made final, for under it the players can do all they would do in its absence, in order to maximize their payoffs in each distribution round. The result, then, is a sort of inverted Buggins's turn: in each round either (a) the richest player is put in the minority by the two poorest, and is made poor, or (b) the richest escapes being put in the minority at the cost of making himself about as poor as he would be if he were put there by the two poorest.

These are, of course, extreme results due to the artificiality of the assumptions. It is easy to allow for this on lower levels of abstraction—an exercise better performed elsewhere and by others.

III

Instead of maximizing the payoff in each round and suffering an inverted Buggins's turn by being put in the minority every third round or so (or in self-defence against this, something nearly as bad), any two players can do better over a number of rounds by *collusion*. They would then form a *permanent majority* with distributive shares of, say, £50, £50, £0, each resisting the temptation to break it up and form a new coalition with the minority player. They might between them go further and agree on a distribution, e.g. £40, £40, £20, which reduced the minority player's incentive to tempt one of them into forming a new coalition. The limiting case of such a temptation-reducing distribution £33⅓, £33⅓, £33⅓, i.e. equal shares.

Another possible, though quite weak, reason for agreeing to equal shares would be the realization by each player that the *average* player can do no better than this over a large enough number of rounds, cyclical redistribution being just a pointless rocking of the boat (see Chapter 3). Whichever is their reason for adopting it, an equal distribution under majority rule is no more self-enforcing then an unequal one, for there is always a latent majority coalition which could make itself better off by repudiating it. Further restrictive assumptions would be necessary to make equality into a stable distribution rule.

To sum up, a pure distribution is always unstable. It tends to be replaced by another one which redistributes the richest share and tends to be replaced in its turn.

IV

In order to protect a distribution from cyclical instability, it must cease to be pure and must be coupled to production. Let there be an initial distribution under which Tom is richest, and a consequent redistribution in favour of the coalition of Dick and Harry. However, in the meantime production takes place. Let factor-endowments be unequal, e.g. let Tom own a goose that lays golden eggs, or let him be cleverer or more energetic than the other players. The effects of production are then capable of undoing the effects of redistribution. Tom can once more get richer than

Dick and Harry, and it will pay the latter to maintain a stable majority coalition against him, continuing to redistribute Tom's share among themselves, as long as, failing such redistribution, Tom's share would grow to be the largest.

V

In a three-person majority rule game, the winning coalition is always the two-person majority. What is it in the bare majority n-person game? Starting with any arbitrary distribution, let a majority of m persons agree on a new distribution D under which they redistribute among themselves the starting share of the minority of $n - m$ persons. The smaller is m, the greater the average share of each beneficiary of the redistribution, while the corollary increase in $n - m$ increases the total available to be redistributed. In other words, the smaller is m, the more attractive it is to join it in preference to any larger alternative coalition, always provided that m is large enough to defeat $n - m$. Consequently, there must be a D' obtained by decreasing m to m', which defeats D as long as the reduced m' is still a decisive majority coalition. The winning D' is obtained where $m' = n - m'$, i.e. the winning coalition is 50 per cent plus a tie-breaker. D' would be voted for by the smallest possible winning coalition, in preference to any D'' a larger coalition would vote for.

If the initial distribution is unequal, a larger payoff is available if the losing $n - m'$ persons constitute the richer half and the winning m' persons the poorer half. Hence, in an auction for the tie-breaker vote, the poorer m' can always outbid the richer $n - m'$, unless (as we have seen in the three-person case) the latter, in self-defence, agree to a redistribution under which they are made about as poor, subject to a threshold, as they would be if they passively let themselves be put in the minority.

PART TWO
PUBLICNESS: SOLUTION AND RESULT

'... amongst these creatures, the Common good differeth
not from the Private'

THOMAS HOBBES, *Leviathan*

6

THE FOUNDATIONS OF
VOLUNTARINESS

If there is no inevitable public goods dilemma, and the content ion
that there is one—a basic proposition on which hinges the
superstructure of modern political thought—is a delusion, why is
society organized as if private contracts were impotent to commit
people to certain critical kinds of co-operation, and why does
command play the role it does? For let it be admitted for the
moment that the Hobbesian argument is a mere rationalization of a
state of affairs brought about by causes wholly alien to it; that
though Leviathan is sovereign, this is no confirmation of a theory
claiming that people need and want it to be sovereign. But then could
the 'real' operative causes be only matters of historical coincidence,
bringing about the centralization of power, as a different coincidence
might have led to its decentralization? Or are there endemic
features in society which explain that the monopoly of force within
it, far from decaying in time, persists with no tendency to a reversal
to the state of nature? Is not the durability and steady growth of the
institutions that can be said to be logical consequences of the social
contract sufficient proof of the impossibility of getting people to do
their bit for the public good and to contribute voluntarily to what
each could enjoy without contributing?

Putting it the other way round, if overcoming the conflict
between private and public good is not the irreplaceable function
one thought political institutions had to fulfil, have they any other?
Or are they just a bad habit, a slack letting go of individual
responsibility one had learnt to indulge in but could unlearn?

This is obviously asking too many large questions all at once.
Priority goes to making the case that the type of social interaction
where the enjoyment of a good by all depends on the contributions
of only some is not generally a dilemma. It can have a positive or a
negative issue in the state of nature. The positive issue—public

provision of some of the good—depends, as it properly should, on there being sufficient advantage in providing it publicly, compared to the acquisition of private substitutes.

The least semblance of founding our argument on the decency, far-sightedness, and considerateness of human nature must be avoided. It is often both possible and sensible to envisage solutions to the hardest of non-pure, conflictual co-ordination problems by recourse to people's better selves. If they are reasonable and can see the pettiness of immediate advantage, the superiority of looking 'across the valley', beyond some paltry 'local optimum', at the true optimum on the far side; if they have enough self-respect, good taste, and sociability not to exploit opportunities for free riding, they will not allow possible gains from loyal co-operation to be aborted by perverse incentives to act disloyally.

It may well be that man's better self is more robust than he is given credit for in the bleak theory of public goods. In particular, it may be the case that his better self becomes the more assertive, and his ability to sustain good co-operative solutions the more reliable, the more often it is appealed to by prevailing social arrangements (or, on the contrary, by the lack of arrangements to impose such solutions by command). This, of course, is the Tocqueville view of 'politics as education', or 'learning by doing', the formation of character to fit the role expected of it. Needless to say, it is not a particularly 'upbeat' view, being well suited to support predictions about the corruption, hypertrophy, and decay of public life once a cumulative process of 'institutions that build characters that build institutions' gets off on the wrong tack.

Now a theory which relies on the reasonableness and decency of men to solve fundamental social problems relies on a question of fact having a comforting answer. People might or might not be decent enough to master the problem in hand, but as a matter of empirical fact, we may find that they happen to be. If we do, all is well.

However, there *is* no empirical fact. Since the problem in hand is universally solved in a socio-contractual manner, i.e. by command-obedience, we can never test with respect to any really serious issue whether people could master it by spontaneous reasonableness and decency. There *is* no state of nature. Hence any rival to the 'paradigm' of the public-goods dilemma owes it to itself to be no less austere and bleak in its view of human character and motivation, eschewing all reliance on our better selves lest it be open to the wholly proper objection that no solution to a vital problem is much good that does not withstand 'selfishness' in motivation and single-mindedness in its pursuit.

'Selfishness' and the milder 'self-interestedness' are much-misused terms in both positive and normative enquiry, in decision theory and ethics. Some authors do not hesitate to treat them as synonyms for rationality or for utility-maximization. If concepts could, the latter would wince and squirm for being taken for the former. The various distinctions between them, some elementary and others a little less so, need not detain us now, though we will not altogether avoid them before we are done; Chapter 8 attempts to sort out some of the tangle. For the immediate purpose in hand, our approach will have all the austerity and bleakness the least hopeful view of human nature may require, as long as we restrict individual motivation by the conditions we sketched out and labelled 'single-mindedness' in Chapter 3.

To recapitulate:

1. Each player's choice is motivated by and only by his own prospective payoff.
2. No player expects to play the game with the same players more than a known small number of times, and his play is uninfluenced by extra-game relations.

With their better selves thus held strictly in check, and without contract-enforcement being publicly provided, let people be confronted with the problem of actual or potential publicness in the provision of any good.

Exclusion

The conceptual framework used in restating the conventional approach to the public-goods dilemma in Chapter 3 can continue to serve here. We are concerned with non-self-renewing goods which need some resource contribution in order to be reproduced. The problem arises from a weak *nexus*, and in the limiting simplest case no *nexus*, between individual contribution to and benefit from the good. For any person, a good is non-excluded if he can increase his benefit (e.g. consume more) without increasing his contribution (e.g. pay no more), or decrease his contribution (e.g. shirk at work) without decreasing his benefit (e.g. draw the same pay). Every non-self-renewing good can be excluded from access by a given set of persons at some cost. The exclusion cost of a good can vary widely from the insignificant to the prohibitive. It is some function, both of its intrinsic characteristics and of institutional arrangements. The former depend, in turn, on an 'engineering' or 'logistical' kind of economics, encompassing factor-endowments and technologies for making the good and preventing access to it on some selective basis, while the latter depend mainly on social mores. It may be helpful to elucidate further these diverse influences.

Food and mass merchandise in cities are 'excluded' by the walls and floor-plans of supermarkets, by checkout counters, cashiers, and electronic anti-theft tags. The cost of exclusion is what it is and nobody outside supermarket operators gives it much thought. The alternative to exclusion is to throw the door open to all comers (i.e. all humanity) or to a self-selected class of persons (all who take the trouble to come and visit the store). Enormous changes in social mores would be needed to make such non-exclusion work; existing mores are strongly for exclusion.

The use of a road or bridge may be excluded by toll-gates. The exclusion cost consists partly in access management—barriers, change-givers, attendants, etc.—and partly in the slowing down and periodic jamming of the traffic. If traffic is very light, the first kind of cost is very high; if it is heavy, the second kind is very high. In either extreme case for traffic density, there are strong arguments for building a public road or bridge with the required resources contributed in a manner, whatever it is, that is less closely linked to road-use than the payment of a toll by each vehicle as it passes. In the limit, it is built out of general revenue with an unknown incidence on particular road-users. In any event, both toll and no toll are generally compatible with our mores.

A children's playground in a public square is easy to exclude at the material cost of a fence and an attendant, yet the intangible cost is such that the control of access by the sale of entry tickets, and the building of the playground from anticipated receipts, are unthinkable. Contemporary mores would not tolerate a playground where rich children could play and poor ones look on. The total exclusion cost, including the offence to our sense of the fitness of things, would be high enough decisively to put the playground, if there is to be one at all, in the publicly provided class of goods. School is another, perhaps slightly weaker, case where the intangible 'moral' cost to society of excluding children whose parents are too poor or too indifferent to pay, and who are not bright enough to win scholarships, suffices to put education in the category of public goods—even though the costs of exclusion in the narrower, tangible sense are quite low if not actually negative. (They could be said to be negative in case it is cheaper to achieve a 'given improvement' in the mind of the average child if some of the unmotivated or dumb children, as well as children both unlucky in being born poor and lacking the family background favouring application and discipline, are filtered out by having to win scholarships or by their parents having to pay. Their not being dragged along, retarding the rest, would presumably provide a saving greater than the cost of collecting fees and running tests for scholarships. None the less, even no or negative exclusion cost is unlikely to sway education, or at least a residual core of it, out of the class of publicly provided goods.)

Health servies have exclusion costs whose nature is not unlike those of education. Non-exclusion authorizes misgivings about not discouraging frivolous complaints and about treating, and postponing the death of, the hopelessly ill at a cost they or their families would not support. Given these by-products of non-exclusion in health care, exclusion may save rather than cost money, but this will no more prove a decisive reason for turning all health care back into a private good in the future than it was an obstacle to making most of it a public good in the first place. Many of the most important *de facto* public goods owe their publicness not at all to the 'logistics' of exclusion, but to what we tend glibly to call, for want of a less question-begging word, 'social choice'.

Perhaps the arch-example of mores, of a social sense of the fitness and propriety of things as the dominant factor in exclusion, is the link between work and pay. Working together to some common purpose, to carry out interrelated tasks, can be conceived as an arrangement with some contractual features, where a co-operating group's pay bears some fixed relation to its total input of effort. The ultimate group, the only one of which this is always rigorously true, is all humanity. For any smaller group there are, by definition, individuals or other groups outside it at whose expense our group can, under the right circumstances, free ride or who can, in turn, free ride at the group's expense. Nevertheless, there are market disciplines of greater or lesser strictness which keep the pay received and the work done by a co-operative group as a whole—such as a firm, a partnership, a workshop, etc.—roughly in line with its total marginal product.

No such market disciplines operate inside the group. The marginal product of an individual within a team may not be measurable, or it may be offensive to measure it. Often, individual members of it share and share alike, or in proportions depending on seniority or other criteria not directly dependent on individual contributions. Everyone is deemed to have given an implicit promise to do his bit. The reliability of these promises is a public good. Each team member benefits from the promise-keeping of the others without having to keep his own, for as long as he shirks decorously and does not defy appearances, his pay will continue. Exclusion—no pay for no work, less pay for less work—depends on monitoring individual efforts by the team, which collectively bears the cost of individual shirking. (The result in equilibrium is the same whether the 'team' is employed by a 'firm', or is itself the 'firm'.) The cost of monitoring is only partly a matter of the logistics and engineering of performance-measurement and the deployment and motivation of supervisors. My claim is that in the vast majority of cases of team effort these 'objective' costs play no important part in the non-exclusion of the shirker.[1] Weightier is the deterrent effect of the social niceties, the dislike of pettiness, the sheer embarrassment of looking over someone's shoulder, imputing to him less than wholly fair conduct, making invidious comparisons with mates, applying inegalitarian yardsticks leading to no less inegalitarian sanctions, and so forth. This is perhaps the main reason why pay structures depend so much on exogenous symbols like diplomas and degrees, or 'objective' factors like seniority— distinctions among team members whose effect on value added is often debatable or even negative—while those undistinguished by such differentials get, within the limits of reasonableness and decency, equal pay for equal presence rather than equal pay for equal effort. It is the high 'cost of exclusion' in this social, rather than engineering, sense that mainly makes the link between efforts

---

[1] Taking a different view, Alchian and Demsetz (1977), 73–110, reason in terms of the 'metering' costs of assessing the efforts of individuals in team production, confining such costs to what I would call the 'logistics' of exclusion. What type of obstacle to exclusion matters more is, of course, a question of fact.

and rewards within a team tenuous, and confers upon individual wages and salaries a degree of 'publicness' which is largely ignored by public goods theory.[2]

Taking a continuum of 'degrees of publicness', going from the wholly private to the wholly public, and imagining that the universe of goods can be arranged along this continuum in any manner we choose, two imaginary limiting cases mark either end. At one end, everything is obtained privately by contracts of exchange. Each person either gets what he wants by individually paying for it or finds himself excluded from access to it. The marginal cost of acquiring a unit of the good is generally not less than the marginal cost of producing *and* excluding it. This case underlies the classical liberal idea of social organization as a spontaneous market order which maximizes the probable material welfare of any randomly chosen person.

However, the elegance of the reasoning behind this idea of every benefit matched to a contribution by the market mechanism is marred by the Achilles heel (which classical liberals fully acknowledge) of some 'irreducible minimum' domain of social choice dealing with the provision of public goods. They pertain to the rule of law, the protection of the realm, and, depending on the pragmatism of the particular version, to 'essential public services', a 'social safety-net', and certain positive and negative externalities which do not lend themselves to the assignment of negotiable 'rights' and hence to market solutions.

These, then, comprise the legitimate functions of the state, and may constitute a loose definition of the 'minimal' state. Their list is stipulative. It is in some fashion *prior* to, and not the product of, a 'social-choice rule', least of all the type that aggregates preferences. (The exception is if the result of the aggregation is 'fixed' in advance by an appropriate loading of preferences. There may, for instance,

---

[2] There is what economics and political science have come to call an 'agency problem' whenever the composite objectives or '*maximands*' of principal and his agent do not fully coincide; cf. Fama and Jensen (1983). There is, to take a crude example, an agency problem between every employer and his employees, the former wanting from the latter at least a certain effort for a certain wage, the latter generally preferring to exert a smaller effort for the given wage. There is, in our example in the text, an agency problem of the same sort between the team and any one of its individual members. This aspect of the delegation of tasks to agents is perfectly recognized by contemporary theory. What is not recognized is the 'public-goods problem' involved in the 'exclusion' of the shirker. Failing exclusion or a credible exclusion threat, the 'agency problem' becomes uncontrollable.

be a society with a distribution of preference profiles such that it will under no sensible aggregation rule declare to want more than certain 'essential public services' or more than a wide-meshed, rudimentary 'social safety-net'. Nor would it call for enlarging the list of public goods in the quiet expectation of comfortable free rides on some of these goods. No doubt the weakest side of the classical liberal theory is that it seems to assume, *Deus ex machina*, the possibility and even the likelihood of a society which has such minimal public-goods preferences, or would have them but for the 'demagogy' of 'politicians'.)

The opposite extreme of the continuum of publicness is also stipulative and normative, albeit in a more heroic and uncompromising fashion. The list of public goods does not spring from any Achilles heel, any principle of exception. Everything is provided publicly 'to each according to his needs'. Contribution is required 'from each according to his ability'.[3] For any one person, there is no dependence whatever of the benefits he enjoys upon the contribution he makes. He can accede to enhanced conceptions of his needs; he can then consume correspondingly more and 'culturally higher' goods at no marginal cost to himself. His contribution varies only with his ability, or his representation (including his possible concealment) of it. As two forces pull in opposite directions, to greater individual needs and smaller individual contributions, with no explicit 'social choice rule' to reconcile the gigantic public-goods problem that this creates, the result must tend towards a chronic inconsistency at the collective level between too high consumption and too low production. Consistency is saved by the fortunate circumstance that the rule regulating benefits and the other rule regulating contributions operate outside time and space, in the 'realm of abundance'. Exclusion is happily irrelevant and the socially painful exclusion cost of treating goods as 'commodities' and subjecting them to the cash nexus need not be borne.

Anything between these two Platonic ideals of privateness and publicness is, of course, a 'mix', a distribution across the spectrum of publicness in some pattern. It might look tempting to seek the determinants of the pattern in marginal equivalences between the cost of providing each good publicly and the cost of production and exclusion of the same good provided privately. Moreover, since for

---

[3] Marx (1875; 1968 edn.), 321.

many goods there would be no marginal equivalence and some would be provided only publicly, others only privately, explaining the respective lists of goods and their outputs would have to run in terms of production and exclusion-cost functions of the private substitutes of the public goods, with due allowance for the elasticities of substitution of each for every other. (Every good is, of course, a substitute for every other to *some* extent.)

Pushing the reasoning a little, it becomes evident quickly enough that, as is to be expected, the price and output of every good depends on those of every other, both private, public and in between (e.g. 'subsidized'). From this it is only a step to defining that 'mix' of publicly provided and market exchange goods which is efficient and welfare-maximizing, given the production possibilities, individual preferences, the method of their aggregation, and the distribution of income. This step, I think, should be firmly resisted if only for the reason that *any* mix, from the wholly public to the wholly market, can be defined as the welfare-maximizing one if we impute such (tangible and intangible) exclusion costs as will make that particular mix come out as the result. Provided all exclusion costs are high enough, a pure socialist regime, with everything provided publicly and no production for market exchange, is the most efficient one. Since the exclusion cost is not 'known', but is 'revealed' by social choice, there is nothing to stop us from imputing that value to it which makes it worth while publicly to provide the publicly provided good; in fact, no other imputation seems possible. Any mix is the most efficient one by virtue of the tautological nature of exclusion costs.

Though it is only a little less vulnerable to this type of critique, we will address a more modest objective. Instead of seeking to define the equilibrium pattern of public and exchange goods that would be efficient and hence rational for society to choose and force its members to contribute to, we will first exclude social choice; we will reason in a state-of-nature context, devoid of any rule whereby non-unanimous decisions become binding on both consenting and dissenting members. We will then suppose that on an ideal Day One, the day of allocating productive resources to alternative uses for a number of succeeding days, an indefinite number of projects are suggested, each for publicly providing a quantity of a certain good for a given non-excluded group of persons. Prospective beneficiary members of the group own equal shares of available productive resources and are free to contribute or not to each project, chosen singly. The question to answer is: what conditions must such a project fulfil in order to be successfully launched? The conventional social-contract answer, of course, is that since any such project has the essential characteristics of a public-goods dilemma, voluntary contribution (on the assumptions of single-mindedness, which is our agreed platform) is irrational, hence the conditions of success cannot be found within the rational-choice 'paradigm'. It is this conventional answer we seek to replace with a more general one.

Free Riders and Suckers All

Let us take it that a successful project of public provision for the group N has N beneficiaries, of whom k (the 'suckers') contribute and the remaining $N - k$ (the 'free riders') do not. Though we will be resorting to this simple Manichaean distinction, it is in fact too easy and obscures the continuity of shades in social roles; even if we will make no direct use of it in the analytical part of the argument, this continuity is important and should have a place in the backs of our minds as we go on. Except in limiting cases, which are not easy to realize, being a sucker may be no total loss; nor is being a free rider necessarily a total 'getting away with it'. If a person's contribution to a project of public provision and his consumption of the publicly provided good are both variable, it is possible to move towards more and more perfect free-rider status (a) by contributing less, (b) by consuming more, or (c) by some of both. Conversely, the status of absolute sucker is approached via (a) a higher contribution, (b) lesser use of the publicly provided good, or (c) both.

A person who, starting from one type of status, keeps adjusting his contribution or his consumption or both towards the other will 'flip' at some point, changing over from sucker to free rider or vice versa. The thin conceptual line separating the two, which he crosses in effecting this passage, is the '*locus* of fairness'. It is a set of 'fair' combinations of contribution and benefit. There are infinitely many such combinations, and selecting the set of 'fair' ones in general, let alone applied to the circumstances of a particular rich or poor, young or old, healthy or ill person, is a problem in what we might call 'moral accountancy'. Evidently, it can have as many solutions as there are moral accountants.

There are literally countless criteria for telling those who are abused (contribute too much, given the benefits they derive) from those who abuse them (benefit too much, given what they contribute). The hypothetical occupier of the *locus* of fairness, who neither abuses nor is abused, may be rare or non-existent; on either side of him there are all shades and degrees of suckers and free riders. The contrary would be curious. For private exchange is so designed that contribution and benefit should be balanced individually, while in public provision they are balanced globally for a group, and neither can nor are intended to be matched for each person. Some may just happen to come off fairly, or none may; all others are treated either too well or not well enough.

The absence of any mechanism that could keep individually adjusting contributions and benefits to each other means that by most criteria and most of the time a scheme of public provision will validly be judged redistributive, more or less heavily taking from some and giving to others; if by a fluke a criterion were found that momentarily saved this from being the case, in a moving environment a different criterion would be required a moment later. Not all who judge a scheme redistributive would also judge it unfair. The notion of fairness is shapeless enough to fit a scheme both because it is and because it is not redistributive. Nevertheless, the mechanism of public provision is such as to keep provoking the making of these judgements, whichever way they fall out. The burden of the argument is that 'free rider' and 'sucker' are, if looked at closely, more ubiquitous social roles than we tend to imply in ordinary discourse. Having said this, and continuing to bear it in mind, for practical purposes one must not push relativism and moral accountancy all the way. In arguing the rationality of a course of action—to contribute or not to a project of public provision—one needs identifiable 'payoffs', rather than a multiplicity of shades of moral judgements upon outcomes that shade imperceptibly into one another.

In simplifying, we will use symbols denoting the following meanings:

x good available in and for market exchange (x_1, x_2: quantities of x);

y	good available by public provision to non-excluded persons (y_1: quantity of y);
N	a group of N non-excluded persons who all share equally in the benefit if the good y is provided. No non-N benefits;
k	a subgroup of k persons in N who all contribute equally to the total cost of publicly providing y_1;
γ	the contribution of each person in k; 'subscription';
$\bar{k}$	the threshold value that k must attain at a given *ex ante* γ for the project of publicly providing y_1 to be successful; $k < \bar{k} \to y = 0$. *Ex post*, k and $\bar{k}$ are equated in every successful project by the pro rata adjustment of subscriptions;
$N > 1$ ⎫ $k \geqslant \bar{k}$ ⎭	the good y is publicly provided, the good x is produced for exchange. We will call it the 'mixed regime';
$N = k$	condition of 'fairness';
$N - k$	subgroup of free riders in N;
k	subgroup of suckers in N if $N - k > 0$;
$N = 1 \to$	only the good x is produced and every person is a one-man band. We will call it the 'exchange regime'.

While under command–obedience relations the contribution γ would be a poll *tax*, in the state of nature it is a voluntary *subscription*. The rule of the 'game' is that when a project for publicly providing y_1 for the group N is put forward, subscriptions of γ are invited. All who subscribe do so without knowing how many others are also subscribing. Knowing the nature of the project and γ, however, all have some more or less precise estimate of $\bar{k}$, the smallest number who must subscribe for the project to be successful. If it is undersubscribed (i.e. $k < \bar{k}$), subscriptions are not called up and the 'exchange regime' prevails; each person gets the private good x he produces, or the private goods produced outside the group N that he can exchange for x. Both x and all private goods exchanged for x are substitutes of y to varying degrees.

   If the project for organizing y fails due to undersubscription, it can be reproposed, but only under significant penalty: for instance, a waiting-period of some length has to be accepted before the group N can try again to organize the provision of y. Without this condition, no risk would be attached to failure by undersubscription, for non-subscribers could costlessly repent and subscribe the morning after. If the project is oversubscribed, γ is reduced pro rata. An alternative rule to apply in this case would be to provide $y_1 + \Delta y_1$ of the good y, i.e. to organize public provision on a more lavish scale. However, we will not admit this alternative, both because we can define the condition of success with greater economy without it and because the provision of Δy_1 can always be treated as an accessory project proposed subject to y_1 and to be accepted or rejected on its merits, rather than as an overshooting of the target.

An asymmetry is implied in the rules. The gain of the free rider can be net, absolute: he can get something for nothing. The loss of the sucker, however, need never be total loss: he does not have to give something for nothing. If he contributes to public provision, he derives *some* benefit, albeit on unfair terms. He is exploited, but it is *a priori* compatible with sanity for him to prefer a 'mixed regime' where he pays an unfair γ for public provision to an 'exchange regime' where he keeps γ and devotes it to private goods. As is the habit of asymmetries,[4] this particular one plays a central role in determining whether the public-goods 'dilemma' is inherent or not in 'publicness' and in the consequent loosening of the nexus between contribution and benefit.

Stacked, Interlocking, and Straddle Rankings

Having reconsidered the nature of the 'payoffs' in public-goods provision, and bearing in mind that in reality they are not discrete outcomes, but shade into one another by degrees, we are reaching the heart of the matter, the ranking of the possible public-goods 'payoffs' in the preference-orders of 'single-minded' persons. At least in the present context (though not in every 'game' context), it would be running away from the real questions to treat the rankings of payoffs as 'given' by tastes or dispositions, much as we treat goods in consumer choice or states of affairs in social-choice theory—as matters about which *non est disputandum*. Instead, the rankings in the public-goods 'game' must be endogenous, grounded in the analysis of the problem a rational person, who uses payoffs

---

[4] Remember the role of the 'Hobbesian Asymmetry' between attack (always in a pack) and defence (always solitary) in making peace in the state of nature impossible.

as instrumental goods, as means to 'utility', must try and solve when confronted with the binary choice 'subscribe' or 'not subscribe'.[5]

In our N-person group, we are considering the choice of moves of a person A which will result in certain 'payoffs' depending on how the other N − A persons move; let these other persons be represented by B. B's move can be considered as A's probability estimate that any randomly chosen member in the group will move as B; the limiting value of this probability is 1, standing for A's certainty that the *whole* group moves as B does. In Figure 11, however, B can simply be the other player in a two-person game; the game serves as a reference framework only and is not meant to yield a solution.

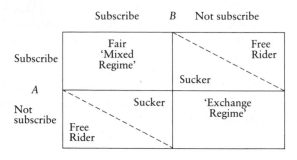

FIGURE 11.

The four different payoffs of the characteristic public-good game can be ranked in 24 different orders. Of these, 21 would be either downright nonsensical or would make sense only if the conditions of 'single-mindedness' were violated. (For intance, A's preferring to pay for something rather than getting it for nothing is either nonsense or is not 'single-minded' because it presupposes some concern for B getting the 'sucker' payoff as a consequence, or seeks virtue associated with his own payoff, or reflects an aversion to the moral outcomes or social consequences of taking a certain payoff

---

[5] The same requirement is set in different terms by Elster (1986), 11 and n. 12. He states, commenting on Schelling's treatment of the 'multi-person prisoners' dilemma', that the utility payoff to a given individual from co-operating, given that others do or do not co-operate, ought to be *derived* from 'the basic technology of collective action', rather than treated as a datum available for the solution of the problem.

rather than a less favourable one.) Only three of the possible rank-orders are prima facie not insane and also single-minded. Each payoff in each of the three rankings is labelled below with A's move, 'subscribe' or 'not subscribe', of which it is a possible alternative outcome. Thus, s_1 and s_2 are the high and low payoffs to A from 'subscribe', ns_1 and ns_2 the high and low payoffs from 'not subscribe'. In each ranking, then, there is a different linkage between the two high and the two low payoffs of the two respective moves:

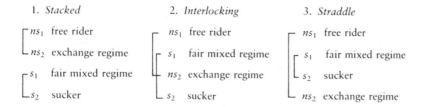

1. *Stacked*

- ns_1 free rider
- ns_2 exchange regime
- s_1 fair mixed regime
- s_2 sucker

2. *Interlocking*

- ns_1 free rider
- s_1 fair mixed regime
- ns_2 exchange regime
- s_2 sucker

3. *Straddle*

- ns_1 free rider
- s_1 fair mixed regime
- s_2 sucker
- ns_2 exchange regime

In the first type of ranking, the two alternative payoffs that may result from not subscribing are 'stacked' on top of the two payoffs that subscribing may produce. In the second ranking, the alternative pairs 'interlock', not subscribing producing the best or third-best, subscribing the second-best and worst payoffs. The third ranking has the possible payoffs from not subscribing in best and worst place; these 'straddle' those from subscribing, placed second- and third-best.

There is nothing further to be said at this stage about persons whose payoff ranking is stacked or interlocking (though some such people, motivated by other considerations than the preference-order of their public-goods payoffs, will come back on the scene in Chapter 8). Whatever B may do, an A with such payoff rankings will always value the payoff from not subscribing higher than the payoff from subscribing (his ns_1 is higher than his s_1; his ns_2 is higher than his s_2). His 'dominant strategy' confirms the prediction of the public-goods dilemma: in public-goods situations where the level of contribution and the value of the publicly provided benefit in the 'mixed regime' (i.e. some public and some private goods) are such as to engender this preference-ranking, A will not contribute voluntarily to public provision. Of course, this is merely an implication of ranking payoffs in a certain order. We do not *know* whether there are many or any persons with such preference-rankings, nor whether there are contribution-to-benefit relationships in the world that would make such rankings rationally compelling and the 'not subscribe' strategy consequently dominant.

On the other hand, a great deal more can and needs to be said about the 'straddle' ranking. It imposes no dominant strategy. Putting it less technically, there is no telling, from a mere look at the ranking, that the *pair* of payoffs to A from not subscribing stands higher or is worth more than the *pair* from subscribing, or vice versa, for any one of the two alternative moves B may make: 'best' is paired with 'worst', 'second-best' with 'third-best'. Hence, voluntary subscription is at least an admissible solution; a group where the straddle ranking is significantly represented in the members' preferences may or may not publicly provide a good for itself, but at least its attempt to do so is not condemned by the logical interdiction laid down in the public-goods dilemma.

Our programme adopted above, however, was not to treat preference for payoffs as falling from heaven like 'tastes' for final (consumption) goods and 'dispositions' to final, non-instrumental values. They must, to make sense, be *derivable* form instrumental rational-choice criteria applied to the fundamentals of public provision. Both subscription *and* non-subscription under such conditions should be the product of the 'straddle' which imposes no dominant strategy, but *allows* one or the other.

The possibility of voluntary public provision under 'single-minded' motivation depends on two successive tests:

1. Are conditions such that the 'straddle' is the rationally compelling preference ranking?
2. Given the straddle ranking, are conditions such as to make 'subscribe' a better move than 'not subscribe'?

Of the two tests, the second is set up in Chapter 7. Before attempting the first, however, it will pay us to explore what beckons as a bold short cut.[6]

---

[6] The essential idea of such a short cut was suggested to me in a passing remark by Mr Alan Ryan.

No Free Riders, No Suckers

If the rules of the 'game' are what we say they are, its four payoffs arise out of the inequality

$$N \geqslant k \geqslant \bar{k} \geqslant 1 \qquad (1)$$

for only if (1) holds can there be a 'mixed regime' ($N > 1$, $k \geqslant \bar{k}$), with free riders and suckers ($N - k \neq 0$), and with the possibility of reversion to an 'exchange regime' ($N = 1$). But it should be a simple matter to fix γ in such a way that

$$N = \bar{k} \geqslant 1 \qquad (2)$$

excluding the possibility of the 'free-rider' and 'sucker' payoffs, and admitting only two alternatives, the 'fair' mixed regime if all subscribe or the pure exchange regime if less than all do (the 'group' then shrinks to a single person).

In plain English, what we are saying is that if in a community all members want a bridge over the river, the way to persuade each to contribute might be to fix the per caput contribution γ low enough to make the money run just short of that needed for completing it from bank to bank *unless all contribute.*

Unfortunately, such an arrangement would be too easy to defeat. Any one group member who under such conditions is the first to declare that he will not contribute, and if need be lends his declaration added credibility by one of the many devices for 'pre-committing' himself to a course of action (e.g. making an expensive side-bet, forfeiting something precious if he subscribes), has a very good chance of getting the others to subscribe his share in addition to their own, lest the whole project should be aborted for want of a relatively small sum. The same would be true, albeit a little less so each time, of the second declarer, and the third, and so forth. With each additional declarer, γ is getting progressively higher, $\bar{k}$ lower and $N - \bar{k}$ (the greatest number of free riders a public-good project can support given that each of a critical minimum number $\bar{k}$ of suckers is prepared to contribute γ) growing, until the process stops at the point where suckers no longer find it worth while to accept a marginal increase in γ.

Clearly, as γ rises, it gets less and less attractive for a diminishing number of suckers to save the project from an increasing number of free riders, so that with other things equal the probability of at least k voluntary subscriptions forthcoming must be falling. The per caput subscription that maximizes this probability, i.e. one the group or its organizers should choose if it would rather have the project succeed than fail, must thus be low enough to encourage subscription, yet high enough to provide a safety margin against the risk represented by attempted free riding, since if there is no room for it the latter can spoil all.

The notion of a 'safety margin', however, is itself a little question-begging. We are not dealing with a given natural disposition of a population, the observed statistical frequency of free riders within a community, but with rational calculation that tips the scales in favour of free riding. If the fixing of γ were a matter of public negotiation, any group member could try and negotiate it upwards by one of two tactics: he could either lie by claiming to be keener to pay than he was in the hope that others will be encouraged to follow his false lead ('suckering' them into paying a high enough γ to let him free ride); or he could lie by claiming lack of interest, 'pre-committing' himself not to pay ('suckering' the rest into compensating for this with a high enough γ). With successful pursuit of these tactics producing a rising γ, there would be both increasing resistance by the rest of the group to any further rise and an increasing probability that further attempts at widening the margin for free riding would defeat themselves by causing undersubscription, hence no public provision at all and nothing to ride free on.

The per caput subscription γ eventually fixed for a given public-good project can either be seen as the outcome of trial and error, *tâtonnement* by negotiation, or as the product of a decision on behalf of the group (e.g. by its habitual or *ad hoc* 'leadership', by a subgroup promoting the project, or by the 'emergent consensus' of public opinion), reached as if it took the assumed outcome of hypothetical negotiation into account. In neither case may the actually chosen γ be one that demonstrably maximizes the chance of an adequate number of subscriptions, for it cannot be demonstrated that there is a single particular γ that satisfies this requirement. However, the chosen γ will in any case be greater than the value that would satisfy the expression (2) above and (i.e. that would exclude all possibility of free riding). The 'short cut to fairness' under voluntariness is not feasible.

Finally, any negotiation, or any probability judgement about what the negotiation would yield if it took place, whose effect is to determine what shall be the admissible number of free riders consistent with an adequate level of voluntary contribution by the rest, presupposes that the per caput subscription γ is naturally variable (for if γ is fixed and the total cost of public provision is also fixed, there is no room for negotiating about the admissible number of free riders). This is clearly the case with variable sums of money or variable hours of labour; there are, however, important public-goods problems where the individual contribution is naturally fixed. If a group attempted to secure for its members such 'moral public goods' as reliance on promises, contract compliance, the safety of unguarded property, trust in unmarried girls being virgins and married ones faithful, a person could either contribute or not: little would be added to the public's trust in virtue by respecting *some* contracts, not stealing *all* unguarded property, telling the truth *often*, keeping faith *now and then*, and being virgin *a little*. Arguably, only the *full* exercise of such virtues by *enough* members of a community will really provide the respective moral goods as public goods, to be relied on by all.

Whether the uniform contribution promised by each subscriber is a decision-variable or a natural fact of life, for voluntariness it must be such as to deny the *certainty* that anyone's subscription to contribute *is*, or *is not*, required for making up the decisive number of subscribers. 'Certain to be required' allows easy blackmail; 'certain not to be required' leaves no reason to contribute. The straddle ordering produces no interesting result in a non-stochastic environment; only uncertainty makes it come into its own.

The Straddle Ranking: A Necessary Condition

1. 'Free riding', ranked highest, is impossible to beat or to match. None of the other three payoffs can possibly be as favourable (provided the player is 'single-minded').
2. The 'fair' mixed regime, ranked second-best, is superior to 'sucker' by virtue of their respective definitions; under the former, a person gets more for the same, or as much for less, than under the latter. 'Sucker' gets the mixed regime at unfair odds, which is implied to be worse than getting it at fair ones.

3. The 'fair' mixed regime is superior to the market-exchange regime by virtue of the hypothesis that there *is* a public-goods problem. If it were not, the person whose preferences we are considering would never be prepared to devote any of his resources to obtain public provision of a given good on 'fair' terms in preference to getting substitutes in market exchange, no matter how many or how few others of his group were willing to devote theirs to it; the question of how to get the voluntary co-operation of others would not arise if it were not desired.

4. The remaining piece needed for justifying the straddle is to establish that under certain conditions being a 'sucker' is superior to having the exchange regime.[7]

As the public good is, by definition, to be provided for a whole group, the latter is the proper starting-point. From the group we will have to find our way back to the individual member who is the sole master over the way he values outcomes. We want to end up knowing whether (assuming these were the only two outcomes to choose from) he would rather contribute to public provision on *unfair* terms, or opt for an exchange regime where he got what he paid for.

One may feel free to regard the group N as homogeneous in having some common interest in the public good y. From here, we will take it that there is a utility function $U(x, y)$ such that as U increases, at least some person in N feels better off and none feels worse off. Moreover, we will treat U as a cardinal index number, as if it were, save for its dimensionality, the utility of a representative member of N. We define the mixed regime m, the exchange regime e and the conditions of desired publicness of y:

$$U(x_1, y_1) \equiv U_m$$
$$U(x_2, 0) \equiv U_e$$
$$U(x_1, y_1) > U(x_1, 0) \qquad (1)$$
$$U(x_1, y_1 - dy_1) = U(x_1, 0) \qquad (2)$$

A weaker alternative to condition (2) would be to assume that the marginal utility of the public good increases steeply up to some threshold quantity and diminishes steeply past that threshold. This conveys, less rigidly than condition (2), that the public good has a

---

[7] The following section had the benefit of valuable advice I received from Mr F. Seton.

critical supply; less of it causes crowdedness and jeopardizes non-exclusion, more produces questionable additional benefit.

The sole resource available and needed to produce either good is C, the production function is $C(x, y)$ and the resource budget at the disposal of and shared equally by all in N is $\bar{C}$. We assume:

$$C(x_1, y_1) = C(x_2, 0) = \bar{C}$$

When in a mixed regime y_1 is produced, the cost of x_1 is cx_1, hence the cost of publicly providing y_1 is $\bar{C} - cx_1$. To establish the utility dimension:

$$U_e = \bar{C}$$

The hypothesis that there is a public-goods problem to be solved implies:

$$U_m \geqslant U_e \rightarrow \frac{U_m}{\bar{C}} > 1 \qquad (1)$$

The hypothesis can be interpreted intuitively: if the group N had a collective mind, it would be 'collectively rational' for it to opt for the mixed regime and produce x_1, y_1. However, since we take it that N has no collective mind, whether this will be done is presumed to be decided by separate individual minds.

While all N persons share equally in the benefit U_m and in the cost of the exchange good cx_1, only a subset of k persons in N share the cost of the public good $\bar{C} - cx_1$. It is 'collectively rational' for the subgroup k to contribute $C - cx_1$ if their portion k/N of the total benefit that accrues to the whole group exceeds the cost they alone bear:

$$(U_m - U_e)\frac{k}{N} > C - cx_1$$

alternatively:

$$\frac{U_m - U_e}{C - cx_1}\frac{k}{N} > 1 \qquad (2)$$

The inequality (2) expressed the case of *general dilution*. Whatever the dilution factor k/N, it is 'collectively rational' for the subgroup k to contribute if the dilution is at least offset by the cost–benefit relationship which I will (very loosely) baptize the *'productivity of publicness'* factor $U_m - U_e/C - cx_1$. (The 'productivity of privateness' is unity, for it is the *numéraire* or yardstick.) A low dilution-factor may permit toleration of a relatively modest productivity of publicness and vice versa.

A different way of putting it is that if the advantage of providing a good publicly rather than getting by with privately exchanged substitutes is not very great, a high proportion of the beneficiary community must share in the cost if each contributor is not to be worse off than in the exchange regime. The opposite, of course, is the case when providing the public good is so advantageous that it would be preferable even for a small proportion of the community to contribute, and to carry a large proportion of free riders, rather than make do with the exchange regime.

Though these are statements of the obvious, they help to drive home the point that whether public provision is 'collectively rational' for a subgroup of 'suckers' (voluntary contributors) depends on two ratios: one reflects the 'productivity of publicness', the other the general dilution factor k/N, showing the fraction the contributors get out of the whole benefit accruing to the non-excluded group due to their contribution. Intuitively, one may see the dilution-factor as the measure of the handicap inflicted by non-exclusion upon the attractiveness of contributing. (With exclusion, there is of course no dilution; only contributors benefit and neither suckers nor free riders exist.) The handicap of dilution must be offset by what I call, for lack of a less objectionable term, the extra 'productivity of publicness'. The greater is the latter, the more dilution by free riding a project of public provision can bear and still remain preferable for the body of 'suckers', *taken together*, than the exchange regime.

The two ratios combined must be not less unity. This is a necessary condition for any member of the group N to accept playing the role of sucker (i.e. staying in the subgroup k) in the public-goods situation described by inequality (2) above, if the sole alternative is to have the exchange regime. Whether it is a sufficient condition is an open question; we will consider it presently. Meanwhile, two implications of the necessary condition are worth pointing out.

1. Voluntariness of contribution introduces a *selection mechanism* for sorting out attractive from unattractive projects of public

provision. While many or all may be deserving for one reason or another, only those stand a reasonable chance of spontaneous realization whose publicness confers upon the group concerned a substantial additional benefit compared to non-public substitutes obtainable under an exchange regime. The selection mechanism implied by the combined 'productivity-and-dilution' ratio in inequality (2) would screen out frivolous projects and somebody's mere good ideas,[8] no comparable screening mechanism operates under command–obedience relations.

2. The absolute *size of the group is not directly relevant* to voluntary contribution being rational (in the sense of being an admissible, non-dominated strategy); it is not N but k/N that matters. There is a type of 'parochial' motivation (cf. Chapter 8, p. 198) under which k/N may, in turn, be influenced by N. But the reason why this may be so does not lie in any straightforward contribution–benefit calculus.

The Straddle Ranking: A Sufficient Condition

Assuming for simplicity that members of a subgroup bear equal costs and enjoy equal benefits, unless the necessary condition for a subgroup of 'suckers' to be better off when contributing to a mixed regime than having a pure exchange regime is satisfied, it cannot be preferable for an individual to be part of the subgroup. The necessary condition for k and for *any individual in k* is the same. However, this is not sufficient to make the individual actually prefer being in the subgroup.

In looking into reasons justifying a preference, we must bear in mind that such an enquiry is subjecting the individual to an artificial thought-experiment. He is not being asked whether he would wish to be one of his group's suckers, or would rather not subscribe given the combined chance of free riding (if enough others subscribe), or the exchange regime (if they do not). He must instead close his mind to the two major payoffs—free riding and

---

[8] I am not prejudging whether the mechanism would screen projects too harshly, too leniently, or just as it should. It seems to me that for both epistemic and ethical reasons we must be agnostic towards concepts of the socially optimal ('efficient') output of public goods, with respect to which the actual output could be judged too small or too large.

the fair mixed regime—and decide which of the two minor payoffs—sucker and the exchange regime—he would rather have if the more attractive major payoffs were somehow excluded. The problem he must solve in deciding what is sensible for him to prefer is perhaps best located by 'bracketing' it with ranging shots, i.e. with limiting special cases.

One such limiting case is 'no dilution'. Let y_1 in the 'mixed regime' be a good to which all must contribute or else none of it will be provided. A police cordon where all must firmly link arms, traffic which will only flow if all drive on the same side, a shared secret that all must keep, look like being such goods; there are others of which 'all or none' is not literally true but a good enough approximation. The contribution of each member of the group being required for the entire benefit to accrue, and *the failure of one spoiling it for all*, any one individual's contribution bears the same proportion to *his own* benefit resulting from it as the total contribution bears to the *total* benefit. There is no dilution, and k/N in the general inequality (2) becomes N/N, i.e. unity. From (2), an individual will prefer to contribute to such a good provided:

$$\frac{U_m - U_e}{C - cx_1} > 1 \qquad (2a)$$

This is the same condition as for the 'collective rationality' of the whole group. It is also the condition for the case where $N = 1$, the one-man band. Contribution is both collectively and individually preferable to the exchange regime as long as the 'productivity of publicness' is greater than that of 'privateness', i.e. of the exchange regime used as the yardstick. (Evidently, a one-man band may find it impossible to contribute at all by himself, since public provision has an implicit scale aspect.) If the concept of an efficient or 'socially optimal' scale of public provision were to be admitted as meaningful despite the attendant problem of moving from a voluntary to an involuntary distribution of the burden of required contributions, it might be said that the socially optimal scale is reached where the diminishing 'productivity of publicness' reaches unity.

In another special case, let y_1 be not a man-made, but a God-given public good, such as daylight at noon. An individual's attempted contribution to it would be totally wasted: lighting his candle would not make the day any more luminous. There would be 'infinite dilution', and it would be better for the individual to contribute only if:

$$\frac{U_m - U_e}{\bar{C} - cx_1} \frac{0}{N} > 1 \rightarrow \frac{U_m - U_e}{\bar{C} - cx_1} > \infty \qquad (2b)$$

—a silly condition.

Finally, take the case of what passes for archetypal and figures as an unstated assumption in most orthodox discussions of public-goods problems. Justifications of taxation and treatments of 'publicness' or 'collective action' which demonstrate the quasi-impossibility of voluntary contribution usually contain this unstated assumption. For short, I will call it the case of 'conventional dilution'.[9] It postulates that since—share equally, the part a contributor can hope to capture for himself out of the increase in group benefit *due to his own contribution* corresponds to 1/N, i.e. the reciprocal of the size of the group. The general dilution factor *k*/ N takes the value 1/N and the sufficient condition for 'sucker'

[9] For the vast majority of public-goods theorists, this special case is the only case; oddly, they hardly ever envisage others; hence my term 'conventional'. Rigorous demonstrations that the larger is the group, the smaller is the individual incentive to contribute or the greater is the shortfall of actual public provision compared to its 'efficient' or 'optimal' scale, rest on the properties of this case; cf. Chamberlin (1974; 1976), who seems to regard it as typical but, unlike most others, recognizes that at least one other case is possible. Among the rare exceptions, one who clearly sees that it is a special case among a multiplicity of others is Hirshleifer (1983). He calls them 'social composition functions'. My 'conventional dilution' corresponds to his 'summation function'. (He does not, however, seek to present a general function that would correspond to the 'general dilution' of the present book.) There is also a recognition that the nature of the public-goods problem is different from the prisoners' dilemma in Frohlich, Oppenheimer, and Young (1971). A notable advance in clearing up the question is accomplished by Hampton (1987), whose contribution is further referred to in ch. 7 with regard to indivisibility.

A further argument asserts not only the received wisdom that large-number public-goods interactions degenerate into prisoners' dilemmas but that in such dilemmas repetition (or continuity) of play may not help either, because the non-exclusion inherent in public-goods interactions makes retaliation in a game against the free rider of the preceding game impossible. Cf. Conybeare (1986), 151. In strict logic, however, it is not non-exclusion that makes retaliation impossible (for there may be other ways of punishing the free rider than by excluding him), but anonymity of the free rider. Clearly, in a small group it is easier to spot the free rider and sanction him in one of many possible ways once he is identified than in a large group, where he can hide in the crowd. It is to this extent that the small group is favoured in public-goods problems. But this is a different argument from the mistaken one which (at least implicitly) claims that the larger the group, the greater the dilution.

being individually better than 'exchange regime' is:

$$\frac{U_m - U_e}{\bar{C} - cx_1} \frac{1}{N} > 1 \tag{2c}$$

This, of course, is an almost impossibly demanding condition. Significantly, as k/N turns into $1/N$, the numerator becomes constant and the denominator alone remains variable. The dilution becomes directly and solely dependent on N, the absolute size of the group. This must have been the intuitive spring of the belief that while voluntary contribution by rational persons is wholly unlikely, it is a little less unlikely in small than in large groups.[10] But in the context this is hardly more instructive than to find that while pigs are wholly unlikely to fly, they are a little less unlikely to outfly woodcocks than eagles.[11] Once they are cast as pigs, it seems pointless to determine whom they might outfly. If they see the effect of their own contribution on their own share in benefits as in (2c), circumstances must be quite extraordinary for it to seem better to them to act the sucker. The straddle ranking is then a freakish rarity.

The unstated assumption which turns potential contributors into pigs who won't fly is now ready to break surface. In 'no dilution' (2a), the 'marginal product' due to any one contribution is equal to the total product, for the withdrawal of any single contribution would spoil or abort the public good altogether: the group benefit $U_m - U_e$ would disappear. In 'infinite dilution' (2b), the 'marginal product' due to any one contribution is nil. The public good is there regardless of whether anyone contributes. In 'conventional dilution' (2c), the marginal product due to one more contribution is no higher than the average product per contributor. This is because the public good in question is continuously divisible and can be increased or decreased by driblets. Each contribution to its production is alone decisive for an increment, independently of other contributions. The ith contribution is solely responsible for the ith increment and *only for that increment*. No contribution is pivotal or decisive for the *whole* good or any *large lump* of it. With k contributors, withdrawal of one would reduce the total product or group benefit by no more than the factor $(k - 1)/k$, and the

[10] Cf. Olson (1965), 36.
[11] As Hardin pertinently puts it: 'If the incentive [to contribute] is negative, one will not contribute no matter *how* negative.' Hardin (1982), 44.

reduction in the withdrawing ex-contributor's own benefit would, of course, be only the $1/N$ part of this, presumably small, reduction. Under almost no conceivable circumstances would it pay him to make the contribution.

Once it is made explicit, the assumption of perfect or near-perfect divisibility of the public good and the consequent *irrelevance of its scale* and of the number of contributions to it, with each contributor adding the average product per head, looks a quite special one. I should certainly not wish to build the 'logic of collective action' upon it.[12]

The relevance of scale seems to be inherent in the notion of

[12] The 'logic', based on assumed properties of public provision which, if they corresponded to reality, would give rise to what I call in the text 'conventional dilution', dictates that there shall virtually never be any voluntary collective action. In reality, however, voluntary collective action proliferates. This could mean that the alleged 'logic' is false, or that collective action is virtually always illogical, or that some other reason found outside the logic of collective action overcomes the reason furnished by the 'logic'. Thus, the latter remains valid but happens in many cases to be suppressed, dominated by something else. This something else is the notion of 'selective incentives', a central concept in Olson (1965) and the subsequent literature inspired by this line of thought. If the selective incentive is a *private* good and it has *market substitutes*, it is very difficult to undertand its supposed role. The gist of the Olson argument is as follows. Workers would not, if they followed the 'logic' and paid no heed to anything else, ever belong to a trade union, pay dues, and obey its disciplines, for the benefit from the very small increase in union strength that the contribution of any one worker could bring about would be diluted over all other workers, the share accruing to the individual contributor being negligibly small and in any case smaller than his contribution. However, the union runs a funeral insurance scheme offered selectively to union members only, and this 'selective incentive' makes the average worker contribute.

This explanation is unintelligible unless bolstered by the assumption that the union has some unbeatable cost advantage in providing the funeral insurance (or other selective benefits). Workers' contributions must cover *both* the cost of union activities *and* of funerals. If he obeyed the 'logic', however, a rational worker would not contribute more in terms of money and non-monetary efforts and sacrifices to the two activities, taken together, than the funeral insurance premium he would have to pay for the comparable policy of a non-union insurer. Under competitive conditions, this would just cover the full cost of funerals, leaving nothing over for subsidizing 'real' union activities, including the cost to the worker of having to obey the union and engage in 'collective action', such as striking. To survive as a funeral insurer, the union would have to become just that and would have to cease any 'real' union activity.

Another way of putting this is that in terms of the 'logic' the individual worker would be prepared to pay dues that did not exceed the competitive price for the 'selective benefit' or its market equivalent substitute, but he would not find it rational to do so if, as a side condition, he was also required, at some further cost to himself, to engage in 'collective action' and walk off the job even when he preferred to go on earning wages. If he nevertheless obeyed the union's strike call, it was for a reason unexplained *both* by the 'logic' of collective action *and* the selective incentive.

publicness. In a subsequent section (Chapter 7, p. 160) the case for regarding the scale of supply of publicly provided goods under given 'cultural' conditions as being determined by the size of the beneficiary group is argued in detail. In the formal analysis of the present chapter, one of the conditions defining the public goods problem (condition 2) is a threshold size of the public good y_1: withdrawal of dy_1 from it would render the whole useless. This strong condition evokes the bridge spanning the river from bank to bank: pinching off even a short length would leave a useless, incomplete bridge. Less intransigent threshold or indivisibility conditions might well be more realistic, but at all events dimensionality seems to me inseparable from the very concept of publicness. Given the size and character of the community, there are few goods one can offer to each and very member of it *for free in driblets*, for doing so would make a mockery of non-exclusion unless *enough* driblets were offered to add up to a critical total.

Be that as it may, the rules of the 'game' that help to define the general dilution factor k/N in inequality (2) above provide that when a project is proposed to a group involving the public provision of the good y_1, there must be $k \geq \bar{k}$ voluntary contributors, each subscribing γ, for it to go ahead; if undersubscribed, nothing happens. Assuming it goes ahead, there are k suckers and $N - k$ free riders. The best of all worlds, of course, is to be in $N - k$, and when the 'game' is played out any player may in fact gamble on his falling into the $N - k$ subgroup where he can have his cake and eat it. Before the game is played, however, we need to know how he would rank two of its minor, least attractive possible 'payoffs', assuming he could have only one or the other. Would he consider being a sucker more attractive than the exchange regime, where he gets to keep his subscription γ and can exchange it for the private goods it will fetch?

If, miraculously, he could have the certain knowledge that he is one of $N-k$, he would by implication know that k others are subscribing anyway, hence his own subscription would add nothing to total group benefit. Its 'marginal productivity' would be nil, and only the quite absurd inequality (2b) above would be a sufficient condition to make him prefer being a sucker to no purpose. Conversely, if equally miraculously he knew for certain that he is one of k (and k is not greater than $\bar{k}$), his subscription (like that of any other suckers in k) would make all the difference between having the mixed regime and the corresponding group benefit, or having the exchange regime. The sufficient condition for his preference for 'sucker' over 'exchange regime' would then be the quite undemanding inequality (2a).

Admitting that he knows neither that he is one of $N-k$ nor that he is one of k, what is it sensible for him to suppose, given that it is *a priori* no worse and could be better for him to order his possible payoffs on a reasoned basis—no matter how scant the evidence from which he must reason—than by drawing matchsticks?[13]

If, arguing from the principle of there being insufficient reason to hold any *other* hypothesis for as likely (let alone more likely) to be true, he supposed that his chance of being one of the $N-k$ subgroup was $(N-k)/N$ and his chance of being one of the k subgroup was k/N, the *sufficient* condition for his preferring 'sucker' would, of course, coincide with the *necessary* condition expressed by inequality (2).

Equiprobability II

The same form of equiprobability which in Chapter 5 was found to be necessary for a rational person to believe that bare majority rule will be best for him turns out to provide a pivotal condition for a rational and single-minded person willingly to accept the role of sucker. As in certain novels, 'the resemblance is wholly coincidental', and if parallels are to be drawn it is perhaps fair to say that Equiprobability I, leading to preference for the barest majority rule, supposes ignorance about one's community, and unworldliness, of a taller order than Equiprobability II. The latter is a hypothesis envisaged by A that if a given project of public provision requires that the proportion of subscribers be k/N, the probability of any random B subscribing is also k/N. This hypothesis is purely a landmark, a formal point of reference to aid reasoning. It has no suggested truth-value, and it will be up to A to invest it with a different probability if there is some ground for doing so, depending

---

[13] For qualifications that limit the general validity of this 'purely Bayesian' stand, cf. Suppes (1984), 210–12. Let us note, however, that while choosing by drawing matchsticks can have defensive merits against a canny opponent, reasoned choice which does not have these defensive qualities retains its *a priori* superiority in 'games against nature' where no opponent is playing *against* you, or at any rate not with a reasoned strategy of his own.

on the nature of the public-goods project in question, and the information he has about the tastes, needs, and interests of the Bs. The equiprobability hypothesis is best seen as a reference-point in a probability spectrum which A would compare to the specific probability attaching to a given project (which may itself be less than, equal to, or greater than equiprobability), such comparisons supporting or not a reasoned preference for 'sucker' over the private good of the exchange regime. It is not suggested that A does make this comparison, but that his conduct can be rationalized as if he did.

A does not in fact *know* what is best for him, unless he knows what the Bs will do; knowledge of what the Bs would do if they opted for what was best for *them* could, in a sense (the sense of 'Nash equilibrium') define A's best, but he has to substitute probability judgements for the missing knowledge. For a start, let the Bs represent an independent variable he ignores. Suppose that they are all led, blindfolded, to a bowl full of black and white marbles, each B taking one. If he took black, he must subscribe to a given public project, if he took white, he must not. A is then made to choose a marble with his eyes open. Whether a black or white marble has the higher value for him depends on the distribution of the marbles held by the Bs, which he must estimate as best he can if he wants to make a reasoned choice. Broadly speaking, if he thought most of the Bs held black marbles, he should take white, for his subscription would not be required for the project to be realized and for him to benefit from it. Conversely, if he thought too few Bs might be holding black marbles, he should choose black (and subscribe), for at worst nothing happens as a consequence and the pure exchange regime remains available, and at best the project is realized in a mixed regime.

Equiprobability II is the case where the bowl was filled with black and white marbles in the proportions k/N to $(N-k)/N$; by taking their marbles blindfolded, the Bs are led to the 'mixed strategy' of subscribing with a probability $p = k/N$. For any value of p between 0 and k/N, the black marble is worth more to A than the white if his possible payoffs are ranked in the straddle order. 'Subscribe', in other words, is his 'dominant strategy' in the face of B's 'mixed strategy' of subscribing from 0 to k times out of N; for if A subscribes his expected payoff is either 'sucker' (the mixed regime on unfair terms) or 'nothing happens', depending on how the B's broke between k and 0, whilst if he does not subscribe both of his expected payoffs are 'nothing happens' no matter how the B's broke.[14]

On the other hand, if p is not bounded by the range $0 < p < k/N$ but can assume any value $0 < p < 1$, hence, also $p > k/N$, A has no dominant strategy. A merely ordinal straddle ranking of his payoffs which tells us which he prefers but not by how much does not fully define his best course of action. Its full definition calls for the cardinal utilities of A's payoffs and the fully numerical probability of the collective mixed strategy of the Bs. For the wheel to come full circle, one must then consider that instead of taking marbles blindfolded and acting on that, each B is really an A, trying to work out what he had best do in view of what everybody else might do. This, in turn, begs the question of the mutual consistency of people's expectations. We attempt to shed a little more light on these matters in Chapter 7.

---

[14] We say, in effect, that as part of the game there is a possible subsidiary game in which B may vary ('mix') his strategy only in the range between subscribing k/N of the time and not at all. In this game, A *always* ends up as well or better if he subscribes, i.e. he has 'subscribe' as a dominant strategy. This subgame fits into the larger main game in which B may freely vary his strategy between subscribing less than k/N of the time and more than k/N of the time. Here, A has no dominant strategy; the calculus of expected utility-maximization will recommend to him one strategy or the other according to the probability of B adopting one strategy (or strategy-mix) or the other.

7

CONSTRUCTIVE RISK

The classic position[1] in social-contract theory, public finance, and welfare economics has tended to be that public goods are defined by non-excludability and jointness of supply. It was not always very clear whether it was both characteristics together that conferred the quality of publicness on a good, or whether non-excludability was responsible for some and jointness for other aspects of publicness, each separately being capable of causing different, more or less intractable, problems. In any event, however, causation was to run from intrinsic characteristics of the good to its publicness.

On examination, few goods are found to have the peculiar properties that would make them intrinsically public. Even the notorious lighthouse whose signals every passing ship could see as well as every other regardless of whether it had paid any lighthouse dues, and whose usefulness to one ship was in no way diminished by another ship's also benefiting from it, could be argued out of the public realm and 'privatized' with the aid of imaginary light-scramblers and unscramblers (the latter given only to ships that paid dues). Its 'jointness' would fall victim to the progressive crowding of the sea-lanes in the area due to too many ships being induced to pass that way by the usefulness of the beacon's signal.

Our tactic in the last chapter with respect to exclusion was to reverse the order of causation. Instead of being public because it was non-excludable, a good became non-excluded because the 'public' wanted it so. Its intrinsic non-excludability, if any (or more precisely its high exclusion cost in the 'logistical', 'engineering' sense), was one possible factor among others in the decision to provide it publicly for a given group. Its 'social' and indeed 'moral' exclusion cost may have been another. But, except for special cases, it rarely looks convincing to explain a group attempting to organize public provision of a good in terms of its high exclusion cost.

---

[1] Cf. Samuelson (1954).

Causation generally runs more easily the other way. There is no reason why *any* good, regardless of its intrinsic characteristics, should *not* be publicly provided if somebody—typically, though not at all necessarily, the members of the group to be included in the benefits of provision—will contribute the required resources. High enough exclusion cost made up of moral and social intangibles can always be imputed so as to make such an enterprise worth while in a trivial sense.

Subscription to the enterprise may or may not be non-trivially worth while in two senses. On criteria that are quite vulnerable[2] to attack, it may be 'collectively rational' for the group. On somewhat more impregnable grounds, it is individually rational if individuals, assumed to reach their decisions in certain ways and on certain grounds, prove it so by subscribing voluntarily. In the state of nature that is the scene of this part of the present book, it is this second sense of worthwhileness that concerns us. In formulating a sufficient condition for the straddle ordering of alternative payoffs in public provision, we have come some way towards a theory of voluntary, state-of-nature contribution to public goods. The rest of the way gets progressively easier as we go.

Having turned the classic public-goods argument upside down with respect to exclusion, we shall now expose jointness to the same treatment, to see what extent it will lend itself to it, and with what consequences.

All or None

Jointness is the property of a good which enables one more person to use, consume or enjoy it, rely on, or otherwise benefit from it without the consumption, reliance, benefit, etc. of any other person being thereby reduced. If there can be a man-made good in truly joint supply, it is either available or not. The idea of making more of it available contradicts the idea of its jointness. If such goods can

---

[2] The vulnerability is the same as that afflicting any group, collective, or 'social' concept of 'better'. Either utilities must be interpersonally comparable and integrable, permitting such findings as 'some people's gains outweigh other people's losses', or a state of affairs must not be worse for any member if it is to be better for the group. Failing either of those conditions, a change is collectively rational, good or worth while, only on the authority of someone's say-so.

have increments, they have them at a borderline where this jointness has ceased.

Contract-enforcement may illustrate jointness over a bounded range. All contracting parties benefit from enforceability and from the belief of others in it. This benefit in terms of greater *compliance* by all 'believers' is undiminished as the same or additional parties conclude more contracts in *reliance* on it. However, as contracts proliferate, so do (though perhaps not in proportion) defaults and litigation. At some point, the apparatus of judging and enforcing judgment gets sufficiently clogged up, expensive, unreliable, and slow for contractual commitments to be taken less seriously and contracts no longer to 'mean what they used to'. Crowdedness of enforcement, in encouraging lax compliance or downright default, may perversely induce greater crowdedness. Everybody's benefit from reliance on the practice of contracting is impaired. The borderline of 'jointness' has been passed and an increase in the supply of enforcement, or in that of non-public substitutes, becomes meaningful. Much the same may be true of civil security being, after a point, compromised and swamped by rising criminality, calling forth a rising supply of substitutes, self-help, private guards, vigilanteism, and insurance.

On scrutiny, jointness turns out to be merely a special case of indivisibility, linked to it by 'uncrowdedness'. A one-lane bridge over a watercourse is in joint supply to all users as long as they are few. As traffic gets heavier, jointness stops; each additional vehicle reduces the average benefit derived by all, due to crowdedness, longer waiting, accidents, and so on. Broadening the bridge and adding a second lane, allowing vehicles to pass both ways, restores jointness. That this is the case is due solely to the impossibility of adjusting the bridge's capacity by driblets to traffic growth. The smallest practicable increment is one more lane and when that gets crowded, one more again, each lane recreating jointness over a certain range, and each further phase of traffic growth erasing it again.

The converse, however, is not always true. A good may come only in indivisible, fixed 'lumps', yet it might never be uncrowded and each additional user would diminish the enjoyment of existing ones, no matter how few. A lovers' lane or any place where two is company and three is a crowd are cases in point, and so are less romantic 'positional goods', privileges, and honours which may well be indivisible yet are always 'crowded' to some extent the moment they have more than one occupant. Indivisibility alone *permits* jointness; but it does not entail it.

It is quite clear how the indivisibility of a good has the direct consequence that for any level of individual contribution to its cost some minimum number k must contribute in order to enable a group of N persons to benefit from it, while once k have contributed, the remaining $N-k$ might as well not contribute unless to affect distributional issues of 'fairness'. To the extent that this is the case, the benefit that an individual can expect to derive from his own contribution to the group good is powerfully 'leveraged'. Instead of having (implicitly) to reckon with some patently destructive dilution factor (such as $1/N$, the reciprocal of group size, which would be applicable under perfect divisibility of the public good and constant returns to contributions), it is typically a much more moderate one (k/N, the proportion of the group carrying the burden for the whole group) that an individual has to allow for when deciding whether it would pay him to volunteer for the role of sucker. This general dilution-factor functions as the measure of probability—in looser everyday parlance, the risk—that the failure of any randomly chosen member of the group to subscribe to the cost of the group good would cause the group good to fail.

Do we conclude, then, that wholly indivisible goods stand some, at first sight quite reasonable, chance of being publicly provided out of freely subscribed contributions, whereas the chance of wholly divisible goods being so provided is incomparably smaller (and for most practical purposes negligible)—so that for the latter sorts of goods 'divided we fall' and the forbidding public-goods 'dilemma' remains the appropriate paradigm?

What our scrutiny is about to show is that while this is formally quite true, it is also fairly unimportant, for once divisible goods 'go public' they lose much of their divisibility. Publicness may well be caused by indivisibility in the engineering-logistic sense (the bridge that must not be shorter than the width of the river). Much of the social infrastructure is presumably public because it is to some degree indivisible. In the probably more general socio-economic sense, however, it is publicness that *causes* indivisibility. This is a logical consequence of the form of the problem: the size of the non-excluded public and its standards of expected provision being exogenous constants at least within limits, the supply dimension of the good, or at all events the threshold size it must at least have, is by implication fixed. Its physical characteristics, notably its eventual divisibility in terms of the logistics of production, do not really affect the issue.

The supply of bought meals is divisible in all kinds of ways. The number of restaurants, their tables, the number of meals, and the contents of each meal are all variable by fine increments. Let, however, a free mid-day meal be offered in the works canteen to all employees who choose to come; in a canteen under a certain size, with too few tables and meals below a conventional standard, there might be so much jostling, having to come very early or very late, bribing of waitresses, frustrated queueing, and grumbling by discontented employees that the meal, considered as an attempt at non-excluded provision, could not qualify as a public good. There is an unflattering analogy with animal husbandry: when feeding a herd of swine or cattle, there is a minimum length of trough, size of feed-lot, and quantity of grain or fodder, failing which the animals push, spill, and trample the feed into the mud; below a threshold size of supply there *is* no good.

It is of the essence of non-excluded, public provision that the familiar mechanisms for adjusting supply and demand to each other *ex post* are ruled out at least in intent. If they do creep back in (as they sometimes do in the form of 'pull', side-deals, the bartering of favours, fiddling, queues and waiting lists, bribes, under-the-counter service, and, last but far from least, quasi-exclusion by the assignment of priorities), leading to the establishment of limited and controlled access according to merit, deserts, or some other criterion (in the presence of significant effects from this kind of demand-adjusting device), provision of the good is not 'non-excluded' and properly 'public', though its privateness may be disguised by the figleaf of no overt price or low price.

At a given level and style of civilization, with habitual norms and practices in the use of private substitutes, a community is likely to have reasonably specific ideas about the standard that public provision of a good must meet. There is only so much truancy, juvenile delinquency, gang intimidation of teachers, and scholastic non-achievement that is still compatible with the concept of free public education for all. If the 'supply of education', however one may contrive to put a measuring-rod against it, falls short of the community's notion of the minimum needed for coping, unplanned corrective mechanisms of diverse efficiency tend to be set in motion. Part of the non-excluded group—probably the richer and/or brighter—may 'exclude itself' altogether, or form a separate 'élite', inclusive group and informally annex the 'good' schools. Another part—probably the dullest and/or those with the worst family backgrounds—may be effectively excluded and relegated to a separate publicly provided 'good', consisting of a less ambitious or substandard education in the worst schools.[3] Alternatively, contributions to the cost may be raised to lift the level of supply to (or above) the threshold consistent with publicness, or short cuts and reforms tried to alter the nature of the good and fit its supply to the demand without raising the cost. In any case, a degree of indivisibility of the (physically no doubt easily divisible) good 'education' will have been demonstrated: once it is made non-excluded, if all do not get it, none do, at least not in the intended sense and manner, and to the culturally determined standard of expectation.

Medical care, almost infinitely divisible in terms of its logistics, likewise tends to become indivisible to a degree once it is no longer meant to be rationed either by money or by medical discretion and sense of proportion. Unless there are enough doctors to cope with everyone's demands for attention more or less instantaneously, nobody is assured of proper attention, though many will in fact get it. Failing a publicly provided, free health service of a certain minimum dimension, there must be hidden (or perhaps even overt) exclusion mechanisms which screen out a part of the demand on some ground, satisfy frivolous complaints with placebos, and keep others at the bottom of waiting-lists. Literal non-exclusion, however, literally means all or none; all or none in turns means some, albeit standard-bound, fixed minimum size of supply; and that, of course, means indivisibility at least up to a threshold.

To anticipate a very reasonable objection, let us admit to two kinds of indivisibility. One is of the logistical sort: half a bridge is

[3] Obviously, even in disgraceful schools, many children—to the great credit of their teachers, parents, and themselves—do manage to become reasonably educated. This is not inconsistent with the diagnosis that in such schools education is not, properly speaking, a public good, for it is vitiated by more or less covert, or at least unwittingly created, 'exclusion mechanisms' which direct more of the supply to the good pupil and less to the bad one. This can be the case even with the most devoted and even-handed teachers.

no bridge, a half-pair of boots is useless. Unless the whole cost of the natural unit of the good is found, it will not be usefully provided. This is 'definite indivisibility', easy to perceive. The other kind is 'vague indivisibility', where the useful unit of the good in public provision is hard to define, moot, a matter of appreciation. The exact dimensions (how large a room, how many tables and waitresses, how much crockery, how much food and what sort) the free meal in the works canteen must have to pass for 'public', non-excluded in the intended meaning of non-exclusion, and given the standards of the group of people to be served, are not sharply drawn. The criterion the unit of the good must meet is adequacy, and the good is vaguely indivisible because 'adequate' is a vague term. This gives rise to a paradox invoked by Hampton (1987). She uses the example of 'a heap' of stones. Whether a given pile of stones is adequate to pass for a heap is not self-evident. Supposing that there is doubt about the matter and it is worth something to each of a group of individuals that the pile should be a heap. Would each or any of them take the trouble to add a stone to it? The conventional wisdom is that none would, each arguing that either the pile is already a heap as it is, or it is not going to become one thanks to just more stone. In other words, the vagueness of the indivisibility of the desired heap deprives the kth contribution of the critical, pivotal character it has for 'definitely indivisible' goods. Potential contributions would consequently lose the incentive provided by the probability that without them there might be fewer than k contributors, causing failure.

Their reasoning, however, would be irrational in the sense of being self-contradictory. For if they were asked whether they were certain that the pile is already a heap, and they said no, we could ask them whether it would become one for sure thanks to two more stones, or three more stones, etc., to n more stones. If there were no finite n stones, no matter how large n was, that would for sure make a heap (i.e. if only an infinitely large unit would constitute a 'good' and have value for them), the problem could be dismissed as a false one. If, on the other hand, adding a finite number Δn stones would be agreed as 'sure to make a heap' and $-\Delta n$ sure to unmake it, the person so interviewed would have admitted to some implicit probability distribution that a given stone within the range $-\Delta n$ to Δn *is* the stone that makes a pile a heap. Unless the person could reasonably account for a belief that there is a black hole, a discontinuity over some part of the probability range he has so defined, he would have reasoned as if he held that adding *any* stone up to the nth will add *some* increment of probability Δp to the truth of the statement that the pile is a heap; his expected benefit from contributing that stone would be the value to him of the heap *times* Δp. The converse would be true if he withdrew a stone.

While for a sharply outlined, 'definitely indivisible' good there is a single number k denoting the number of contributions required for the good to be produced at all, for a fuzzily outlined, 'vaguely indivisible' good this is replaced by a probability distribution of numbers whose mathematical expectation is *ex hypothesi* k. Passing from a sharp to a blurred outline of the indivisible good does not deprive the contributors of the incentive to contribute if they had any to start with. There is still a set of contributors whose marginal product equals the total product in such a way that if *any* member of the set withdrew his contribution the good would fail to be provided.

Under 'definite indivisibility' this set is the subset k of the non-excluded population N, and the *a priori* probability that any random member of N is also a member of k is k/N. Under 'vague indivisibility', the subset is itself a probability distribution around k. But this should prima facie not deter the individual from contributing, provided he would have done so if k had been a single number; his maximizing reasoning would simply become a little more sophisticated to reach an analogous conclusion. If the contributing subset needed to produce the good were in fact larger than k, his chance of being a necessary contributor would be *pro tanto* larger than k/N, and vice versa. Consequently, using in a maximizing calculation the certainty equivalent of the probability distribution of the subset of required contributors would entitle an individual to expect as good or as bad a result in terms of his benefit *less* his contribution as he would have got if he had calculated with the single number k. This result might have to be modified for utility-maximizing (rather than net-benefit-maximizing) individuals whose utility was not a linear function of their net benefit. If the latter were the case, they might attach more weight to the loss they would bring upon themselves by being the cause of the failure of the public good and of the falling back to the exchange regime than to the gain from not contributing to a good that was going to be produced anyway, since in reality it needed fewer contributors than the certainty equivalent of a distribution of more or less probable values of k. It may be that the presence of many such individuals in N would, on balance, bias the overall result in favour of contributing to 'vaguely indivisible' public goods, but the bias seems to me too conjectural to insist upon.

It is hard to think of a conveniently divisible good which, once it is made freely available to some group of non-excluded persons, does not become 'vaguely' indivisible, at least within limits broadly set by 'culture' and custom. Good manners seem infinitely divisible, but unless a large enough proportion of a (locally defined) group subscribes to a code of good manners, reliance on it will not serve as a public good to the whole group, for that would require some threshold probability of anyone meeting with predictable good conduct on the part of anyone else (including, of course, strangers). That one more person in the group forgetting his manners, one more stroller spreading litter in the park, one more apprehended offender[4] being let off with impunity should spoil the social amentities, the agreements of the park, or the security of unguarded property, so that one moment all benefit and the next none does, is admittedly a contrived construction to put on public goods. So is the role given to the last straw in breaking the camel's back.

Nevertheless, if a critical load of straw can break the camel's back, there must always be a critical nth straw to complete the critical load; the fact that we do not confidently assign a single number to stand for n, but implicitly treat it as a probability distribution, does not make the notions of criticalness and of thresholds any less valid. If all other straws are to be carried as planned, the possible loss of utility in case they cease to be carried, and the rising probability of the loss in fact being incurred as additional straws are added to the load, are conceptually perfectly clear. Applying the concept in practice may be a difficult calculation and blundering about it easy; but this is immaterial to questions of validity and may even be irrelevant to empirical issues as long as there are enough blunders *either side* of the 'right' answer to cancel themselves out. The necessity to treat the problem in probabilistic

---

[4] The person who forgot his manners, the litterer, and the thief are 'negative subscribers' to the corresponding public goods; so is the polluter, the defector, and the traitor. The alternative formulation, in which they are *positive* subscribers to public *bads*, is if anything more tortuous.

terms, moreover, can be made into a virtue by harnessing the solution to the effect of risk.

Non-exclusion of a given group, brought up to certain standards of civilization, entails a certain, however indistinctly defined, threshold. Supply cannot be allowed to fall below the threshold if the good is to function as a public one. Hence, for its provision to be possible from the resources of the group, some minimum number of 'subscriptions' to contribute is needed. The supply a lesser number of subscribers could provide would either be useless (the feed would be trampled into the mud, the bridge would not reach the other shore) or contrary to the intent of the enterprise in that it would bring about recourse to devices of covert exclusion and quasi-exclusion. The 'lump' of the good corresponding to the critical threshold supply is, of course, liable to have the same handicap as the pile of stones that was a heap, or the load that would break the camel's back: it is hard to say for sure exactly how large it is. Evidence to support various hypotheses about it could come from experience, worldly wisdom, public debate, and public-goods lobby politics from the parish pump to the national level. Given the evidence, such as it is, it will be a probability distribution in people's heads and quite possibly a somewhat different one in each head—without this fact making a particular solution any more or less likely.

'Uncertainty'

We do not usually know for sure what is in people's heads. However, this is no licence for ascribing to them unexplained dispositions, propensities, and aversions which can be turned to support almost any claim concerning behaviour. Attributing to people uncaused leanings, 'animal spirits', and gut reactions is a rampant practice in situations involving uncertainty and 'risky' choices, where choosing could be said to be rational if it seemed consistent with 'probability of utility' comparisons among mutually exclusive outcomes (payoffs). There are two non-instrumental, non-derived, 'final' propensities, in particular, that tend to be imputed to people in such situations, both confusing, or so I believe, because they reflect confused thought.

1. People deal in certain ways with *known* probabilities; they are

supposed to deal differently with *unknown* probabilities (because they 'dislike uncertainty', refuse to make decisions on inadequate data', 'prefer rational evaluation to blind plunging', etc.). In fact, almost anything they might do could be explained by and blamed on 'uncertainty'.

In this type of claim, there is first a confusion between frequency (or statistical probability) and the far more general concept of the (necessarily subjective) probability a person attaches to a hypothesis being true. It makes a certain sense to speak of a frequency as 'known'.[5] If applicable to the hypothesis, a known *frequency* is one possible and perhaps the major element among many that a person may choose to consider as evidence when judging the *probability* that the hypothesis is in fact true. It is this probability, formed in the mind of the person concerned, on such evidence as he has, that is alone relevant to his reasons for and against his *acting* on the hypothesis. It is neither 'known' nor 'unknown'; these are quite inappropriate categories to apply to the *probability* of something being true.

'Unknown probability' (except in the frequency sense) is either an unintelligible linguistic absurdity or (more charitably) it is the symbolic expression of the *refusal* by a person to estimate the truth-value of a hypothesis. He may justify his refusal with the penury of evidence, his incompetence in getting any more of it, and in evaluating that which he has. All this is perfectly acceptable as long as judging the hypothesis is an inconsequential parlour-game he may elect to engage in or not, at *no opportunity cost* either way.

When, however, consequences affecting the person and involving benefits and costs (including forgone benefits and avoided costs)in the widest sense are inseparable *both* from acting *and* from not acting on a hypthesis of consequences, the alleged refusal to assign a probability to the hypothesis is either pretence and self-delusion—for by his choice of action or inaction the person has 'revealed' that he was implicitly using the particular probability judgement that would have justified his choice—or a renunciation of the exigencies of rationality as a methodological assumption. In the latter case, the claim we make about 'unknown probability' is, in reality, a claim that in certain situations otherwise rational persons try and run away from choices, start throwing tantrums,

---

[5] A frequency is known *ex post* and under appropriate conditions it can be interpreted as a 'known' statistical probability *ex ante*.

dig in their heels, or bury their head in the sand. This is not a claim one can contest, but nor is it one critics of probabilistic decision theory would own up to.

The other confusion is to treat certain changes in probability as quantitative, others as qualitative, by slipping in a more or less covert assumption of non-continuity. The claim that 'uncertainty' makes for a wholly different behavioural world from 'certainty' is of this sort. If the probability of a proposition being true is represented by a cardinal[6] index running from 0 to 1, the Hegelian fallacy about a 'change of quantity' becoming a 'change of quality' would, in this context, be to argue that as the index rises from 0.9 to 1 something happens that is quite different in kind from the effect of its rising from 0.8 to 0.9. Likewise, a fall in the index from 0.1 to 0 is a very different matter from its decline from 0.2 to 0.1. In both the shift from 0.9 to 1 and from 0.1 to 0, 'uncertainty' is replaced by 'certainty', and the choice whose consequences are 'uncertain' is 'different in kind' from that whose (sole) consequence is certain. To say this is either an empty verbalism having no bearing on how we in fact try to make the best choices we can, or an escape into a realm of gratuitous assumptions about non-rational choices under which 'anything goes', and for all one can tell there are no determinate solutions.

2. The other great unexplained propensity is not so much to switch behaviour (e.g. from rational to irrational or from calculated to ritualistic and reflex-reactive), but to 'switch *maximands*' while still pursuing maximization as the criterion of rational behaviour in the face of 'uncertainty'. When the probabilities of a certain decision producing certain consequences or payoffs are either 1 or 0, at each limiting value (one consequence is certain, all others are excluded), the best decision is the one that maximizes utility. In neo-classical decision theory, this is still the best decision when the several probabilities of alternative consequences are distributed *between* 1 and 0, for the simple reason that utility is defined as that

---

[6] Ordinal probability (*a* is more likely than *b*; 'by how much' is left unstated) is limited in its explanatory force in the same way as ordinal utility is. Each can justify (determine) a choice only if the other weakly favours it anyway. If one of two gambles yields *a* or *c* and the other *b* or *c*, the greater ordinal probability of *a* can justifiedly decide in favour of the first gamble if *a* is weakly preferred over *b*. Similarly, ordinal preference for *a* justifies the first gamble if *a* is at least equiprobable to *b*. However, if *a* is preferred but *b* is more probable, ordinal indices cannot tell us which of the two gambles to take.

168 PUBLICNESS: SOLUTION AND RESULT

dependent variable of the payoffs (or consequences of decisions) which the decision is meant to maximize. Given the probabilities, the best decision 'reveals' the respective utilities.[7] (The converse is the case when it is the utilities that are given.) It can be said, for instance, that if a person would rather take 20 dollars than the even chance of 10 or 50 dollars, he reveals a utility function where the marginal utility of the payoff diminishes at a certain rate as the payoff increases. If it did not, we could not affirm that refusing the mathematically more than fair gamble was the best, 'maximizing' decision. Colloquially, we can also say that the shape of the utility function reflects risk-aversion, prudence, a reluctance to gamble; these attitudes are the *visible symptoms* of the endeavour to maximize utility when it is declining at the margin.

In addition, however, one often encounters purported explanations of behaviour which contend that while people may maximize utility under certainty (and, in certain versions, also in the face of statistically measurable risk), under 'genuine uncertainty' they just do not (though what else they do is left unclear); or if they do, it is subject to constraints, boundaries, vetoes. Alternatively, they do not maximize utility but something else; they minimize 'potential surprise', maximize the minimum outcome, minimize potential regret, anxiety, and so forth. Sometimes 'uncertainty of the relevant probabilities' and 'aversion to risk' are put forward as the reasons why some other *maximand* than utility should be assumed, and maximization of expected utility discarded, as the sufficient condition of rational decisions—as if expected utility-maximization were not expressly designed to encompass precisely these features of choice with uncertain consequences.

In sum, these propensities and special behaviour-assumptions in the face of uncertainty are not complementary, but alternatives to expected utility-maximization. One cannot hold *them* and *it* at the same time.[8] The reason for making this point firmly and at some length (though still far too briefly for a subject to which a book or a whole shelf of books could hardly do full justice) is that sticking

[7] This was the approach of Ramsey's famous essay 'Truth and Probability': Ramsey (1931).
[8] For a contrary view, cf. Elster (1986*b*), 29 n. 16. More precisely, Elster expresses the wish that one could meaningfully state the intuition, which he believes to reflect a genuine element of reality, that risk-avoidance is not simply double-counting what is already stated in utility-maximization, but may in some sense be additional to it.

to expected utility-maximization as the explanatory hypothesis imposes a salutary discipline on what can and cannot be advanced in a theory where all hinges on the participants' probability judgements of each other's actions. The core of such a theory is sketched in the next section

A Spontaneous Solution through Risk

The straddle ranking of the four alternative payoffs that two strategies, 'subscribe' and 'not subscribe', may yield permits rational play without imposing a dominant strategy. Player A expects his best or his worst payoffs if he does not subscribe, and his second- or third-best if he does. Neither pair is *a priori* better under expected utility-maximization (though the inside pair would presumably be better, and subscribing always right, under the kind of risk-minimizing propensities discussed in the preceding section). Since the ranking alone does not enable the player to weigh the outside pair ('best or worst') against the inside pair ('second-best or third-best'), his choice between subscribing and not subscribing is at first blush indeterminate. Actual choice, of course, is always determinate in the trivial sense that it must have had sufficient cause, if only the fall of a spun coin. To restrict possible causes and shut out whimsy, we assume that the player seeks the strategy or move that will maximize his utility, or that he behaves near enough as if he did.

Each move is 'risky' in that each involves some probability of a major and some other probability of a minor payoff. The expected utility of each move is the sum of the expected utilities of the major and the minor payoff. Such sums and their difference-comparisons are unintelligible if the payoffs themselves are comparable only in terms of better or worse, greater or smaller, i.e. in terms of their ranks in an ordering. A player's utility-maximizing choice with uncertain payoffs is conceptually intelligible only in terms of level-and-difference comparisons (cardinal utility) and fully numerical probabilities, though it need not be supposed that he must actually assign the numbers and perform the calculation to achieve a reasonably successful approximation to what he would, on longer reflection, identify as his best choice.

We denote the elements in A's choice as follows:

US the expected utility of the 'subscribe' strategy S to A;

s_1 the utility of the 'fair mixed regime' (major payoff);

s_2 the utility of 'sucker' (minor payoff);

UNS the expected utility of the 'not subscribe' strategy NS to A;

ns_1 the utility of 'free ride' (major payoff);

ns_2 the utility of the 'exchange regime' (minor payoff);

k/N the proportion of 'suckers' in the group needed for the mixed regime ($k = \bar{k}$ after adjustment of per caput subscriptions);

p the probability that any randomly chosen member B subscribes;

p' the probability of the 'free ride' payoff.

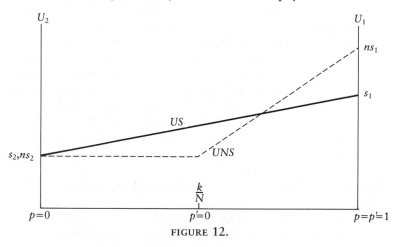

FIGURE 12.

The expected utility US of the strategy S is the sum of the expected values of s_2 and s_1. Both vary directly with p. With $p = 0$ (no B is expected to subscribe) s_1 has no expected value, while the value of s_2 is its opportunity cost ns_2, for the subscriber is sure to keep his subscription and resort to the exchange regime of private goods. As p increases, US rises *pari passu*. One can either say that this reflects a tiny but growing chance of the 'fair mixed regime', or that 'sucker' involves terms of diminishing unfairness. At a low p, US is mostly the sucker payoff; at a high p, it is mostly 'fair mixed regime'. When $p = 1$, US is s_1, for the subscriber is sure of fair provision. Thus one can write:

$$US = (1 - p)s_2 + ps_1$$

The expected utility UNS of NS is likewise the sum of the expected values of ns_2 and ns_1. The nature of free riding is such as to require some contribution before there can be any free riding or, in probabilistic terms, $p' < p < 1$. Where all Bs are expected to subscribe, A is sure of the free-rider payoff if he chooses not to subscribe: hence in the limit $p' = p = 1$. Conversely, where 'too few' Bs are expected to subscribe, A has little or no chance of the free-rider payoff, i.e $k/N > p > p'$. In general terms:

$$p' = f(k/N, p)$$

A specific form of this hypothesis is that p' increases with the excess of p over k/N, rising from nil when $p = k/N$ and converging on p when $p = 1$. This reflects the argument of Chapter 6, p. 155, and is reflected in Figure 12. However, any weaker hypothesis would suffice as long as it stipulated that $p' < p$ when p was low and $p' = p$ when p was high—a condition which can be taken as axiomatic. Under any hypothesis about the determination of p', the expected utility of the not-subscribe strategy NS is

$$UNS = (1 - p') ns_2 + p' ns_1$$

Expected utility-maximization by A is represented in Figure 12, where the utility of the minor and major payoffs is marked on the vertical axes U_2 and U_1, respectively, and p and p' are marked on the horizontal axis. Where US is higher than UNS, it is better for A to subscribe, and vice versa.

Between $0 < p < k/N$, A plays in what earlier (p. 155n.) we called a subsidiary part of the main game. If he subscribes, the chance of his and the Bs' subscriptions together reaching the critical threshold required for the mixed regime on 'sucker' terms increases from 0 to 1 as p rises from 0 to k/N. Over this range, the expected utility UNS of the 'not subscribe' strategy is supported only or mainly by the assured utility of ns_2; 'subscribe' dominates.

Opening up the probability range of the Bs subscribing all the way from 0 to 1 puts A in the generalized choice position of what we had called the main game. At low probabilities of the Bs subscribing, he is better off subscribing, at high probabilities he is better off going for the significant chance of ns_1, free riding. UNS cuts US from below, some way to the right of the threshold value

k/N of the probability of subscriptions. The weaker the hypothesis, the closer would come this inversion-point to k/N.

Once past the inversion-point, not only is it better not to subscribe, but the excess utility so secured keeps increasing as p tends towards unity. The greater is the probability of all Bs subscribing, the greater is A's incentive to try free riding, and vice versa. This accords with the intuitive interpretation of subscribing as buying the mixed regime on unfair terms for fear that on fairer terms it might not become available at all. The lesser the risk of this being the case, the lesser the point of paying to avoid it. The risk is 'constructive' in that it reduces the discrepancy between what is 'collectively' and individually rational.

All Cretans are not Liars

There is a central range of probabilities of the members of a group being prepared to contribute to a 'mixed regime', i.e. to the public provision for the whole group of a certain good. Over this range the group is believed to break broadly two ways. A significant proportion are thought to accept being suckers, the remainder are expected to try their luck on free riding. A, whom we assume to hold these probabilistic judgements about his fellows, may go either way 'depending on the numbers', i.e. depending on the utilities of his payoffs and the specific probability he attaches to each. For some values of these variable numbers, 'subscribe' will maximize his expected utility. Spontaneous co-operation in associations and interest-groups, voluntary contributions to collective purposes, charity, carrying the burdens of leadership, honouring commitments, and respecting norms when it is inconvenient to do so can accordingly be consistent with single-minded utility-maximization, provided the 'productivity of publicness' furnishes sufficient incentive. No recourse need be had to more varied mixed motivations, nor to assumptions about certain 'games' being replayed, about informal sanctions, private enforcement and 'man's better nature'. Not that there is anything wrong with such assumptions. In some ways, what is wrong is not to make them, for they are patently more realistic than snow-pure single-mindedness. However, a theory which can get by on the latter and needs none of the former has, I think, both some intrinsic interest (for it is widely believed that voluntary contribution is inexplicable on that basis alone) and could be helpful in assessing the effect of adding more realistic and less austere assumptions about motives. Some attempt to do that is made in Chapter 8.

For the present, however, the theory must also come to terms with itself outside the central range of probabilities. At the extremes, where we approach certainty of the fair mixed regime (all subscribe) or of the exchange regime (none subscribe), the logic of the straddle framework—and the coherence of the advice to be read off the diagram in Figure 12—comes under some strain. At values of p approaching unity, nearly all group members are expected to subscribe and the utility-maximizing move is to do the opposite. Does it really make sense for A to expect all or nearly all the Bs to act contrary to what, from where he stands, looks the best choice? Could the Bs be sufficiently different from him to explain their strange behaviour? They cannot really be, for A is any member of the group chosen at random to play opposite the Bs; he is one of them and could swap roles with any randomly chosen B.

The apparent paradox would disappear if the Bs did not 'subscribe' but were 'taxed'. There would then be perfect coherence between everybody contributing while his utility-maximizing move was not to contribute. Any (single-minded) reason to *want* to pay taxes, however strong or weak to start with, must fall victim to a very high probability that enough others are paying anyway and free riding on their contributions is assured. Taxes, however, are typically paid for reasons other than one's share in the public goods and services financed by one's own payment. Being socio-contractually commanded to pay can explain why all pay, though given that they do, none has any incentive to pay. In the uncoerced state of nature, however, both 'all pay' and 'none pays' are hopelessly self-contradictory. If all pay, none would, and if none pay, all would.

We seem to be caught in the paradox of the Cretan Liar. When he declares that all Cretans are liars,[9] his lie is construed to mean that none are liars. However, in that case he, too, is telling the truth and all are liars. The solution of this paradox is to refuse to step into logic traps, dismissing them instead as figures of speech. (If the Cretan says that all Cretans are liars, only some are; some may be

---

[9] The paradox is attributed to the semi-legendary 6th-cent. BC philosopher Epimenides of Knossos, who was himself a Cretan.

telling the truth and he may be one who does.) The same solution suggests itself for our state-of-nature public-provision problem: 'all subscribe' or 'none does'—and even the slightly weaker forms where nearly all do or hardly anyone does—are really figures of speech, for, taken literally, they destroy the stochastic environment with its 'constructive' risk, which is an antecedent condition of the solution.

In order to see this, let us recall that the straddle ordering, with the minor payoff from 'subscribing' ranked above the minor payoff from 'not subscribing', was not one of our assumptions, a kind of given 'taste about which there shall be no dispute'. Instead, it was *derived* from calculating, single-minded instrumental rationality in the face of certain characteristics of a given public-goods problem. As such, it was very much open to 'dispute'. Broadly, the productivity of publicness had to offset the dilutive effect of publicness for 'sucker' to be preferred. Dilution was a stochastic value, having to do with the probability of an individual being a part of the decisive subset of 'suckers', who must carry the free-riding complement of the group in order for public provision for all to happen. The more this probability approaches 0 or 1, the harder it is to accept the straddle ranking in general and the 'sucker' payoff in particular. Anyone holding an extreme expectation about his fellow group members, either that nearly all will or that hardly any will contribute, is cutting the ground under the hypothesis that would make it rational for him to rank the payoffs in the straddle order.

Inconsistent Expectations

Consideration of the Cretan Liar problem, placed in the context of private contribution–public benefit, helps to clarify the role of inconsistent expectations held by 'players' in the straddle 'game' about each other's likely conduct. The sole positive solution with mutually consistent expectations is one where k out of N players hold that the probability p of anyone else subscribing is k/N or less, hence it is preferable to subscribe, while $N - k$ players hold that p is k/N or greater, hence it is better not to subscribe. (The strict division is not at $p = k/N$, but at a somewhat higher probability, defined by the intersection of US and UNS in Figure 12, corresponding to somewhat more suckers and somewhat fewer free riders. It sems more natural to assume, however, that if members of a group formulate a probability about each other, it is in terms of the sucker–free rider distinction, i.e. the focal k/N.)

Mutual consistency is merely a landmark to assist reasoning. It happens to correspond to a positive solution (public provision will be carried out on the planned scale), but it is not a necessary condition of it. There is nothing in our scheme that would act upon individual probability-judgements to help make them mutually consistent. Inconsistent expectations can give rise to a positive solution without any absurdity being involved, as long as the inconsistency stops well short of the Cretan Liar paradox. If k or *more* members of N expect k or *less* to subscribe, public provision is likely to be successfully undertaken. Conversely, if k or *more* expect k or *more* to subscribe, the project is likely to fail due to undersubscription. There may well be opportunities for post-game adjustments, for trying again. But nothing suggests that positive solutions cannot arise out of mutually inconsistent expectations in the first place. Many probability-judgements can turn out to have been simply wrong and, for all we can tell, that may be the end of the matter, at least until another mixed regime to provide another good is placed on the agenda of a given group.

APPENDIX: STRADDLE OR CHICKEN

Some of the key propositions and relationships I use in the arguments of Chapters 6 and 7, and some of my conclusions, have been anticipated in an important paper by Taylor and Ward,[10] which came to my attention belatedly, when the text of the present book had already been completed. Acknowledgement of their precedence, and a brief account of some of the divergences between our respective approaches, must therefore be accommodated in this appendix. (References to the Taylor and Ward paper are preceded by TW, to the present book by J.)

[10] Taylor and Ward (1982).

I

For TW, non-excludable and indivisible goods are public. For J, publicness is often a social decision, having little to do with the intrinsic characteristics (excludability and divisibility) of the good concerned. It is publicness (i.e. non-exclusion) that causes (or strongly contributes to) indivisibility, which is often more 'social' than 'technical'.

TW warn that the traditional identification of the public-good problem with the prisoners' dilemma is largely groundless. Other game structures, and especially the game of chicken, correspond better to reality. The preference-ranking of possible public-goods payoffs in chicken is, from best to worst, 'free ride', 'public good', 'sucker', and 'private good', i.e. the alternative payoffs from contributing straddle the alternative payoffs from not contributing. Unlike in the prisoners' dilemma, contributing is not a dominated strategy: it may well be individually rational, utility-maximizing. The clinching argument against the realism of the preference-ordering that causes the prisoners' dilemma (TW, p. 354) is that only in chicken is free ride a feasible alternative. In a non-coerced, state-of-nature public-goods situation, both the prisoners'-dilemma-type and the assurance-game-type preference-ordering of the alternatives would imply that either nobody contributes or all do. Free riding would be impossible in either case. Since the solutions of many actual uncoerced public-goods interactions do include free riding, the preference ordering must place 'sucker' above 'private good' ($CD > DD$), for otherwise the ordering would contradict the solution.

In the present book (Chapter 6), the corresponding straddle ordering is not *inferred* from actual solutions, but *deduced* from the positive effect of the extra utility of publicness and the negative effect of the dilution factor that obtains between an individual's contribution and the benefit that he personally derives from it. The preference order is a matter of rational calculus, with the straddle order being a consequence of the parameters having the right combined value. The nature of the parameters is such that they will tend to have the right value if public provision is sufficiently superior to the exchange regime of private substitutes.

II

Apart from the derivation of the preference-order by inference in TW, by deduction in J, the solutions of chicken and straddle, though similar, are reached by different types (or different 'protocols') of interaction. In a two-person game of chicken, the player allowed to move first can, by not subscribing a contribution, put the other player in a position where his best option is to subscribe, the first player getting 'free ride', the second 'sucker'. If there is no sequential rule, either player may try and pre-empt this bold strategy by committing himself in advance and beating the other player to not subscribing. This shifts the problem from the game to the pre-game. Considering that if both players were to commit themselves not to subscribe, the public good would not be provided, they may both settle for the less bold strategy. While 'both pre-committing' and 'neither pre-committing' are equilibria, they are not stable: each player would gain by deviating from the position provided the other maintains it. A co-ordinating contract would not normally be self-enforcing in chicken any more than it is in the prisoners' dilemma (although some self-enforcing tendency would arise in continuous or repeated interaction).

For three-person chicken games, TW show that pre-commitment by one player not to subscribe makes it certain that the other two will subscribe: they define (TW, p. 355) n-person chicken by the property that each player has an incentive to pre-commit himself not to subscribe. This, however, may not be a workable definition unless n is small enough for any one player's pre-committed strategy to represent a significant threat to others, capable of causing them to 'chicken'. For pre-commitment is not a good strategy in itself, but only through its probable effect on other players. It is by shifting the latter's strategy towards subscribing that the former profits from his own pre-commitment, which earns him the top payoff, i.e. free riding. If the other players' strategies remain unaffected by it, pre-commitment to any particular strategy is at best pointless, at worst a sacrifice of one's freedom to choose a strategy in the game instead of choosing it beforehand in the pre-game—a sacrifice which may be costly if it deprives the player of the benefits of the latest information.

Clearly, the larger is n, the more the posturings and declarations of one player would be ignored by the $n - 1$ others and the more the game would lose the face-to-face character which is the essence of chicken, where the effect of the pre-committed threat strategy of one player upon the uncommitted strategy of the other derives solely from the visibility and mass of the former. Failing that, pre-committing not to subscribe is not better than simply not subscribing, and may be worse. Pre-commitment then becomes the dominated strategy; and, as between the other two uncommitted strategies, neither dominates. The working of the n-person chicken of TW should then come to resemble the straddle in J. As against this, TW consider that pre-commitment by some, adjustment of their strategy to it by others, is valid regardless of the absolute value of n, which seems doubtful.

In the straddle of J, a player does not expect his choice of strategy to influence the choice of the strategies of the others: causation runs from the probability of the Bs doing S (or NS) to A doing NS (or S). The straddle, in other words, is not a true game in that the strategies of the *B*s are 'parametric' for *A*. He does not expect them to depend on *his* strategy, though his depends on *theirs*. In the chicken of TW, causation runs the other way; the *B*s are cowed or bluffed into contributing (*S*) by *A*'s non-contribution (*NS*).

III

The distinction between few-person chicken and *n*-person straddle is implicit in the J account of how the subscription per head γ may be determined (J, p. 142). If it is pitched so low that *all* must subscribe lest public provision is to fail, *one* hold-out can, by pre-committing not to subscribe, blackmail the others into subscribing a little more than γ each. His choice is conspicuous and has great impact. This is the bluff, bargaining, and blackmail play particular to chicken. Once a handful have played this and γ has been raised high enough for the subscriptions of only *some* others to suffice, pre-commitment not to subscribe by each additional player ceases to be conspicuous and has a progressively smaller effect on the likelihood of total subscriptions being sufficient.

IV

The straddle can be converted into 'chicken with pre-commitment' by having a large *n*-person group coalesce into a small number of homogeneous subgroups, each choosing a binding strategy for its members. There would, however, be an obvious problem of defection and unravelling of the subgroup if there is no coercion. Hence, it is doubtful that getting back to small numbers by amalgamating many persons into a few cohesive coalitions is a legitimate device to employ in an assumed state-of-nature environment; for making the common strategy binding for all members of the coalition in the absence of third-party enforcement is itself a public-goods problem needing to be solved, and cannot be used to bring about the solution.

V

If the sequence of strategy-choices (or pre-commitments to them) are not controlled by a protocol, revolving-door, or queueing device, too many players in TW chicken may decide not to subscribe, or pre-commit not to, all at once, causing public provision to fail by mistake. TW admit two possibilities. People are either 'risk-averse' (TW, p. 362) and steer clear of commitment strategies, in which case all may subscribe and none ride free; this solution would be unstable. Or people are 'risk-loving', to the effect that too many commit themselves not to subscribe (TW, p. 370). Only if the latter contingency occurs will voluntary provision of the public good fail altogether (ibid.), though—we might add—the group would then have strong reasons for trying again, with many of its members tempering their 'love of risk'.

In J, there is no exogenously supplied risk-aversion or risk-love. Risk is not a 'good' or a 'bad' for which there are given 'tastes', but a certain constellation of contingent utilities combined with the probabilities of their occurrence. (TW. too, revert to a congruous, rational-choice-type analysis in Section VII of their paper.)

VI

In the straddle, the solution is constructed around the probability of any member B of the non-excluded group N being in the decisive set k who must all subscribe. This probability depends among other things on k/N. In the reference case of equiprobability, it *is* simply k/N. The solution is generally independent of the absolute size N of the group seeking to organize public provision of a good for itself.

In TW, the somewhat analogous key probability of any group member pre-commiting himself not to subscribe is some function of N and some *other* function of k. It has a separate elasticity with respect to each and the elasticities vary independently of each other (TW, pp. 368–9). Thus, even in the face of a constant k/N, the key probability in question can change either way if both k and N rise or fall in the same proportion. The characteristics in question appear to be unexplained independent variables (in much the same way as 'risk-love' and 'risk-aversion' come exogeneously from a black box). This leads TW to fairly inconclusive speculation about the effect of group size on the probability of co-operative solutions.

VII

In TW's chicken, if less than k subscribe and public provision fails to take place, the subscriptions appear to be totally lost (TW, p. 368, table 3). In J, upon undersubscription the subscriptions are simply not called up (returned if 'paid' in advance). The difference is important; it is prima facie surprising that under TW's assumptions of total loss, the preference-order is not that of the public goods (or 'prisoners' ') dilemma, with 'sucker' the worst outcome and non-subscription the dominant strategy.

8

AN ETHICS TURNPIKE

Having derived certain results, such as they are, from the deliberately austere assumptions of single-mindedness, we should now take a more relaxed view and deal with men who, albeit wholly rational, are open to most (though not all) of the wide range of possible motivations which look capable jointly to govern conduct. At the same time, we must try to eschew the kind of trivial generality where whatever is is, and whatever is done must have been done for a sufficient reason.

Utility-maximization, widely interpreted, is simply making one's action conform to one's motivation. So conceived, it is entailed by rationality. The category of rational actions must, at the very least, exclude the action of knowingly choosing other than the best available alternative. 'Best' has the empirical content, if any, that we had put into 'motivation'. Only if the hierarchy of his motives (including the ratios of any trade-offs that may be acceptable between them) is specified in sufficient detail can we sensibly say, in the face of a choice he has made, that a person did *not* do the best he could for himself according to his own lights.

'He preferred X to Y', however, is very rudimentary information. It is silent on how the preference-order depended on the quantity and on the probability of X and Y. *Any* X, no matter how puny or improbable, preferred to *any* Y, no matter how big, strong, or probable, is an absolute, 'lexical' ordering; it excludes trade-offs between variable driblets and variable probabilities of X and Y. Genuine lexical orderings, i.e. orderings of goods that are literally priceless, must be quite rare. Yet the discourse of choice theory often runs, no doubt unwittingly, as if preference were absolute, and X priceless in terms of Y, or at least as if acceptable rates of substitution between X and Y were so far away from their available rates of transformation as to leave trade-offs out of the question. It may be that if trade-offs were more in the foreground of analysis and people were consequently represented as more sensitive, more trigger-happy in their choices as prices, quantities available, and probabilities of accrual varied, public finance theory would pay less attention to finding and distributing the burden of contributions for certain public goods that must be provided, and more to the choice between public goods and private substitutes. This, however, is a digression whose pursuit must be left to another occasion.

If motivation is left unspecified and the utility function is only symbolically described, any action can be asserted to maximize utility. Chosen, preferred, and utility-maximizing all become synonyms we cannot tell from each other, though the concept of maximization will not lose all formal significance. 'Wanton destruction of one's good maximizes one's utility' is a coherent statement, that we judge as sensible against a background of just the right trade-offs between the good destroyed and such other 'goods' as the sense of power, the pleasure of a gratuitous gesture, the demonstration of being above material considerations, and so forth. It is obviously hard, though perhaps not impossible, to deny altogether that a sane man could harbour the sort of preferences that could make self-inflicted damage utility-maximizing for him.

Whether we want to enter into conjectures of this kind depends on the level of abstraction we seek and on our willingness, or lack of it, to be specific about the motivations we attribute to people.

The success of a body of economic theory which gets by very well with a purely formal concept of utility and chooses to ignore specific motivation (it does not matter what people want provided they seek it consistently) suggests that formal 'utility' did not swallow up 'motives' altogether without cause. Yet for all the progress that stands to the credit of this approach, it seems to me impossible to say all that needs to be said in many areas of the study of choice, solely in 'utility-speak' or 'preference-talk'.

Take, for example, the choice of 'risking one's life to save another's'. How is this phrased in the two languages? In preference- or utility-speak, the choice reveals a higher ranking, or excess utility, of saving another's life over the relevant opportunity cost, i.e. over not risking one's own. In motivation-talk, we uncouple the tautological identity between the *reason* for the act and its utility. The act of risking one's life can be ascribed to a specific motive, which is conceptually distinct from the utility of the act or the utility of its consequences. The act may then signify that 'duty overrode preference', or perhaps that 'rule-obedience has put a constraint on utility-maximization'. Moral philosophers might find these terms of reference more congenial than pure utility- or preference-speak. In what I irreverently call preference-speak, I could never say with impunity 'he preferred X but chose Y'. Yet the information that gets lost by not saying this might well be important and valuable.

Imputing specific motives to participants in social life must go hand in hand with reducing the all-inclusive generality of preference or utility concepts, for otherwise choice would end up overdetermined.[1] Were utility left wide open, to swallow up all reasons for human action, there could obviously be no place left for a variety of motivations. For moral philosophy and economics to cohabit once again as in their golden age, it might well help if distinct non-utility, extra-preferential motivations could find room next to utility in explanations of choices.

The project of accommodating both in some common frame looks worthwhile. However, its execution runs into the tangled and disputed frontiers between what must at all events be left to utility and what had better be allotted to (other) specific motivations. The uninstructed have long identified a person's utility with the fulfilment of his *selfish* ends. Sometimes this has been carried to the heroic simplification of equating 'rational' with 'selfish'. Such pairings of utility and selfishness, selfish and rational, are untenable if treated as definitions, and a muddle if treated as synthetic conclusions. This would be so even if selfishness were a workable, well-defined attribute, allowing actions to be sorted into useful, significant classes by reference to it. But it is not much good at classifying actions, for only a small part of all actions could qualify as either selfish or unselfish. The immense majority of commonplace choices are neither, or not noticeably so. Their one obvious motive is ethically neutral. It is to transact 'the ordinary business of life'—a motive coming close enough to the intuitive content of the idea of utility, hence one we would certainly not want to purge from it on the grounds that it does not meet the test of selfishness.

The major failing of selfishness as a sorting criterion, however, is its obscurity and weakness. Perhaps one can come closer to giving it

---

[1] Conversely, if the content of utility or preference is restricted, without 'meta-preferential' motivation being introduced to supplement and bolster it, choice will end up underdetermined. Those who choose all the same will qualify for A. K. Sen's aptly named class of 'rational fools' (Sen, 1976–7).

a clear and hard meaning by saying that acting selfishly is acting as if we gave no thought to the wishes and interests of others. It could then be the case that all anonymous arms-length transactions must fall into the selfish class. Yet this would be an unacceptable use of 'selfish': for selfishness implies the possibility of unselfishness, but how can one unselfishly buy a pound of sugar off the grocery shelf? How must one give thought to the wishes and interests of cane-cutters and grocers to save this act from being selfish?

As such usage of selfish will not do, it is presumably necessary that one should both know, be able to affect, yet choose to ignore, the wishes and interests of others. All our face-to-face Pareto-non-optimal choices should no doubt be put in this class, for it is surely selfish not to please someone if we could please him at *no* cost to ourselves.

What about cases, then, where we could do so at *little* cost? On reflection we discover that in indefinitely many of our actions we take no account of manifest, identifiable third-party interests or desires, without anybody, including even the third party in question, being inclined to rule the action selfish. Using my right of way rather than yielding to the other driver, taking the last empty seat in the bus, claiming attention on a first come, first served basis are at worst acts lacking in courtesy. They are generally unclassifiable by reference to selfishness and do not by a long way become selfish acts except by virtue of some disproportionate harm I inflict, or the disproportionate deserts of the rival claim I ignore. It is the other vehicle being an ambulance rushing to an emergency, or the standing passenger being a cripple, that makes my act selfish, while in their absence I was merely exercising rights and following rules, though I did ignore others who would have wished me not to do so.

Selfishness, then, is conceptually posterior to, and contingent on, a set of pre-existing, recognized rights and rules, customary laws, and ethical precepts, and could hardly have entered into the shaping of that set in any significant way. As a second-order regulating principle nearer to manners than to morals, parasitic on more fundamental principles, it is not cut out to serve as a basic dividing-line between utility-maximizing actions and actions best understood in terms of other motivations.

The passing reference to Pareto may put the reader in mind of his distinction (though it is one that is perhaps best forgotten) between 'logical' and 'non-logical' actions and their 'springs and roots',

184 PUBLICNESS: SOLUTION AND RESULT

interest for the first sort and *the residuals* for the second.[2] The
project to distinguish actions meant to be utility-maximizing, from
others rooted in non-utility motives, echoes this Paretian classification
without, of course, conceding that it has anything to do with 'logic'.

Interest, no doubt more so than selfishness, may be a workable
criterion in deciding how to deflate the utility function which has
grown too all-encompassing for comfort. In doing so, one must not
slip into reasoning from interest (that which secures our utility) to
utility (that which serves our interests). A widely approved tactic
for breaking this circle is that of Rawls, who, in his 'thin theory of
the good', employs an 'index of primary goods' as the appropriate
maximand in a context where people do not know in detail who
they are and what they want, hence their utility function is as yet
unknown. In such a context, a rational person's interest is defined,
independently of utility, as the maximization of (the expected value
of) his index of primary goods.[3] It turns out, however, that
'primary goods' are too broad, too permeable. They let back in the
all-embracing, quasi-tautological utility one hoped they would help
to banish or cut down to size. Primary goods are said to consist of:

Rights and liberties   *mostly not alienable*[4]
Powers and opportunities   *mostly not alienable*
Income and wealth   *mostly alienable*
Self-respect   *not alienable*

A large, if not the largest, part of these goods cannot be alienated,
sold, or even transferred without consideration to others; some, in
addition, are not measurable. This is true *par excellence* of self-
respect, which Rawls considers of central importance.[5] A non-
transferable good can nevertheless be substituted for another good
in a person's index, endowment, or budget, and there may exist
substitutions which leave him no worse off. The person may be able
to effect such intra-personal trades within his own endowment,
e.g. use up an 'opportunity' by turning it into 'income' or gain some

---

[2] Pareto (1923), chs. IV–X in the 'Treatise of General Sociology'.
[3] Rawls (1972), 62, 92, 142–3. Note his category of 'selfish motivation',
advancing one's interest as one pleases, regardless of others, without respecting some
boundary constituted by mutual agreement with others: for Rawls, this is the 'state-
of-nature' or 'no-agreement' principle of interest (p. 124).
[4] Property rights, which are characteristically alienable (transferable) unless
specifically restricted, do not seem to be part of the 'rights and liberties' category. If
they were, what would be left over for the 'income and wealth' category?
[5] Rawls (1972), 440.

'power' by giving up some 'liberty'. He may even give up his self-respect for a demeaning profit. It can make perfect sense to impute to such a person, conjointly with the understanding that certain trade-offs between pairs of his primary goods are inherently feasible, a recognition of the marginal rates of substitution at which he would just find it agreeable to proceed to given trade-offs. What, however, a non-transferable good cannot do is become the object of an interpersonal trade[6] against someone else's good. Consequently, there is no ascertainable rate at which more of such a good—say self-esteem—could be had in exchange for less of another.

In the absence of such a rate, it is impossible validly to deny, for example, that wanton destruction of some quantity of one's own wealth, with *some* concomitant gain in self-esteem, does in fact maximize one's 'index of primary goods'. When the goods that make up the index are unalienable and unquantifiable, almost anything one does with them can be construed as index-maximizing, i.e. 'the best for one's interest', just as in broad utility-speak whatever one does can be said to be utility-maximizing (at least within the limits of consistency or non-contradiction; but one must not place much hope in such limits, for nothing obliges a person to have stable preferences or always to attach the same weights to various primary goods). As long as 'interest' is broad enough to include non-transferable goods among the entities that can serve and enhance it, any action can be said to be in our interest if it can be claimed either to increase the quantity or probability of one of our non-transferable goods or to decrease it while increasing that of another good. This is so because one can always impute a high enough *or* low enough valuation to the non-transferable good which will make the benefit larger than the cost, the gain larger than the loss. Unfavourable internal trade-offs could only be recognized as such by reference to available and ascertainable marginal rates of transformation of one good into the other; if there can be no such rates, the claim that a trade-off was a 'maximizing' one cannot be falsified. We are no better off with broad *interest* than with broad *utility*.

---

[6] A quantifiable but non-transferable good g can have an ascertainable price if it generates an 'externality'. Its possession by A may have an effect upon B, such that he would pay A a 'price' to induce the latter to increase or decrease g if it is feasible to do so.

Homo Oeconomicus

The point of this argument is not to undermine Rawls's concept of 'interest' and his choice of the 'index of primary goods' as the maximand. These are in fact among the less unattractive parts of his theory. Nor would there be much purpose in attacking them, for their relevance is in any case much reduced by his abandonment of maximization of the *expected value* of the index in favour of the maximization of its minimum possible value ('maximin'), a relatively crude rule of thumb under which many trade-offs would be foregone as too risky and ambitious. The purpose of labouring the point that *interest* defined through 'primary goods' is no more immune from tautology than undefined, broad *utility*, because neither can plausibly leave out of account the contribution of unquantifiable intangibles, was rather to prepare the ground for the plea I am making to reinstate poor, much-denigrated, and ridiculed *homo oeconomicus*.

There is no question of expelling humanity and in its place putting up straw men who only undertake such purposeful acts whose consequences can, in Pigou's unforgotten phrase, 'be brought in relation with the measuring rod of money'; who have no intangible interests, aim at no unquantifiable ends, and respect no rules and standards of conduct unless it is because 'honesty pays'. The object is instead to bring back *homo oeconomicus* among the other dramatis personae; more precisely, to have him as one of the several personalities (or dare we say, one of the several parallel preference-orderings?) a given individual may have. In this way, we can use a convenient litmus-test for actions we are prepared to attribute to utility motives. They are actions that have their *identifiable money's worth* in terms of their full opportunity costs, their full expected consequences, or both. (A weaker form of 'full', where *most* of the cost, or the *main* consequence, has its money's worth or can otherwise 'be brought in relation with the measuring rod of money', may have to do, especially since there may be few actions that would meet the strong version of the test. Most will have some, albeit minor, costs and consequences that have *no* money's worth, yet matter morally, affectively, or in some other way.) Actions not meeting this test will require the clear and explicit assignment of other specific motives in order to be explicable in terms of conscious rational choice. Thus, preference and utility may cease to be a tautology, 'the reason for acting as we do'. The utility-motive will stand reduced, reasonably delineated, and much less apt to invade, confuse, or blot out other, interesting motives and interesting sides of the human character.

Three Grades of Rationality

Perhaps it goes without saying, but it is better still to say it, that on the reduced and indeed 'reductionist' definition of utility I propose to fit to *homo oeconomicus*, maximizing it is still rational; diagnosing that it is, in fact, being maximized poses difficulties, but they are perhaps less forbidding than those associated with the broader, more tautology-prone concept; the novelty is that 'rational' may, but by no means must, mean 'utility-maximizing'. Self-sacrifice, self-denial, and more generally conduct determined by *standards*, with little or no conscious reference to *consequences*, are at least potentially rational but would not, under the narrowed utility concept that goes with *homo oeconomicus*, be utility-maximizing.

How, then, should we use the term 'rational' without unwittingly relegating perfectly valid motives for choice to the irrational, but also without implying that whatever sane people do has, for that reason, been done rationally?

For my relatively pedestrian purpose, a brief statement to insure against misunderstanding will suffice; I have no quarrel with and nothing to add to received theory. Many valid concepts of rationality coexist, and, like horses for courses, the sort of action one wants to qualify as rational or not should dictate the choice of the concept.[7]

1. *Coherence.* Rationality as coherence is the lowest-grade and most general concept likely to be useful. It does just a little more than exclude insane actions. It implies the discipline of subjection to the rules of logic, hence, it forbids self-contradiction and intransitivity.

---

[7] Contrast, however, the view of Frank Hahn: 'Economics probably made a mistake when it adopted the nomenclature "rational" when all it meant is correct calculations and an orderly personality'; Hahn and Hollis (1979) 12. This suggests that a single concept, comprised of bits of our three concepts below, would suit, at least as far as economics is concerned.

188   PUBLICNESS: SOLUTION AND RESULT

Preferences must be ordered transitively or not at all—it may not be incoherent *not* to order *everything*. Coherence requires acceptance that mutually exclusive alternatives have probabilities whose sum cannot exceed unity: for coherence must reject manifest wishful thinking. Rationality as coherence must also satisfy another minimal requirement, the willingness to take notice of available evidence in assessing actions in terms of their expected consequences.

2. *Calculation.* More demanding and higher-grade than coherence, rationality as calculation involves not merely the non-violation, but also the best-efforts application of the rules of reason and the due-diligence carrying out of the proper mental processes, notably the evaluation of evidence and the comparison of alternatives, by which actions and their consequences can be judged. 'Calculation' is, I believe, what Herbert Simon[8] calls 'procedural rationality'. A clear, albeit summary, instruction to conform to such rationality is the proverbial *Quidquid agis prudenter agas et respice finem.*[9] In contrast to the weaker 'coherence', which merely forbids the closing of the mind to relevant evidence, 'calculation' may require both that we should examine available evidence and that we should seek out additional evidence, making some attempt at balancing the cost of doing so against its expected value, for however tenuous such balancing is bound to be, it is better *ex ante* than blind action or blind inaction. Simon's 'satisficing' is bounded procedural rationality, where both the acquisition of new evidence and the whole effort of calculation are cut off some way short of the putative optimum. Thus, certain suboptimal but simple rules of thumb, such as 'maximin' or 'minimax regret', can be accepted under the calculation and *a fortiori* under the coherence definition of rationality, though they clash with the more sophisticated correspondence.[10]

3. *Correspondence.* Rationality as correspondence *is* the criterion of the putative optimum. It is the best match a person with given resources and placed under given constraints can arrange between 'cost' and 'benefit', opportunity and consequence. Unlike calculation, which need not be faultless, correspondence does imply the successful finding of the most favourable relation between what we want and what we do; like the shortest distance between two

---

[8] Simon (1976).
[9] 'In all you do, act prudently and consider the consequence.'
[10] Harsanyi (1975).

points, rationality as correspondence is efficient pairing between ends and means. More than formal and more than procedural, it is substantive; it is the strong rationality concept that underlies maximization. If utility is defined very broadly as that which motivates conscious choice, Bayesian expected utility-maximizing becomes synonymous with rationality as correspondence. The latter satisfies both of the classic Weberian concepts at the same time: *Zweckrationalität* is of course direct, first-order means–ends correspondence, while *Wertrationalität* is their second-order correspondence in that the 'values' or 'ends' it seeks to categorize can only be judged 'rational' or not in their instrumental capacity, as means to other ends.[11] (True, non-instrumental ends or 'values' cannot be brought into relation with the category of rationality.) Correspondence, then, is the most demanding, highest-grade concept of rationality we may wish to attribute to actions.

Public-Goods Forks

Let us imagine a random sample of a population of rationally acting persons in the perfect state of nature. Potentially or actually, they are members of various overlapping groups defined spatially, temporally, culturally, by occupation, income, or whatever community of interest is liable to give rise among them to wishes for the public provision, in common for the group, of given goods. This sample of people, therefore, confronts a number of public-goods problems and within our time-horizon will deal with each positively or negatively. We might imagine the sample of persons transforming itself into a society in the course of producing those solutions. Prevalence of positive solutions will condition and dispose the society to be a (predominantly) *political* one, while if most of the solutions are negative, the society will live by exchange

[11] Justifying the proposition that an end is rational is a special instance of the task of justifying belief that a proposition is true; it runs into the 'trilemma' (Fries's Trilemma) of self-justification, circularity, or infinite regress. Hence the search for a non-arbitrary Archimedean stopping-point. Revelation and historical necessity, each on its very different moral and intellectual level, have at times served as stopping-points in such arguments. Some contemporary philosophers believe in the possibility of non-religious and non-arbitrary stopping-points; others deny the call for justification; a few philosophical relativists and nihilists feel dispensed from having a position at all. Cf. the authoritative account, from a Popperian stand, of G. Radnitzky in Radnitzky and Bartley (1987) ch. 14.

regimes and develop, at least for a while a (predominantly) capitalist *market order*.

Three types of causes will tend to bring about negative solutions.

1. Utility motives are weak, because the 'productivity of publicness' is relatively low; the attractiveness of providing the good on a non-excluded basis, compared to getting it or its substitutes in an exchange regime on an excluded basis, fails to outweigh the dilutive effect of publicness.

2. Non-utility motives in favour of public provision are weak.

3. Public provision fails by mistake; non-utility motives are weak and though utility motives would be adequate for a positive solution, mutually inconsistent expectations about each other's actions take the particular form (too many expect too many to contribute, hence too few contribute) which produces a negative solution. Unless one or more of these causes prevail, a certain quantity, intensity, frequency, reliability, etc. of the good will be publicly provided by voluntary 'subscription'; the particular quantity is a 'culturally' determined choice, conditioned by the indivisibility inherent in public provision.

A metaphor and its 'map' might best illustrate the causes at work. One could imagine the members of our 'latent society' all wandering, in dispersed order, down a special road, called for this occasion the 'Ethics Turnpike'. It has a number of exits, each exit standing for a possible contributory cause of a positive solution to a given public-goods problem. A particular exit leads to an ethically congenial destination for a particular class or type of wanderer. Signposts will attract him to take a given exit, by virtue of the corresponding ethical principles or the self-image that inspires his motives; he will pass exits whose signposts attract him but weakly, and go on down the road.

For each such person, travelling down the Ethics Turnpike corresponds to weighing the rational 'strategy' in response to a public-goods problem or 'game'. At each fork, there are different arguments to consider in favour of taking the particular exit to ethically congenial territory and contribute to the public good in common with those similarly motivated, or going on. These arguments are ethical in a loose sense, and present themselves along the Ethics Turnpike in a descending order of moral worth. At the bottom of the road, having passed all exits and remaining unmoved by the corresponding arguments for contributing, a person may find (*a*) that enough others have contributed and he is able to free ride; (*b*) that not enough others have contributed to let him free ride and he would consequently have to make do without the public good, or accept the social contract if all accepted it; or (*c*) that it is best to return to 'Go', proceed down the road a second time, and reconsider the arguments.

On the map of the Ethics Turnpike (Figure 13), three main segments are marked off according to the basic type of person most likely to find his congenial exit along it. The first segment is primarily for the type who fears God or acts as if he did. The second segment has exits to suit those who are not indifferent to how some or all their fellow men are faring, and who value only that (but not *all* that) which people want for themselves or for others. The third is for *homo oeconomicus*, maximizing a narrowly defined utility that varies only with the money's worth of his own payoffs.

Lest it be misconstrued, I must enlarge on the last point. *Homo oeconomicus* behaves as the gambler at the table or the player in the field where 'he knows no brothers'.[12] Having maximized his payoff, he may dispose of it in any conceivable manner; the behavioural discipline is in the getting, not in the using. There is an analogy here with the producer who obeys the dictates of the utility function appropriate for his calling and maximizes some definition of profit, that being the object of the exercise. The choice between disposing of the profit in a 'socially responsible' or hog-hedonistic manner can be construed as separate and posterior. Accountancy, in setting up a profit-and-loss account and an appropriation account, provides a lesson in how the social sciences can make the best use of the fiction of *homo oeconomicus* without having to pretend that he is a soulless monster.

The matching of types of person with exits is, of course, not fatal, but probabilistic. A God-fearing man may fail to obey the rules of rectitude, yet may end up subscribing to the public good under the cumulative weight of standard-bound, philanthropic, and 'economic' arguments, which add up on the way down the Ethics Turnpike.

Each stretch of the Turnpike leading up to a fork is signposted for the attention of the person whose 'standard-bound', 'humanist',

---

[12] By the German rule *Kein Bruder im Spiel*, all brothers play to win, though the winner may choose to share with his brothers after the game.

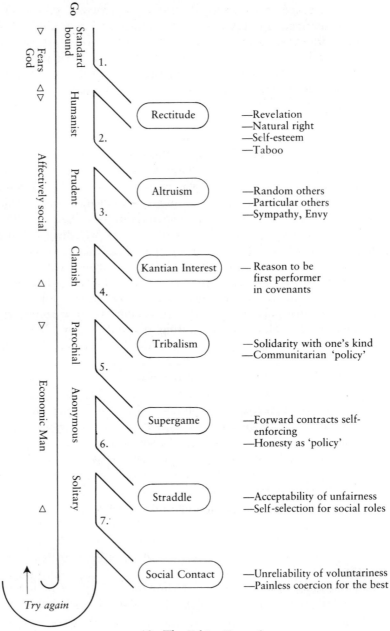

FIGURE 13. The Ethics Turnpike

'prudent', etc. disposition might be attracted by the approaching exit. Thus, he who sees himself as a humanist and thinks that people should, as far as possible, get what they want rather than what moral arguments, or other arguments not derived from their preferences, dictate might wish to listen to altruistic reasons that refer to their satisfactions. Another, who is discriminating in his love of others, may attach much weight to 'tribal' interests but none to the interests of any random member of humanity outside his tribe.

1. The top fork poses the public-goods problem above all to the person whose conduct is strongly bound to standards, rather than governed by preferences or interests—'God-fearing', as a figure of speech, suggests his character. He finds unanswerable, final arguments on Moses' tablets, in natural right, or in some venerated personal authority for doing the right thing, pulling his weight, not abusing the good faith of others, and living up to a code which may be inherited or formed to match and confirm his own self-image. These arguments are meta-rational, shielded from critical scrutiny, and depend only on genuine, non-instrumental value-perceptions. He may also be moved by considerations of reasonableness, equity, and the merits of cases, but these will have a lesser influence, being essentially consequential points of view. The person who lets himself be governed by standards and rules of rectitude is presumably acting rationally in the sense of being coherent; his rationality, however, is neither calculation nor correspondence (unless it is the calculation of the righteous-by-policy, who seeks to *earn* his place in heaven or to escape hell). Such a person selects actions for what they are, and does not consciously seek to value them in terms of probable consequences. In 'game' settings, his strategy is only weakly dependent on the payoffs. The clearest standard-bound behaviour is unconditional obedience to taboos. This is Pareto's 'non-logical action' of the *reflex* type, i.e. one where the subject need not see and does not seek to appreciate the 'point' or purpose of a taboo. Obedience to the commands of religion is partly, but only partly, reflexive, for it is arbitrary to deny that considered judgement may play a part in the beliefs that motivate religious obedience.

Conformity to a code of conduct that proves the justness of one's self-image, that has prestige value in one's eye, is in some ways the most complex and the most interesting of motives for rectitude: a person so motivated would typically seek to maintain as close and stable a relation as his will can sustain, between his actual conduct and conduct he would like to see himself adopt. Success in this enterprise would lead to increased identification of the person with his code, invest the code with the added value of self-esteem, and reinforce the will to conform to it more heroically still. This, one suspects, is often how it comes about that people do not let go of ungrateful tasks and proudly co-operate with others who are manifestly using them.

2. The second 'public-goods fork' is meant to tempt humanists into contributing for altruistic reasons. Their own good depends in some way both on their circumstances and on those of others; 'others' are any fellow men. Ordinarily, however, occasions abound for altering the circumstances of those in one's own proximity, community, interest-group etc., while occasions for affecting the life of random individuals, especially those who are in some respect distant, are infrequent or have to be expressly sought. Hence, 'general' altruism tends, in practice, to be directed at particular people. 'Circumstances' are, of course, a catch-all. They would no doubt have to include the happiness of others, the maximization of *their* maximand. The pure altruist would be guided solely by this: he would wish for others what they wish for themselves, whatever that may be, and would incur *some* sacrifice in his own circumstances to let them get it. The cost he would accept to bear for a given increase in what others wish for themselves is, but for a common unit of measurement, his 'degree' of altruism.[13] This degree is well defined if both the cost to A and the benefit to B is in the form of money or of the same good. (Once they are both altruists and A wants B to have the good while B wants A to have it, problems[14] arise and a third non-altruist person C is needed to satisfy them; all in a closed society cannot be altruists.)

Real-life altruists are probably very seldom 'pure'. A, a non-pure altruist, will incur some cost to let B have what A thinks is good for him and what B would wish for himself if he also wanted to please

---

[13] In close analogy with Edgeworth's 'coefficient of effective sympathy'. The latter, however, has a properly defined common unit, utility, with the utilities of helper and helped being taken as commensurate. For a survey of the contribution of Edgeworth (and others) cf. Collard (1978), ch. 6.
[14] Collard (1978), 9, aptly calls this the 'After You Problem'.

A. Though this is a boring and convoluted formulation, the basic idea is simple enough. It is that altruism and charity are almost invariably 'tied', in kind, earmarked, and paternalistic, for by giving *B* what he would like to see him have (if there is any such thing) *A* gets either as much or greater satisfaction than by letting *B* choose what the latter would rather have.

Everything we say about altruism, its degree, and its purity can presumably be said about envy by changing the sign. It is worth something to an envious *A* that *B* should not have what he wants; while a non-pure envious *A* would be more pained by *B* having certain specific things, that particularly provoke his own envy, than others.

Altruism may help induce *A* to subscribe to public provision of a good for himself *and B* that he would not have subscribed to from non-altruistic motives alone. Symmetrically, fear of envy[15] may induce *B* to subscribe even though he might have been able to free ride; but this deterrent to free riding, like most others, can only operate in conditions of good visibility of *B*, where he and his ᵇᵉⁿᵉᶠⁱᵗˢ are easy to spot.

3. It may look bizarre for an Ethics Turnpike to go some way downhill before coming to the exit for the Kantian Rule. The reason for not ranking it at the very top, however, is straightforward.

There are really two somewhat different arguments recommending obedience to the Kantian Rule. Kant's principle of the 'universalize-able' interest states, in effect, that it is the duty of anyone to contribute to a public good that would benefit him, if he would wish others to contribute. Kant thus appears to argue from interest to morals, but provides no path from universalizeable interest to the service of one's own. He does not seek and nor does he need to prove that anyone wishing to do the best for himself, given what others do, should obey the Kantian imperative. Moreover, the rule 'Do to others what you would have them do to you' cannot without further ado be grounded in anyone's own interest by the argument that 'by so doing *you will induce them to do it to you*'; such an argument could be based on hope but not on reasoned insight into what others *would* do if they followed *their* interest. Hence, anyone who nevertheless obeys the Kantian rule does so on grounds of rectitude, as part of his standard-bound conduct which is not

[15] For the importance of the *fear of envy*, leading to far-reaching strategies to forestall and disarm envy, cf. Schoeck (1970).

rationally calculated to secure good consequences for himself, though it may turn out to do so if others are righteous, and reciprocate. As such, it does rank with and is fully integrated to the highest motives at the first exit, which is made for the God-fearing but is equally congenial for the high-minded atheist.

There is, however, a morally less lofty level on which obedience to the Kantian categorical imperative is sometimes, however incongruously, recommended on grounds of prudence (the word being used to mean, for all practical purposes, broad utility-maximization). If there is a public-goods dilemma or the threat of one, with a non-co-operative solution that all dislike but cannot escape, and Kantian conduct would overcome the dilemma, is it not prudential conduct? The rule being recommended, then, is 'Do to others what you would have them do to you, *subject to* the probability that *this will induce enough of them to do it* to you.'

This rule is cogent, but its condition is too demanding to be often met. As Hobbes has taught us, the obstacle is inherent in the structure of the implicit 'covenant' to be respected. It calls for non-simultaneous performance, half-spot and half-forward. Given a first performer, it is best for the second performer to default; though he may not in fact do so, it is hardly prudential conduct to perform first.

To make the Kantian Rule attractive on prudential grounds, something more is needed. One possibility is to design the scheme of co-operation as an indefinitely repeated series of performances, where it is never in the interest of the second performer to default and thereby abort the 'third' for $(2n - 1)$th performance, whose value to him is *ex hypothesi* greater than his own opportunity-cost of performing one more time. This design is not always feasible in public-goods situations. We will further consider it at a lower exit ('supergame'). Another possibility is to seek out people with 'better natures', hence with more benign, less ruthlessly single-minded maximands, and have them play the roles of second performers. Touched by the trust shown by first performers, such second performers would put some value on not abusing trust, and would reciprocate. Foreknowledge that trust will induce others to shift towards trustworthiness would transform first performance into a rational act in terms of calculation and eventually in terms of correspondence. In all such cases, Kantian conduct would be explicable in terms of 'enlightened' self-interest, i.e. a strategy of

maximization arrived at by relatively sophisticated calculation.
4. Calling the fourth exit 'tribalism' is meant to convey a more than genetic distinction between 'strangers' and those who, in some significant respect, are our own kind. There is always an inexhaustible number of ways of classifying populations, many of which mean little or nothing to the person so classified. Others, however, rest on important affective, linguistic, cultural, or economic relations, and are liable to generate favourable behaviour by members of the class towards each other compared to strangers. Altruism is impartial, random in the selection of beneficiaries within the material constraints set by proximity and occasion. By contrast, 'tribalism' is knowingly discriminating. Much that passes for altruism in everyday speech is really tribalism in this sense. The moral licence to discriminate is provided by the impossibility to love everybody equally, for what is impossible cannot be required. True non-discrimination would be indistinguishable from indifference. An all-inclusive community is a contradiction in terms, while the inclusion of only some necessarily implies the exclusion of others. Whether this defence is wholly convincing, whether it supports restriction of entry into the community, and whether (if discriminate we must) it justifies discrimination in favour of our own kind instead of some other, possibly more deserving, kind must remain open. For this particular Ethics Turnpike, this is how the exit to tribalism works, and it is a comfort (but no more than that) that there is some, however fragile, moral defence for it, so that not all its weight rests on instincts, passions, and reflexes.

A person with a tribal, communitarian, discriminating disposition towards others will give sympathetic hearing to two non-utility arguments for contributing to a public-good endeavour. The first is 'solidarity' with his own group; he will not be indifferent to them having the publicly provided good they want and will consequently accept to bear more of the cost than his own utility-equation would warrant. Solidarity in this sense is formally the same as a reduction in the dilution factor (cf. p. 146–50), which helps determine the value to an individual of his own contribution; the limiting case of *complete solidarity* means that an individual values the marginal product of his contribution that accrues to others in his group just as highly as if it accrued to him, which has the same effect as the case of 'no dilution'.

The second argument is a matter of 'policy', an ulterior motive.

Public provision will have some effect in building and cementing a community around the good so provided, an effect which market exchanges of private substitute goods do not have. If a 'tribally' disposed person is interested in having a tribe (or perhaps several partly overlapping tribes, clans, clubs, associations, unions, and so forth) to belong to, he may find it politic to incur some cost to facilitate public provision, over and above its own merits, as an instrument of community-building.

5. At the fifth fork, there is a set of arguments for contributing, designed to appeal to the kind of *homo oeconomicus* who lives, or at least thinks of himself, in a *parochial* setting. He bears a name, he has a recognized identity, what he does is readily traceable to him; it is observed and gossiped about in the 'parish', and its adverse effects are likely to be held against him. Others in the parish are in a symmetrical predicament, everybody having to bear in mind that 'it is a small world' and everybody else may hold their actions against them. For each, free riding or otherwise taking advantage of the other 'parishioners' approximates, to a variable degree, an act of default on an implicit contract of reciprocity. Whether each or any such contract is self-enforcing is a question of fact and needs scrutiny.

A parochial man must in any case reject the second condition of single-mindedness: he would fail to establish, or he would risk foolishly to upset, the desirable correspondence between his ends and his means if he adopted conduct (i.e. the use of means) suited only to a known small number of future interactions with others. In the parochial setting, he is in a maze of different, continuing, or repeated 'games' (supergames) and extra-game relations with some of the same people. Though each of the latter may find some *ad hoc* reason to default on a reciprocal 'second performance' if the former has performed first, default is a dominant strategy in the 'last game' only. In any game that precedes the last, non-performance is dominant for either player if and only if it is a pre-emptive strategy against the anticipated default of the second player in the last game. If there is never a last game, or if the probability of the nth game being the last one is not high enough, there is *a priori* no dominant strategy in any game from the first to the nth. Immediate default yields to the second performer the windfall utility of one unrequited performance by the first performer, after which the latter presumably breaks off and ceases performing. Hence, the windfall utility is obtained at the cost of cutting off the anticipated stream of future utilities that the continuing relation of reciprocal performances would have yielded to the ill-advised defaulter.

The utility of this stream depends on its unit value, its probable length, and the time discount. The windfall utility is a function, among other things, of the form and the unit in which the first performer provides his performance. If performance is a largish, discrete lump—say, three months' deliveries of a good before the first performer stops delivering on grounds of non-payment by the second performer—default may well pay despite the loss of future deliveries. The smaller is the discrete unit, or the closer the series of first and second performances approximates *mutually contingent, simultaneous* performance by the two parties, the less profitable is default, i.e. the more the reciprocity relation *approaches self-enforcement.*

Depending on these parameters, performance as dictated by an implicit contract of decency and good faith may be individually best both for the first and the second performer. If so, in no single 'game' of a series of 'games' (social interactions of various kinds) is it worth a player's while to *make* it the last game, (e.g. to free ride, to 'take the money and run'). The case against default is likely to be the stronger the more parochial, the more dense is the network of social relations, and the more numerous and diversified are any person's several interactions with any other.

If in two continuous parallel games some of the players are the same, the opportunity-cost of default in *one* game may well be the termination of *both*; and this result, which helps to make the co-operative solution self-enforcing in both, can obtain even if the two sets of players do not overlap, but simply *talk* to each other. Likewise, and for analogous reasons, if one series of repeated games stops, but another starts up and at least some of the same players play in both, *or* even talk to each other, the result will approximate that obtained in one uninterrupted series of games. Finally, several concurrent series of games (parallel supergames), each involving lumpy, discrete first and second performances by some of the same players, will in the limit shade into a single stream of performances, and will tend to have as good a chance of co-operative solutions as if they were a single supergame with simultaneous continuous performances, i.e. with self-enforcing characteristics.

In all cases, the significance of the 'parochial' setting lies in the visibility of each player for the purpose of reciprocity, trust, and sanction for breach of trust. These elements having relevance only in repeated interactions or supergames, the parochial 'face-to-face' or small-group setting is not a factor in making for co-operative solution in once-only interactions. Our earlier conclusion about the general irrelevance of group size to the solution of public-goods problems remains intact if each problem is considered as an isolated single play. On the other hand, a truly parochial setting will, one way or another, help to connect and weave single plays into a network or a stream which acts as a supergame.

When all games are supergames and there is, properly speaking, *no* last game (or only a very low probability of one), the built-in incentives of reciprocity are such that, with only a bit of luck, 'honesty is the best policy' for each player. This happens for ulterior, ethically unglorious motives, of which the apprehensive 'What will people say?' is one of the least glorious but not the least efficient. Compared to the payoff structure that would obtain under single-minded motivation, these motives would make the free-ride payoff less attractive, the sucker payoff less unfair (for more tend to contribute), and 'fair' public provision a shade less improbable.

6. None of the parochial arguments in favour of contributing to public provision will persuade the *anonymous* person who is or sees himself as inconspicuous and indistinguishable from others, so that the consequences of his actions cannot be held against him. If he finds sufficient reasons to take the straddle exit and support a publicly provided good with his contribution (i.e. if he finds that it pays him to be co-operative even in a single 'game'), this would in the given context imply that he ranks his alternative public-goods payoffs in the 'straddle' order.

The individual player in the straddle acts as if he considered that the excess utility of the non-excluded, public good over that of the market exchange substitute (broadly what earlier we called the 'productivity of publicness') is sufficient to counteract the dilution of his contribution inherent in non-exclusion. His expectations of what other members of his group will do in turn determine whether, against the background of his preference-ordering, he will opt for the sucker role or take a chance on the uncertain but more attractive free-ride option. Collective consistency of expectations, as well as certain moderate forms of their collective inconsistency, ensure that under the straddle conditions enough others agree to contribute for public provision to be successfully organized. The likelihood of this solution, brought about by this motivation, is independent of the size of the group seeking it.

However, the persons who have come down this far on the Ethics Turnpike stand a perhaps better chance of raching a positive solution, and of reaching it with a somewhat less 'unfair' distribution of burdens between suckers and free riders, than would be the case on the sole strength of their straddle preferences and expectations about each other's conduct. The reason is that they may well not be single-minded. In addition to the arguments incorporated in the straddle, they may be open to, and attach some weight to, standard-bound, humanist, 'prudent', discriminating, and 'parochial' type of arguments encountered at higher exits. If insufficient in themselves to induce voluntary co-operation, they may yet add enough additional carried-forward motives to the single-minded narrow utility-maximizing motivation for this sum to bias the population in favour of a positive public-goods solution.

Despite the positive bias that it may get from such a cumulative carry-forward, the straddle solution remains stochastic. Though markedly suboptimal outcomes, where public provision fails altogether despite a high 'productivity' of publicness, are unlikely, they are possible.

7. This lack of certainty in voluntariness is a plausible argument in favour of the social-contract exit. It is weaker and different from the classic contractarian argument. The latter is a corollary of the premiss that the public-goods problem is a dilemma in the state of nature, in that although all would rather contribute to a public good than not benefit from it, none will contribute voluntarily, hence none can benefit. It follows from this premiss that none can, on pain of self-contradiction, reject an arrangement (the social contract) under which all contribute and all benefit and without which the desired outcome is simply not accessible. However, the premiss is false: the public-goods problem is not a dilemma in general. Non-contribution is the dominant strategy only under a particular ('interlocking') ordering of possible outcomes which is unlikely to be found when publicness is substantially more 'productive' than privateness. When the publicness is 'productive' enough to generate an ordering (the 'straddle') where contributing on unfair terms ranks higher than going without the public good, there is no dominant strategy, hence there is nothing fatal

and preordained about public provision in the state of nature.

Wanting public goods while refusing the social contract is not self-contradictory; the two can be perfectly coherent. The social contract would ban free riding. If free riding were not feasible anyway in the state of nature, the social contract could be unanimously accepted (it would be Pareto-optimal) because would-be free riders would have nothing to lose by it. Once public provision in the state of nature, and the attendant free riding, is agreed to be possible, the social contract no longer compels unanimous acceptance, for, if nobody else, at least would-be free riders are possible losers under it.

However, they may not be wholly convinced that this is so. Nor will others necessarily regard the sum of state-of-nature motives for contributing, including the probabilistic reasons that would normally yield positive solutions in straddle-type public goods games, as an absolute assurance of voluntary public provision. For them, the function of the social contract would not be to make public goods *possible*, but to make them *certain*. The less a person trusts the good sense of others, their capacity to act in ways that best serve their purposes and to recognize their reciprocal ties to each other, the more he will value the social contract, not as an enabling, but as a certainty-enhancing device.

Admittedly, the expected value or utility of an event is enhanced *pari passu* with the probability that the statement predicting it is a true statement. The expected utility of publicly providing the good g in excess of the utility of the private substitutes it replaces would increase with the probability that the statement 'g will be provided' is true. Certainty is the upper limiting value of this probability. That utility should increase by a discontinuous lump as this limit is approached (or reached) is conceivable, but a violation of rationality as coherent ordering of alternatives. Unlike the binary distinction figuring in the classic contractarian argument between 'g is impossible' and 'g is rendered possible', the distinction between 'g is probable' and 'g is certain', which is the residual claim one can still make in favour of the social contract, is one of degree and its weight depends on the facts of the case.

The superiority this argument concedes to the social contract may be contingent and weak, but it is still superiority, especially for the doubting and the mistrustful, as long as a second argument is conceded. This argument, rarely stated explicity, holds that since the social contract forces us to opt for an outcome we prefer anyway, the coercion involved in it is painless and the socio-contractual cost of the good to a contributor is simply the contribution, no more. This is asserting two falsehoods. The first is that if two solutions are otherwise indifferent, a reasonable person values as highly the solution he would not have been allowed to refuse as the one he need not have accepted. The second seems to imply that such a person will rank the solution actually imposed upon him as the only feasible, hence best, under the social contract. Such would be the case if the public-goods problem was one of pure co-ordination, with a unique distribution of the excess utility it produced. As we know, however, public provision is non-pure, conflictual co-ordination with an infinity of different possible distributions of the resulting benefits and the required contributions. It is surely false that whatever benefit–contribution balance is imposed upon a person, he will regard it as the best he could have got, will never feel badly done by and feel no pain as long as the balance is at all positive.

Contrary to the obvious presumption that it must be the sociable and socially minded person who is the readiest to call for socio-contractual arrangements, there is a case for holding that their main appeal is to the solitary one who is least linked to others in diverse social interactions and the least confident of the capacity of such interactions to yield and maintain workable spontaneous solutions. He is the archetypal isolated individual of Rousseau, with nothing between him and the state. It is in Tocqueville's rueful image of modern mass society, the legacy of the 'old regime and the revolution', with no historic classes, no corporate bodies, no associative structures, no subdivisions, no intermediate layers, and no relations linking them to each other, that isolated individuals feel the greatest need to rely on the all-encompassing social contract.

As a state-of-nature society is sorting itself out along the Ethics Turnpike, and organizes a measure of public-goods provision on a voluntary basis, those believing in the superiority of a less hit-or-miss, more comprehensive social design can advocate it. Mostly, however, they can only wait, biding their time.

8. Others, still missing their favourite public goods and wanting to achieve a greater measure of social co-operation than would come about in the course of a single passage along the various exits

representing the variety of co-operative motives, might at the last exit leave and return to 'Go', in the expectation that with hindsight and the benefit of experience more can be achieved the second time round.

9

THE UNFAIRNESS OF ANARCHY

In the last three chapters I was mainly engaged in demonstrating why and how a state-of-nature society can generate positive solutions to the reputedly hardest of co-ordination problems. It was my contention that it would act as if it used a built-in selection mechanism, implicit in the freedom of state-of-nature persons to make or withhold contributions to proposed common endeavours, which would favour schemes of public provision in the order of their worthwhileness to individual contributors. The likelihood of a positive solution was found to be the higher the greater was the excess of the 'productivity of publicness', that is the advantage of employing resources to provide a given 'public' good over employing them to produce 'exchange' goods—including, of course, private substitutes of the public good. It was this excess which made it potentially rational for people voluntarily to subscribe to schemes of public provision on unfair, 'sucker' terms, contributing resources to produce benefits both for themselves and for free riders.

The disincentive to contribute, on the other hand, was rooted in the dilution of benefits, a concomitant of non-exclusion. Under conditions of publicness, only a part of the benefit attributable to an individual's own contribution can be captured by him, the rest accrues indiscriminately to others in the non-excluded public. What proportion he can logically consider as accruing to him, i.e. what his 'dilution factor' is, depends on the critical breakdown of a non-excluded population (such as a group with an interest in getting the same public good) between suckers and free riders—a breakdown which is just consistent with producing a positive solution. The critical division of the group is one where there are just enough contributions to enable public provision to be undertaken, fewer contributions implying its failure. Dilution must be at least counterbalanced by the differential productivity of publicness in order for the 'straddle' ordering of alternative outcomes, and hence the acceptance of the role of sucker, to be rationally admissible under the narrowly single-minded motivation we ascribe to 'economic man'. Broader, more diverse, motivations could furnish other, additional, and less stringent reasons for contributing; their relative strength and cumulative weight are questions of fact.

State-of-nature society is broadly capable of looking after the production of public goods of sufficient worthwhileness. This conclusion does not prejudge the question of the efficiency or optimality of the resulting balance between public goods and exchange goods—a question which begs others and which for that reason I do not regard as fit to ask. The issue, however, is not the optimality or otherwise of the scale of state-of-nature public goods output. In the conventional theory of the social contract, there can in general be *no* man-made public goods without coercing some or all members of society to contribute to their production. Hence *de facto* coercion to contribute, whichever way it originated, is regarded by contractarians as if it had been unanimously agreed by all, since all *must* have at least some public goods and may wish to have more than some. It was my contention in Chapters 6 and 7 that this theory is a fallacy.

There is, however, at least one alternative 'as if' explanation of the demise of the state of nature. It can be agreed that if it had not been superseded by an increasingly complete 'perfect' state for reasons that are extraneous to the possibility or otherwise of social co-operation, state-of-nature people would have come to adopt arrangements whose ultimate effect would have been the same. Unlike conventional social-contract theory, the alternative explanation neither claims that the socio-contractual outcome is a necessary consequence of seeking to avoid Pareto-inferior states of affairs nor, what comes to the same thing, that simple consistency requires any individual who prefers to contribute to public goods, *provided others contribute too*, willingly to accept the command–obedience relations that alone enable him actually to choose this preferred arrangement. Still less is it an explanation that, if valid, would be valid for any and every rational individual and would, for this reason, suffice to ensure unanimous agreement.

In our explanation, we find no sufficient reason for unanimous agreement to command-based institutions taking the place of the state of nature. Nor do we need it. We can derive the emergence of such institutions from the distributional conflict between suckers and free riders inseparable from the state of nature. Instead of the certainty that unanimous agreement would produce, it is a matter of conjecture and probability that some should adopt certain strategies; that small beginnings should surreptitiously bring about momentous ends; and that new states of affairs should not be chosen by conscious design but should emerge as the composite result of strategies directed at other objectives. The present chapter is devoted to gathering together the presumptive elements of such an explanation.

The reader will recall that, as a solution of the straddle-type public-goods 'game', a group of 'players' breaks two ways, into a subgroup of subscribers and another of non-subscribers. In the normal course of public-goods provision, there will be schemes where 'subscribe' and 'pay the subscription' comprise one and the same irrevocable decision. Stepping up to shoulder the heavier end of a load, going first to break a path, taking the blame for a collective deed, are composite 'subscribe-and-pay' decisions of this kind, as would be the cash-with-order acquisition of a public good by some for all. In other cases, 'subscribe' having been undertaken at time t_0, 'pay' is not to follow until t_1,—the prime instance is the 'promise to keep promises' made at t_0 and the occasion to keep or break an inconvenient promise, occurring at t_1.

Suppose next that in a proposed public-good enterprise of this two-step kind the subscriber subgroup k happens to be greater than the critical minimum $\bar{k}$. Everyone who took the 'subscribe' decision did so in ignorance of what everyone else was deciding. The result, however, is apt to be public knowledge. Since at this point there are visibly more subscribers than necessary and fewer free riders than could be carried by them, free riding is revealed as riskless. Every subscriber, therefore, has an incentive to free ride instead. He will default if he still can rather than honour his subscription. However, each must continue to be the first or among the first to do so and to cross over to the free riders, for the point of his move depends on his leaving behind at least $\bar{k}$ subscribers in the sucker subgroup. Plainly, all cannot be first and it is entirely possible that if there is a rush, too few might be left behind.

If the exit from the sucker subgroup is by a 'turnstile' (or its equivalent), or there is some natural or man-made arrangement controlling the sequence of people passing from one subgroup to the other, all may yet be well. For with each person who is seen to pass, or is thought on a probabilistic basis to have passed, from the 'suckers-to-be' to the 'free riders-to-be', the next person's incentive to pass over is diminished. (In terms of the 'straddle' diagram of Figure 12, p keeps moving to the left and the expected excess utility of the NS not-subscribe strategy keeps getting smaller until it becomes negative.) With a turnstile or other sequential protocol for changing camps, equilibrium between the sucker and the free-rider camp could be reached in a not too disorderly manner (though perhaps involving some jostling at the turnstile) consistent with sufficient residual 'pay' decisions to ensure the successful organization of public provision.

Many non-excluded groups and many public goods schemes, however, would have no natural turnstiles nor the possibility of enforcing disciplined queueing. 'Suckers-to-be' in such schemes might well try to default all at once. Equilibrium could well be overshot in the rush, and the attempt at arranging public provision be aborted—a result unwanted by disappointed though willing suckers no less than by failed free riders.

It would, under such circumstance, be probable that among the number of public-goods attempts vulnerable to the above scenario the subscribers to some should by mutual agreement seek to suppress default. There could, in fact, be unanimity within a 'sucker' subgroup so situated in favour of enforcing commitments once subscribed to; for nobody would have been forced to subscribe in the first place, all doing so for good reasons of their own. Hence, enforcement would merely have the effect of making sure that the *ex ante* intent of voluntary sucker and free-rider strategies was not frustrated *ex post* by the mutually inconsistent attempts of some to secure, with hindsight, an even better payoff than originally aimed at.

Enforcement could conveniently be (and at least in some cases almost certainly would be) entrusted to a group executive, with a mandate limited to see that whoever subscribed paid his subscription (after adjustment, if necessary, for the number of subscribers k being greater than the critical minimum $\bar{k}$). To carry out its mandate, the executive would have the appropriate means of coercion. In such way, through the length and breadth of society a number (perhaps only a small number) of micro-social contracts could be implanted, so to speak at the grass roots, each associated with an enterprise publicly to provide one good[1] for one group.

Abuse, Outrage, Envy

At this point in our scenario certain subgroups of suckers would have willingly accepted to be held to their commitments by enforcement executives formed for the purpose. Despite the availability of machinery, however, there would be no question of forcing free riders to contribute as well. The prima-facie reason is that in the state of nature the free riders have promised nothing and must not be held to undertakings to which they were not party.[2]

The high road to coercion is the contractarian pretension that acceptance by a person of a share in a benefit he did not solicit is tantamount to his tacit acceptance of an obligation to provide a share of the corresponding contribution in the same way as those who did solicit the benefit. A free rider, by availing himself of a public good, is said to concede the public's right to exact from him a contribution on a basis to be defined. If there were a state-of-nature understanding on public goods, in terms of which suckers freely accept to subscribe to some scheme of public provision in explicit recognition that they are paying both for themselves and for others, this contractarian pretension would contradict it; the two are mutually exclusive.

There is, however, also a low road to coercion that can be taken in a fit of absence of mind, without invoking the high anti-free-rider

---

[1] Conventional theory has a single prior social contract which gives rise to a posterior multitude of public goods, their pattern set by social choice, whose provision it alone makes possible. (Hobbes's version is somewhat exceptional, in that he has the social contract tied to a single public good—civil peace.) In our alternative, grass-roots explanation, we have a number of particular public goods of voluntary origin, each giving rise to its associated 'social contract'. This recalls the first sewage systems of new towns in the English Midlands and Lancashire in the Industrial Revolution: usually, voluntary participants in each scheme chose Commissioners, who soon acquired some coercive powers against free-riding householders. This office eventually blossomed out into a fully fledged municipality, confirmed by Act of Parliament and levying contributions (rates) for a growing variety of other public goods. Lest this example be misconstrued, let us readily admit that the sewers, however suitable, are far from being the only place from which authority and subjection can issue forth.

[2] Both English and Roman law recognize the 'privity' of agreements, which bars a third party from acquiring rights or duties under them.

principle of equal obligation for equal benefit. In any group of people, there is often a handful who do not know how far is too far and how to stop short of it. Free riding on any particular public-good enterprise is meant to be tolerated as a consequence of the state-of-nature condition that suckers assume their role voluntarily. But toleration would be sorely tried by the offensive conduct of the odd free riders who overreach themselves. Since they can always consume more of the public good at no or low marginal cost to themselves, they may easily lose the sense of proportion and good measure that consumers of public goods that run the risk of crowdedness should possess in order to find each other's conduct bearable. Heedless of resentment, they may make themselves conspicuous by excessive use of the public good. Equally easily, they may cause scandal by consuming no more than most but by doing in a provocative, flaunting manner what others do more discreetly. Anyone who has been in a crowd that was given a chance to free ride—to eat and drink all they can, to be seen talking to the star guest, to overlook the collection plate—knows how such occasions bring out extremes of behaviour, some people holding back with embarrassed modesty, other outdoing each other in pushy cleverness and noisy self-congratulation at its success. Not only is there a probabilistic basis for supposing that every social group has some conspicuous free riders; there is also some likelihood that due to the dynamics of emulation and the spur of happily getting away with it offensive behaviour should grow more unacceptable until it meets a punitive sanction, or at least some non-punitive check.

For these reasons, one would expect tensions to develop and intensify in some of the groups which have organized public provision of some good for themselves. Abuse of publicness could lead to outrage, continuing abuse to outrage that spills over into action. Somewhere, and at some point, protracted irritation with provocative free riding would set off counter-measures. In the first instance, they would be directed at the worst offenders. One or both of two measures may be resorted to before any others: exclusion and forced contribution.

Exclusion may be limited to purposes of the public good in question; often, however, it may have to be total expulsion from the group, exclusion from a single, specific benefit not being feasible. In the worst case, non-exclusion would have to be given up altogether. Thus, in a work team that shares and shares alike it may be possible to expel the inveterate shirker; but if that should be impossible all members of the team may have to accept being paid according to their individually monitored performances and the salary would have to cease being a 'public good' within the team.

Alternatively, the suckers may force the free rider to contribute in proportion to his benefit, especially as they already have in place the machinery of contribution-enforcement. Where the technical-logistical exclusion-cost is very high, they may consider this the only practical solution; where exclusion is technically easy and cheap, there may be other reasons, rooted in mores, for opting for forced contributions in preference to exclusion.

For the ex-free rider, assuming he were allowed to take the best of the remaining three inferior payoffs, the 'fair' mixed regime, where he contributes like everybody else *and* benefits, would rank as the second-best; 'sucker', where he contributes *more* or benefits *less*, as third-best; and the exchange regime, where he *neither* contributes *nor* benefits, as the worst payoff. Once free riding was barred, he should therefore, volunteer to contribute, securing the second-best payoff. But forcible closing of the free-ride option does not leave any voluntary alternative. It entails the enforcement of exclusion or of contribution. Whichever is imposed on him comes with the added burden of coercion. Even if he were offered a genuine choice, we can no longer say which he would take, for his preference-order under duress may well not be the same as under freedom. But for the implied constraint, he would have ranked either of the two payoffs that gave him access to the public good higher than the exchange regime. It is not evident that this would still be the case if his contribution turned into a tax, extracted under the threat of sanctions by the enforcement executive.

What is clear, on the other hand, is that taxation rather than exclusion would have a strong appeal to the moral sentiments of those who have the option to impose one or the other. Exclusion is discriminatory; taxation is not (or at least need not be). In adopting the latter, they can correctly claim that they are not asking any more of the ex-free rider than of themselves. When he is made to contribute, his situation is merely brought into parity with theirs. Admittedly, there is a potent counter-argument denying this, i.e. that *their* situation was voluntarily assumed, while his is forced. But exclusion, too, would be forced: and between forced disparity and forced parity the latter may well look more equitable.

With this first, yet decisive, step on the low road to fairness, a frontier will have been crossed. Ethically, we are in a different country. At the outset, back in the state of nature, suckers and free riders were unequal in terms of their contributions, but equal in terms of the free choice of their respective strategies. Each could do what he thought best: suckers contributed for fear that otherwise public provision might fail, free riders took the chance that it might not. Now, on the way out of the state of nature, there is both inequality of contribution and inequality of treatment. Some are made to contribute despite themselves; others are still free to choose their strategy and can continue to ride free.

Such incipient movement as began under the impulse of abusive free riding and outrage at conspicuous misbehaviour would now naturally gather momentum. It would help satisfy a sense of fitness and equity, and it would draw more force from the envy inspired by the unfair advantage still enjoyed by the remaining free riders. Resented, but tolerated for a while, the latter would in time be more and more liable to be forced to contribute, whether one by one, class by class (however classified), or all at once. The pace of the process might differ from one social group to another and one public good to another. Once properly under way, however, the 'fair' mixed regime would be its increasingly probable ultimate outcome. Under any other outcome, inequality of treatment and free-rider advantages would coexist with the coercive potential of an executive apparatus whose vocation was to stop people taking advantage of each other—an unstable combination.

Our starting-line on the Ethics Turnpike was the perfect state of nature, everybody disposing of the same force as everybody else, all disarmed or armed to the same extent. By the time society has organized itself and set up its schemes of public provision, ensuring (where the nature of the good made it necessary) that subscriptions shall be duly followed by actual contributions, the imperfect state of nature will have replaced the perfect one for this reason if not for several others: that each enforcement executive represents some concentration of hitherto dispersed power. Its distribution becomes polycentric instead of evenly spread over all members of society.

Justice and fairness now point in opposite directions. Despite a familiar doctrine teaching that one inspires the other, their contradictory posture is not at all surprising. The free rider takes his stand on the ground of justice, protesting against the pretension which equates the right to exclude from an unsolicited and unrequited benefit with the right to force the beneficiary to contribute to its cost. Though he did not choose to pay for the good, neither did he encourage any expectation that he would. That the suckers in a group do provide it to the entire group is strictly their affair. They have the uncontestable right to include or exclude him from the benefit, but only from the benefit they provide. That inclusion is more convenient than exclusion is, once again, their affair. Its inconvenience and cost do not create a right of forcing him to contribute, in lieu of being excluded. The attempt to arrogate to themselves such a right, by pretending that his non-refusal of the benefit amounts to the implicit acceptance of an obligation, is a failure, for no benefit-based obligation can be created by one party imputing to the other a prior promise he has not made.

The free rider's plea, admitting that in justice he can be excluded but denying that he can be made to pay, may very well be insincere and cynical. He looks suspiciously like inviting suckers to a course of action (exclusion) which he knows to be costly or difficult and which he would be the last to welcome. If there were much chance of its being adopted, he would not suggest it. But only in the last resort would free riding, a problem caused by publicness, be dealt with by abandoning publicness. Nevertheless, the free rider's plea is incontrovertible by arguments drawn from justice.

Quite different is the perspective of fairness. It would be best if all contributed voluntarily, and it would still be reasonably well if none furnished grounds for subjecting them to command-obedience. Once, however, some must be forced to contribute, equality of treatment demands that all should be. Admittedly, there is no sure first choice among rival principles of equal treatment. Maybe all should contribute the same amount; or the same proportion of their resources; or what each can spare; or what is warranted by the benefit each derives. Aristotle's principle of 'proportionate equality' may be freely translated either as a linear or as an exponential relation. Indeed, indefinitely many competing principles of equality are latent in any triad of burdens,[3] benefits, and beneficiaries. Some

---

[3] 'Burdens' is the term that fits my particular public-goods context; 'deserts' would convey the nature of the general problem of equality in distribution rather

principles may be ranked ahead of others by the arguments of 'moral accountancy', ethics, or expediency, but one does not for all that entail *more equal* treatment that another and each has as good a claim to fairness as any other.

Be that as it may, treatment according to *some* fair principle would usually prevail over treatment lacking *any* such principle, in so far as what can pass for fairness is acceptable to third parties without supporting argument, while the soulless rigour of strict deontic justice has no such direct appeal—except to those who revere it for what it is, rather than for the particular judgements it hands down. There is, apart from any plausible process leading to the threat of force against free riders, a presumption that the narrowing of the scope of private contracts and the growth of socio-contractual elements in the organization of social co-operation go hand in hand with a tendency, in cases of conflict, for fairness to get the better of justice, and for 'society's' preferences to prevail over standards and norms that interfere with their realization.

Progress towards the 'fair' mixed regime when all contribute would be the faster, the stronger are two special, sectional interests. One arises from the circumstance that not only suckers but also free riders will at worst not lose, and at best gain, when one more free rider is forced to contribute. The sole loser, of course, is the free rider who ceases to be one. When coercion to contribute spreads piecemeal, person by person, category by category, and class by class, the subjection of one more person, category, or class should, for obvious distributional reasons, be supported both by those already subjected and those whose turn was yet to come, even if they recognize, as they may do, that everybody's turn will come before they are done.

This is how, at least in Western Europe, each stage in the late medieval and modern erosion of 'ancient liberties', privileges, and immunities was made possible by tactical alliances between the government of the day and those categories that had already lost or were yet to lose their exemptions. In the contemporary state, this is how the progressive widening of the tax base is approved, if not

better. In *any* equal distribution, benefits are proportional to deserts, and there are as many equal distributions as there are conceptions of deserts. One conception is that the bearer of the burden deserves the resulting benefit; another is that the needy does. Each such conception has a multitude of variants.

positively demanded, by those already taxed and those to be left outside the net for the time being. There is no reason that plain interest in the allocation of burdens should work differently in the state of nature.

The other special interest in fighting free riding would be that of the enforcement executives. Throughout this book, I have leant over backwards to avoid imparting a will and interests to the state—not that I think doing this would lead to false results, but to see the results one gets without it. An important strand in modern contractarian social philosophy, characterized by such authors as Rawls, Ackerman, or Dworkin, seems to me to treat the state (or, more narrowly, the 'government') as reducible to an emanation of the members of civil society, a pure instrument and never an 'actor' in its own right with a discretionary role to play.[4] It is no doubt best to meet this strand of argument on its own ground if one can without serious loss of substance, and this has been my intention. It might seem a break with this precept to impute an 'interest' to the enforcement executive. Nevertheless, since even a mechanical instrument is perfectly capable of having a bias and most instruments do have one, it is pertinent to point out that the enforcement executive justifies itself and grows by enforcement; if in doubt, its bias would be to take a wide rather than a narrower view of who must make what contribution.

The End of Anarchy

There are pedestrian yet fairly robust reasons why a state of affairs with one separate enforcement executive behind each enterprise of public provision should not be stable. 'Enforcement goods' may be differentiated to some extent—discovering, judging, and executing judgment can be distinct—but there is little occasion for differentiation between what it takes to exact payments due for one public good and another. Enforcement executives would derive no advantages from staying apart. Amalgamation should make them

[4] For an older tradition of political thought, the view of the state as a pure instrument for the execution of social choice is too narrow and does not account well for the range of historical experience, of which the state directed by an elected government subject to recall is only a small part. The holistic institutional view explains most types of state at least as well and some, including the totalitarian, rather better.

stronger in force, more influential in not actually having to employ it, and perhaps also more efficient. Shared territory, shared constituencies, and shared public goods would over time induce more and more enforcement executives to merge: as a paler version of the socio-contractual derivation of the state, one could say that if they had not come into history fully merged to start with, their constituents would have chosen to merge them.

With subscriptions turned into tax assessments and with the emergence of a single collection-and-enforcement executive, little by little everybody, unless specifically exempted, would become a contributor to every scheme of public provision. There would then be no sense in nearly everybody paying scores of separate contributions to the same collector. The fiscal system could with advantage be consolidated on the revenue side, with a multitude of anachronistic taxes replaced by just a few. The equally anachronistic earmarking of particular streams of revenue to the provision of particular public goods—in our parable, a relic of selecting public goods to be provided by testing the relevant public's willingness to subscribe the cost of each separately—would also be eroded in practice before finally done away with in principle: receipts and expenditures would both be pooled. The real housekeeping constraint would be to balance global inflows and outflows by working on whichever of the two could best be made to 'give', and never mind a particular accounting mismatch between a certain expenditure and the particular revenue item supposedly meant to meet it. The enforcer-exchequer would thus find itself relentlessly pulled by its innocuous-looking housekeeping function into a policy-making one, for it could not help but involve itself in questions of how to adjust to autonomous variations in expenditures and revenues, and of who shall be pressed, and who let off more lightly—even if some of its policies in these matters were overridden on appeal. There is little doubt that—more than to such role as it had in organizing warfare—the apparatus of the state owed its systematic growth over history mostly to its innocuous-looking housekeeping role, more or less along the lines of our 'exit from the state of nature' parable.

It does not affect the issue in hand whether the state emerging from these processes is conceived as a pure instrument, or whether it is allowed to take on an institutional life of its own in competition for resources and hence in conflict with civil society. For the present

THE UNFAIRNESS OF ANARCHY

analysis, all we need is that, whether it is a blind instrument or an institution with discretionary features, the incremental actions of the state should to some perceptible degree depend on what its subjects want. This condition is likely to be met by most states except autocracies of rare perfection.

Anarchy, if historical precedent is to be taken as conclusive, does not survive. We have considered two received explanations of its fragility, and found both unconvincing. One of them, Institutional Darwinism, is a half-truth. Invoking the theory of biological evolution, it would posit the survival of the fittest, but can only manage to state a tautology, the survival of the survivor. It fails to give good reasons why we should regard the survivor as fit to survive. It does not come to terms with the demonstrated capacity of perverse, parasitic institutions to survive. It is too easy to turn inside out, becoming in the process an Institutional Gresham's Law. In particular, it never tells us why state-of-nature anarchy should have a uniformly poor life expectancy. At bottom, it must rely on an unprovable axiom, along the lines of Hume's affirmation that there must be a sovereign authority 'because society could not otherwise subsist'.[5] Should anyone feel that this is not self-evident—for the only support of the axiom that 'it could not' is that historically 'it did not'—he would look in vain for a theory to account for the facts, that would tell him 'why not'.

In contrast to Institutional Darwinism, the contractarian tradition, at least in its Hobbesian version, does offer such a theory. It derives the dominance of the state over anarchy from the basic premiss that non-coerced contribution to public goods is irrational. Hence, if people opted for the state of nature they would be knowingly renouncing public goods. But they cannot both prefer (certain) public goods and willingly renounce them. Consistency requires that they should want to do away with anarchy. The contractarian explanation has stood largely uncontested for three centuries after Hobbes. Only recently has political economy, using game theory, started to dispute the validity of the contractarian representation of the public-goods problem as a prisoners' dilemma with a dominant un-cooperative solution.[6] It is the thesis of the present book, argued in detail in Chapters 6 and 7, that the very nature of public goods is

---

[5] Hume (1748) 161.
[6] Cf. e.g. Taylor (1976), Axelrod (1984), the authors cited in p. 149 n. 9 (in particular J. S. Hampton), and those in the appendix to ch. 7.

such that non-co-operation in their production would seldom be a dominant strategy.

Our argument indeed is that if the state of nature had not been obliterated due to *ad hoc* causes, it would have been transformed into a society subject to a sovereign state in a piecemeal process, moving crab-wise, largely unplanned. Its motive force would be, not the desire or 'need' for public goods, but the demand for greater fairness in the manner of getting them. Its actual destination, however, might well not be greater fairness.

Lured on by the relative ease of each step undertaken to put right some glaring unfairness, and quite pardonably failing to foresee the cumulative and distant consequences, state-of-nature society would with great probability (to borrow Nozick's phrase) 'back into the minimal state without really trying'. In the course of tidying up and sorting out one unfairness after another, it would have substantially brought about the effects conventional wisdom ascribes to the ideal, comprehensive social contract. Nor is there any visible reason to expect some such process to stop at the notional minimal state, or at any other particular point along the private good–public good, contract–command spectrum.

10

THE RETURN OF THE FREE RIDER

The end of anarchy would be characterized by two shifts in the social environment. On balance, a shift would occur from contract to command, and from probabilities to certainties.[1] The ultimate source of both is the changeover from voluntary to (mainly) mandatory contributions to public goods.

Implicit in this changeover is the grounding of third-party interventions in conflicts increasingly upon principles of fairness rather than of justice. Justice tends to be the salient principle, facilitating acquiescence in third-party interference, when conflicts arise out of prior conventions, agreements, contracts, and attempts at their enforcement. Fairness is salient for social choice, when conflicts cluster around problems of 'who pays what' and 'who gets what' in the absence of prior agreements, calling for resolution of the distributive implications of coerced co-ordination.

The full dynamics of the encroachment of one form of social co-operation upon another, involving the replacement of voluntary by mandatory co-ordination, is patently not going to be derived from the handful of basic abstractions which make up our parable of the rise of centralized power. However, the austere poverty of our raw material has some compensating merit too. The focus on the simplified *a priori* division of society and its constituent groups into suckers and free riders is the most direct way I can think of to uncover the game-like interactions that are set off when this spontaneous division is overridden by the command of social choice. The new environment of anti-free-rider suppression has two key features that play a direct role in the form these games take. I shall call them 'reverse contribution' and 'pooling'.

---

[1] Recall Hobbes's position that civil peace is not the absence of 'actuall fighting', but the lack of *certainty* of its absence: Hobbes (1651), 186. State-of-nature peace on this definition is impossible since there can be no absolute certainty of no 'actuall fighting' if there is more than one autonomous holder of armed force, or other means of war-making.

Reverse Contribution

Publicness, it will be recalled, implies a loosening of the nexus between individual contributions and benefits. When a good is wholly private, the person who uses it is a customer and 'gets what he pays for'. When it is semi-public, he is a beneficiary and pays less than the replacement cost of the good, which can as a rule only be reproduced with the help of some sort of public subsidy. When the good is wholly public, the beneficiary typically contributes nothing towards its reproduction *in exchange* for the marginal unit of his benefit, whatever contribution he may be obliged to make *independently* of his marginal benefit.

There are cases (*a*) where the individual beneficiary of public provision cannot vary the 'amount' of his benefit at his own discretion. Such public goods as national defence, a common language, widespread respect for one system of customs and laws yield a certain advantage to each, perhaps greater or less according to their walk of life. There is no obvious way for anyone, given his situation in society, to get a greater advantage by having a more intensive recourse to these goods. Not only is the good itself indivisible, or at least subject to a minimum threshold, but each individual's benefit from it is indivisible as well.

In other cases (*b*) it is within a person's discretionary power to use more of the good (have more intensive recourse to it), but there would be no point in so doing: he will not want to cross and recross a bridge more often than the number of times his occasions take him to the other bank. Though his benefit from the use of the bridge is in a sense divisible, the marginal benefit is nil.

Finally, however, there are cases (*c*) where the benefit is both divisible and presumably positive at the margin. Grazing one's livestock on the common looks like being such a case. The remarkable thing about common pasture is not that often it is overgrazed: the contrary would be more remarkable. The surprising fact is that it is not *more* overgrazed, i.e. that its abuse mostly stops well short of the point where one more cow could not be profitably kept on it. The owner of an additional head of stock could reap an unrequited advantage to the detriment of the other cattle-owners. Why does a person in such cases forgo the advantage and restrain his recourse, use, or consumption of the public good, instead of pushing it to the limit where no further benefit could be derived from a further increment?

It looks prima facie irrational to forgo a costless benefit. However, restraint in using the public good can in such apparently puzzling cases be assimilated, at the margin, to a contribution to its provision. Where public provision is based on voluntary co-operation, contributing has a certain rationale which was explored in Chapters 6 and 7. In essence, it is a matter of the allocation of risk between suckers and free riders, the former contributing for fear that public provision might fail if they did not, the latter ready to run the risk that it might. This allocation is consistent with voluntary provision of the good. However, if its rationale is adequate for explaining contribution, it is also adequate to explain restraint in consumption in cases where greater consumption would increase the risk of contributions being inadequate to meet it. Moderation in the consumption of a good increases the probability of its continuing successful public provision.

While we do not know the *effective* cause of there being only so many cows on the common, the equivalence at the margin between contribution and moderation in use can, within the right parameters, very well be a sufficient cause of it. Certain 'players' both among suckers and free riders could rationally choose to employ a variable mixed subscription-and-use strategy, e.g. 'This time round I do not subscribe, but restrain my consumption', in place of the pure subscription strategy, there being no *a priori* reason why the mixed strategy should not yield as much expected utility at the margin as the pure one.

Once, however, contributions cease being voluntary, the whole incentive structure changes. Restraint in consumption is rewarded by a uniformly zero average and marginal payoff, for it does not affect the probability of the good being provided. This probability has previously been fixed at the maximum (i.e. certainty) by social choice: taxes and tax expenditures are certain to be what they are, whether or not a given individual exercises moderation in profiting from a given public good. Rational individuals would therefore, switch the 'use' component of their strategy from 'restraint' to 'no restraint' and increase their consumption of any public good whose marginal benefit to them was positive. They would attain equilibrium at a level of consumption or intensity of use of each good, where the marginal benefit was nil due to saturation or, more characteristically, due to the indivisible public good becoming sufficiently 'crowded' for rationing, queueing, jostling, spoiling, or analogous constraints to deter any greater use.

Publicness in the provision of health care (whether in the form of outright gratuity, or in the form of insurance where the individual's premium is in the nature of a capitation fee and adjusts imperfectly, if at all, to an increase in the individual's consumption of health services) is widely believed to cause higher demands for it at all but the very highest income levels than would be the case if health care were a pure exchange good; demand is only held in check by seemingly chronic 'crowdedness' in many sectors of the free health service, for example, of the United Kingdom. *Mutatis mutandis*, the same is true of university education in those countries, notably France, Italy, and Spain, where fees are merely nominal and admission to most faculties is a right (or, in public-goods language, 'non-excluded'). Recourse to welfare services, including even a reputedly too ready reliance on unemployment benefit in preference to arduous search for inconvenient and inferior employment ('getting on one's bike'), belongs to the same class of phenomena.

In the nature of the case, there are many *ad hoc* explanations for the endemic character of excess demand for this type of good. Some of them contend that but for the parsimony of governments in fixing the scale of public provision, there would be no excess demand. This is not the place to try and judge the merits of such contentions. All we need say is that contrary to state-of-nature conditions where restraint would be rational, 'over-use' of public goods which are subject to crowdedness would be a rational strategy for the user. Hence, the cast-iron social-choice assurance that the good *will* be provided is a *sufficient* explanation of over-use and crowdedness, though we may not know whether it is the *right* one. At least it predicts quite well what seems to be happening across the board.

When contribution to public provision is mandatory, its unrestrained use up to the constraints of crowdedness[2] is best understood and referred to as 'reverse contribution'—as if the

---

[2] At what precise point, level, or degree does crowdedness become really constraining? The question has the same 'catch' in it, and calls for the same type of answer, as the one about the camel's back or the heap of stones. For the vague notion of 'too many' to function as a threshold, there is no logical necessity to find the precise number of straws that *will* break the camel's back, nor of the stones that *will* amount to a heap. Cf. p. 162.

excess use over and above the rational state-of-nature level of use were a partial withdrawal of the contribution that had been exacted from the user. While the contribution is mandatory, the reverse contribution is discretionary. It is, loosely speaking, a revenge strategy for 'getting one's own back'.

Pooling

In the state of nature, the *list* of public goods, comprising the specification and the scale of provision of each, would be the set of group-game solutions, a separate solution being found for each good by the respective group of 'players'. (Separate solutions need not, of course, mean that they are independent.) After the exit from the state of nature, the whole list is decided by one all-inclusive set of 'players'. Social choice is sovereign over the list and over each item in it (except if the choice rule provides for an exempt domain and the good falls within it). Hence, even if aggregate public provision is not determined anew each day in a plebiscitary fell stroke, but is built up piecemeal, sovereignty over the list means that it is what it is because social choice did not decree otherwise. Moreover, contributions are not assessed and exacted separately for each good, but jointly for the entire list: if a person contributes to one man-made public good, he contributes to all. The principle of pooling operates both in deciding what shall be provided and in allocating the costs to be borne: all can have their say and all must do their bit, regardless of their interest in particular items on the list.

Unless the constitution ('choice rule') provides for a dictatorial subset of society whose chosen public-goods list always prevails over the lists everybody else would choose, the 'socially chosen' list is essentially some 'summation compromise' among the entire set of preference-expressions for alternative lists. I will assume that the choice rule is of this kind, that everybody expresses preference (e.g. votes) for the list he really likes best (I use 'preference' non-trivially), and that the nature of the summation compromise is such that some (whether small or large) change in preference-expressions will, if anything, produce some change of the same sign in social choice. One man, one vote combined with some, albeit sluggish, rule of decisiveness will characteristically ensure that the socially chosen list will be sensitive to some degree to everybody's preferred list. Take, for illustration, a case where two classes of goods, public order and social welfare, are provided on a certain scale for A and B. A attaches greater importance to order; B to welfare. In the typical summation compromise, a list of public goods will be chosen, such that A would feel better if more goods conducive to public order were produced, if need be at the expense of welfare-promoting goods; B would have the converse reaction. Once they have both pushed their 'reverse contribution' strategies to the point where both order-goods and welfare-goods are 'crowded', A would gain more if further order-goods were added to the list. Once more, the converse is true of B.

If y (for order) and z (for welfare) were 'excluded' goods obtained in private exchange, we would look for an area of mutual advantage within which A could make B better off at no cost to himself by giving him some z in exchange for some y, and vice versa for B, so that they could trade profitably subject to resolving the bargaining problem of how to share the advantage. Usually, however, no such mutually profitable adjustment of people's holdings or intake of goods is possible when the goods are public. If either of two goods y and z is 'uncrowded', it is always better simply to use more of it without giving up any of the other good for the privilege. Hence, there is no area of mutual advantage and no basis for trade. If both goods are 'crowded', but at least one of the two yields non-transferable benefits, once again there is no basis for trade. (For instance, if z is sickness or unemployment insurance, and both A and B are already drawing all the benefit they can from it, in conformity with the principle of reverse contribution, A cannot cause B to get even more by passing on to him some of his own entitlement. Consequently, B cannot profit from renouncing some of his entitlement to the other good y in favour of A, even if y is transferable.) Only if both y and z are inter-personally transferable can trade create a Pareto-superior outcome and improve the benefit the two goods yield to society. Presumably, however, transferability and non-exclusion do not go together, since it is impossible for transfer to procure a benefit in the absence of exclusion.

Failing trade in non-excluded goods, every individual must make do with the 'pooled' public-goods list, no matter how unsatisfactory he finds it. It sounds paradoxical that while the pooled list can well be Pareto-optimal, i.e. impossible to change without hurting somebody, it may yet leave every individual worse off than they would be if each could draw up his own list within a fixed resource budget.

In reality, of course, there is no paradox, for society cannot have *both* non-exclusion *and* individually tailored patterns of public-goods provision. The two conditions would be contradictory even if each public good were produced in response to preference-expressions and contributions voted for that particular good separately. Pooling, with everybody getting free access to the same list of goods and contributing independently of how much he needs and how well he likes each, is a corollary of publicness and of the whole list being decided by one and the same decisive set (e.g. the majority of voters) under the social-choice rule. Yet when the decision has implications that are mandatory for all, no other way of drawing up the list of public goods may be workable: could it be left to the aged to decide about old-age pensions and long-term health care, given that the burden of contributions does not fall on the aged alone?

The Game of 'Ask'

The question that ends the preceding section is obviously rhetorical but not wholly pointless. Since it is better to be repetitive than misunderstood, let us consider once more how and why public provision under *any* social-choice rule is, by its nature, redistributive with or without deliberate design to that effect on the part of the provider.

In the state of nature, providing public goods redistributes in the somewhat simplified yet palpable sense that all benefit but not all contribute, there being some prima-facie shift of benefit from suckers to free riders. Less obviously, but nevertheless effectively, an allocation of burdens may be redistributive even when all are forced to contribute: any 'fair' mixed regime is redistributive according to some criteria if not according to others—by certain norms of fairness, it would be unfair if it did not both provide *and* redistribute.

An allocation of burdens can be recognized as non-redistributive if it satisfies certain conditions of neutrality that are agreed to be minimally sufficient: its redistributive character is relative to those agreed conditions, whatever they are. If two rival sets of conditions contradict each other, no allocation may satisfy both. One possible neutrality condition would stipulate that the burden of contributions be allocated to produce the distribution of real income (or happiness, or whatever else is supposed to lend itself to distribution) that would have prevailed in the pure exchange regime. To approximate, let alone achieve, this result, however, it would not be enough to fix taxes in such a way as to leave everybody's relative post-tax share unchanged (if there is such a way). Income or happiness is presumably reduced by taxes and increased by publicly provided goods. Because of non-exclusion, the hand that fixed the taxes cannot also fix the individual benefits. The most it could do would be to fix taxes or other contributions in the light of the likely benefit each contributor can be expected to derive from the list of public goods, after allowing for the benefit itself being dependent on the level of post-contribution income. Pretending that a certain allocation of contributions, combined with a certain list of public goods, produces this result or something close to it would be certainly brave, if not preposterous. Other, significantly different, neutrality conditions could be excogitated. But they would be merely trying the reader's patience, for finding plainer, more easily satisfied conditions would not really affect the basic issue, which is that it is not in the nature of a social-choice mechanism to search for, and home in on, the target of neutrality; while hitting it without aiming to would be an extraordinary accident.

Distribution effects relative to the shares all would get in a pure exchange regime, are intrinsic in the movement away from the exchange regime. Gainers from such effects have, by definition, reason to prefer them to neutrality. Only the losers have any incentive to resist them. The nature of non-fatuous social choice, however, is that under any conceivable aggregation rule defining what shall be a decisive set, and hence whose favourite state of affairs shall be accepted as the socially chosen one, it will normally generate distributive outcomes favouring a corresponding decisive set in society.

Under bare majority rule, for example, a bare majority is always able to choose a distributive outcome out of the range of feasible outcomes which favours it, or some subset within it, at the expense of the minority, whose preferred outcome it was able to overrule. Far from tending towards a distributionally neutral list of public goods and pattern of contributions for producing it, social choice will, if anything, act to ensure that they shall not be neutral.

The point that public provision is *sui generis* redistributive is distinct from the more widely understood one that it is a particularly potent tool if deliberately employed to that end. Taxation according to some measure of the 'capacity to pay' combined with public provision according to some measure of 'need' is the grandfather of most deliberate redistributive policies. Social-choice rules, as we have seen, are predisposed to employ public provision in deliberately redistributive ways, by virtue of permitting the resulting set of gainers to overrule the losers. For this reason, a marginal expansion of public provision has a greater likelihood of being 'socially chosen' if it is deliberately designed to have a redistributive effect favourable to a potential decisive set, than if its redistributive effect is, so to speak, left to chance.[3] Evidently, public provision need not be a positive-sum game to allow the gainers to outweigh the losers. Provided it is divisible, it is a perfectly straightforward task to divide a zero or negative sum so as to produce a preponderance of gainers over losers, as long as it is the preponderance of their numbers that matters, and there is no rule against making one individual lose more than another gains. Fairness rules, far from prohibiting it, may positively call for such results.

Ordinarily one should expect both the unintended and the deliberate redistributive effects of public provision to be at work. The reason I insist on the conceptual distinction between the two is that I can abstract from the second as ordinarily understood, and still derive the same results: public provision will expand, command will encroach upon contract, and free riding and its attempted suppression will be a typically open-ended process even in the assumed absence of policies aimed at modifying the distribution of benefits and burdens in a welfarist and egalitarian (or any other) direction.

Let us now suppose the equal feasibility of two 'political' states of affairs, reflected in two extreme 'mixed regimes' and (on the principle of 'he who can do more can do less') of all less extreme

---

[3] It is always loose talk, if not worse, to say that society prefers to provide a certain public good by taxing itself. What 'society prefers' is to do so in a certain manner, producing a certain redistributive effect from which the right people gain and the right ones lose.

mixed regimes falling between the extremes. At one extreme, the list of public goods is short and most resources are devoted to exchange goods; the converse is true at the other extreme. We will call the first the Minimal and the second the Maximal State. The actual regime between the two limiting ones is socially chosen. The state is a pure instrument registering and executing social choices. The choice of regime changes if enough individual preference-expressions change in the same direction. This translates into the state being to some degree sensitive to what individuals demand. The more agile the choice rule, the more sensitive is the state; if there is provision in the rule for a 'mandate to govern', a short, revocable, yet renewable mandate makes for greater, a long, irrevocable mandate for lesser, sensitivity.

There are individuals who, given the actual regime, prefer moving towards the Minimal and others towards the Maximal State. (This does not, of course, prejudge whether they would like to go all the way, but that is not relevant.) Each has reasons and motives for his preferred direction; some or all of the ethical motives surveyed in Chapter 8 may well be at work, albeit influenced by the fact that certain 'exits' become either mandatory or forbidden under the operation of the social contract. Everybody is supposed to have expectations of the value to him of various possible public goods, given the contribution he expects to have to make; individuals may or may not reckon that their own contributions would have to vary if the list of public goods varied. There would presumably be at least some 'ideologically' neutral, single-minded narrow utility-maximizers playing 'economic man'. They would be indifferent between going towards the Minimal or the Maximal State, except if, and only to the extent that, they expected a change in the overall scale of public provision to have good or bad redistributive effects for themselves. I will take A and B to be two such neutral 'economic men'. Of the two, moreover, I suppose A to reckon on no redistributive advantage from a changed scale (length of 'list') of public provision, nor to have any preferences for a different composition of it.

The free-riding benefit that public provision offers to some at the expense of others is twofold.

1. One sort arises from a change in the composition of public provision in one's favour. Since the same 'pooled' list of public goods is available to all non-excluded members of the public, a

given individual (such as *B*), having adjusted his consumption of each good by 'reverse contributions', may still derive more benefit from his marginal consumption of certain goods (including perhaps potential public goods that could be but are not provided) than of others. Given the list actually provided, the addition of some he liked and the suppression of others he liked less would increase his benefit; the increase would not require more resources to be devoted to public goods.

2. Depending on how the burden of resource contributions is shared out, providing a given list of public goods redistributes income, utility, or happiness from some people to others (note that taxation need not be progressive, proportional, or for that matter conform to any pattern at all, for this to be the case; a weak or simply indeterminate nexus between contributions and benefits will do). A marginal increase in public provision matched by a marginal increase in contributions could increase redistributive gains and losses: gainers could gain more, and losers lose more. However, many public goods are likely to be indivisible ('lumpy') both ways, collapsing if compressed, but resisting expansion. Therefore, one may never get an all-round marginal increase in public provision as a whole which would leave its composition unchanged. Instead, one can envisage each increase as a newly provided good, e.g. some additional defence of public order, or some new welfare service. If for a given individual the new good is a random addition to existing ones, he is as likely to like it better as to like it less than the average. We can then take it that his expected free-rider benefit, if any, from such a random addition to public goods is due to the larger *scale* of public provision and owes nothing to its changed *composition*.

In terms of these two distinct sources, (scale and composition) of free-rider benefit, indifference between moving towards the Minimal or the Maximal State signifies that the person concerned expects no gain or loss as the relative size of the state expands, unless he expects the expansion to involve a non-random change in the composition of public goods.

Let *A* and *B* be indifferent to the scale of public provision in the above sense. They expect to break even on redistribution. In addition, being 'economic men', they have no ideological bias either. They are neither rugged individualist plutocrats nor welfare-parasite social-fascists; if there were only two kinds of axes, the ideological and the venal, they would have no axe to grind. If everyone was like them, in terms of the conventional theory of the creeping welfare state, no force would be left to sustain the advance of the public sector and the retreat of free contracts. Nevertheless, their rational interaction would still produce unambiguous impulses to keep society moving towards the Maximal State.

This result can be deduced from fairly innocent assumptions.

1. Every member of society can, once in every time-period, demand of the state to amend the list of old public goods by making one specific change in it. The new list is the sum of these demands, aggregated in the manner laid down by the social-choice rule. Any individual has three options: to ask for one more good, to ask for one less good, or not to ask at all. Asking is costless to the individual concerned, its cost being borne by society. If need be, this assumption can be justified by the likelihood that political entrepreneurs expect to profit from diagnosing, articulating, and pressing home individual demands for public goods. For instance, if some members of the public appear to find public order, and others welfare services, inadequate, there will soon arise a candidate, a lobby, or a party of order, and one of welfare, each promoting the provision of more public goods conducive to satisfying the respective constituencies (which freeride on the back of society as far as the cost of rewarding political activity on their behalf is concerned).

2. An individual expects at least as great or greater incremental benefits if his demand for one more public good is met than if his request for suppressing one is agreed. This condition holds if his average benefit from the good he would like to add and the one he would like to suppress, pro rata to their resource costs, is as great or greater than his own share of the cost.[4] I assume this normally to be

---

[4] Let $\bar{C}$ be the total resource cost of producing either the whole good y or the whole good z. Whichever is produced, the individual's contribution to the cost is $c = f(\bar{C})$. His benefits from y and z, however, are $b_y \neq b_z$. He will weakly prefer y to be added to the list of public goods, rather than z to be suppressed from it, if

$$b_y - c_y > c_z - b_z$$

and since

$$c_y \equiv c_z$$

we can write

$$\frac{b_y + b_z}{2} \geqslant c.$$

the case, except if there are public goods that are so useless or are so wastefully produced that an individual could hope personally to gain more from their suppression than from the addition of his favourite new good. This is perfectly possible, especially if the state proves to be a very imperfectly controlled 'instrument' of society and takes on a life of its own. But a list of public goods, originally selected on the basis of the 'productivity of publicness', must go downhill a long way in quality and cost-efficiency before the exception becomes important and demands to 'roll back the state' start to be directed at practical, specific targets instead of being the worthy general principle that has seldom committed anybody to give up any particular public good (or service).

3. Given that everyone else is making the same calculations as the individual in assumption 2, everyone is more likely to ask for one more good than for one fewer. Under any social-choice rule that obliges the state to be sensitive to demands, the probability of good y being added is as great or greater than that of good z being suppressed in response to an individual's demand, for it will tend to be reinforced by the similar demands of many other individuals. In the contrary case, for example, if society were very parsimonious in what it instructed the state to do, an individual might do better to use his 'right to ask' for getting rid of a public good he did not much like, and save his share of its cost, than to waste it on a vain request for a good he liked very much but that no one else was requesting. (The familiar objection, that one individual's voice, lobbying efforts, etc. are not going to change the probability of anything one way or the other, is of course as valid or invalid with respect to asking one thing rather than another, as with respect to any other attempt at getting one's way through the political mechanism. Since many people do make such attempts all the time, the objection cannot be altogether valid. The reason is presumably to be sought among the very motives that can make it rational for a person to make a voluntary contribution to a public good despite the dilution in his resulting benefit.) Assumption 3 is probabilistically supported if assumption 2 holds: for if a randomly chosen individual weakly prefers 'asking for more' to 'asking for less', then more individuals will tend to ask for more than for fewer public goods and any individual who wants a longer list of public goods has a greater chance of finding his demand 'socially chosen', provided the two

sets of goods that can be added and suppressed are suitably restricted.

If, as under assumption 1, 'economic men' have certain limited and formalized political strategies to choose from, and assumptions 2 and 3 are more likely to hold than not, there is (*a*) as much or more of a free-rider benefit to be had from changing the composition of public provision in one's favour by an expansion than by a contraction of the list of public goods; and (*b*) the demand for expansion is no less likely to be successful. The strategy of 'asking for more' would consequently weakly dominate 'asking for less' for both player *A* and player *B*. This would leave both of them with two admissible strategies: to ask (for more) or not to ask. In each time-period, each player must decide the strategy he will adopt without knowing what the other will have decided.

The resulting game of 'Ask' in a two-person form is represented in Figure 14. The payoff in square 1, where both ask for, and in a certain proportion of plays get, more of their favourite public goods, corresponds to a movement towards the Maximal State. Square 4 is the possibility of preserving a pre-game Minimal State; it is also consistent with a movement towards it, propelled by extra-game impulses, if any. In neither square 1 nor square 4 does one player get a free-rider benefit at the expense to the other; we will abstract from whatever they may get from non-players if there are any such. Square 2 produces the sucker payoff for *B*, for the composition of the list of public goods becomes less favourable to him. As the list gets longer, too, the contributions of the two players increase. This is neither good nor bad for either player; we know that they are both indifferent to a change in the *scale* of public

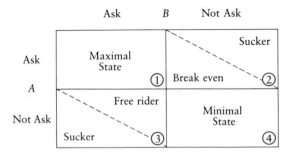

FIGURE 14.

provision, its redistributive effects being neutral for them and affecting only other people. A, however, is also indifferent to the change in the *composition* of public provision. Hence, in this square, A just breaks even; if we assumed that he too had a favourite public good to lobby for, our thesis would become stronger but more banal. Finally, square 3 is the classic situation where A gets the sucker payoff and B gets a free ride on him; the composition of the public-goods list gets worse for A and better for B, while both contribute more to it since it has lengthened. A's ranking of the squares (i.e. of the payoffs he would get by landing in the square in question) is therefore 1 = 2 = 4 > 3. All he must do is to ward off the risk of square 3: his 'ask' strategy consequently dominates his 'not ask' strategy, although he would just as soon have minimal as maximal provision, and does not believe that a change in the composition of public goods could make him better off. The reason for this apparent paradox can be intuitively seen by considering that in asking for more A expects no positive new benefit, but seeks to insure against B asking for and getting more of what he wants. The latter would get a free-rider benefit at A's expense unless A successfully pressed home a demand of his own, restoring the previous balance in the *composition* of public goods, albeit on a larger scale. The predicament of A is that of the man walking up the down escalator: he has to keep climbing to stay in the same place.

While A shows a degree of disabused indifference, the payoff rankings of B indicate that he is hopefully striving. He would go for the free-rider benefit, putting the squares in the following order: 3 > 1 = 4 > 2. But his more differentiated preference-order, springing from his more optimistic view of what politics can do for him, does not impel him to adopt a strategy any different from that of the more sceptical A; B too must 'ask' no matter what strategy he expects the opposite player to adopt. With or without much conviction, they have to play symmetrically. The solution of the game, therefore, is the Maximal State in square 1, where, as in Alice's Caucus Race, all have won and all must get a prize. However, this solution is a stable equilibrium only in the dynamic and not the static sense; after each 'play' the players will be impelled to 'ask' again, and will keep moving in the same direction until stopped by some extra-game cause. The movement toward the Maximal State is like the Caucus Race in this, too, that not only must all get prizes, but there is no particular place where the race is supposed to stop either; it goes on unless and until the Dodo stops it.

The Game of 'Deficit'

Assumption 1 above, as the astute reader will have noticed, was lop-sided. It gave individuals a chance to influence social choice on the benefit side of the public goods relation, but not on the contribution side. It is almost as if the underlying approach tacitly presupposed that accounts must balance anyway, that willing the ends is as good as willing the means, and that though individuals may manage to get free rides, for society as a whole benefits cannot increase without contributions increasing. On this tacit supposition, a social choice of more public goods *eo ipso* is also a choice of higher taxes, however levied. But this supposition is gratuitous in logic, and contradicted by experience. No social choice entails another unless there is a decisive set of individuals such that, given the entailing choice, they would always opt for the entailed one. There is nothing that would necessarily induce a decisive set of people to match an increase in public provision by an increase in taxes; opting for it may or may not be attractive to the minimum number of individuals needed for a decisive coalition; but unless he *wishes* to, nothing *obliges* an individual to aim at consistency between benefits and contributions. The essence of publicness, as we have been finding all along, is in fact that there is no individual obligation to balance the two.

I propose, therefore, to make the assumptions of the preceding section more symmetrical by enlarging the options available. An individual will now be able to ask for one more or one fewer public good, but also for lower or higher taxation. If he asks successfully, taxation will be lowered or raised for him and everybody else. Perhaps arbitrarily, I will also assume that there is a fairness rule under which he cannot ask for something for others without asking for it for himself, so that in practice no one will choose to ask for *higher* taxes.

Since asking is still costless to the individual, I will take it that a 'mixed strategy' of asking for more goods and for lower taxes dominates the 'pure' strategy of merely asking for more goods. On the other hand, asking only for lower taxes would also be admissible as a pure strategy. It would dominate and replace the strategy of asking nothing.

The game of 'Ask' can now be redesigned to give us the game of 'Deficit', represented in Figure 15. It is played by the same two persons A and B. In the three squares 1, 2, and 3, the outcome is a deficit for three alternative reasons: because there is movement towards the Maximal State, because B gets the sucker payoff, or because B gets a free ride. In square 4, the deficit may or may not be avoided, depending on whether tax reductions are balanced or not by an autonomous movement towards fewer public goods; the payoffs in this square are at least not inconsistent with a tendency to a balanced-budget Minimal State—though twentieth-century experience does not encourage expectations of such an outcome, nor does consideration of the incentive structure of the game.

As in the 'Ask' game, and for the same reason, A does not expect to be noticeably better off if, as would be the case in square 2, he got the new public good he asked for. Unlike the 'Ask' game, however, in the 'Deficit' game he does not fear to be worse off if, as in square 3, B gets the new public good *he* asked for. The reason is that in this game A's contribution does not have to increase to help pay for B's increased benefit. As we will see presently, the free ride B gets is not at A's expense. It looks, therefore, as if disabused A does not much mind what happens and which square turns out to yield the solution of the game; his most likely ranking of the squares is $1 = 2 = 3 = 4$, suggesting that he has no dominant

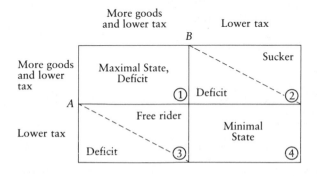

FIGURE 15.

strategy. On the other hand, B is still his eager and hopeful old self and ranks the squares as he did in the 'Ask' game, meaning that his mixed strategy always seems best to him no matter how he expects A to play. If so, the game solution can only lie in squares 1 or 3, though we cannot say which of the two is more likely.

Square 1 is the familiar image of the uniformly beneficial political process, with 'more of everything'; more public goods with prizes for everybody, greater deficits, and progress towards the Maximal State. In square 3, expansion of the state's activities is less even-handed. It is biased towards a class of public goods that are close substitutes (e.g. all defence-related, all order-related, or all welfare-related goods) or that are mostly demanded by a particular class or segment of society (represented by the demands of B). Inasmuch as public provision now grows in a particular direction rather than in all directions at once, it could be that the deficit produced by this outcome is smaller. The cumulative problem it eventually creates may, however, be greater if, as may well be the case, society takes more seriously, and attempts to honour, a public debt which still looks manageable, while it would find ways of defaulting in practice if service of the debt were manifestly beyond its means and strength of will.[5]

In going all out towards the Maximal State, society's resources are committed to producing an ever-widening range of public goods. At the same time they are also committed to meeting the claims upon private goods on the part of the owners of the cumulative public debt that is being piled up in the process. There may not be enough resources to honour both commitments. Nobody in particular is responsible for them to be honoured. Real-life 'maximal states', unable to get a mandate for changing their course—an inability that could be easily predicted by consulting the 'Ask' and 'Deficit' games, if it were not predicted anyway by

[5] The greater the public debt relative to national income, the greater is the proportion of national income pre-empted by its service. The public debt grows each year at a rate determined by the year's deficit. Given this rate, the ultimate possibility of honouring the debt at all depends on the rate of growth of national income compared to the rate of interest on the debt. Should the interest rate be higher than the growth rate, even a modest annual deficit must in time produce a closing of the 'debt trap', where current debt service exceeds total income, and the interest simply cannot be paid. The lower the annual deficit, however, the more distant is the evil day when default in some fashion becomes physically inevitable. For the arithmetic, see Bispham (1987).

plain worldly wisdom[6]—can and often do get this looming inconsistency between resources and commitments resolved for them by inflation. They need not even consciously invite inflation, but can just lie back and submit to it. Without anybody having to break a promise and repudiate a debt, inflation impersonally takes care of the cumulative deficit and the claims arising from it.

The beauty, if one may call it that, of the free riding permitted by the 'Deficit' game is that, unlike the ordinary public-goods free riding with its *interpersonal* redistribution from losers to gainers, it produces an *intertemporal* redistribution. B gains today without A losing today. It is only by introducing a time dimension that we can locate the losers at all. They are the future selves of A or B or both, in some proportion that is difficult, if not impossible, to forecast intelligently, and of course their children, to an extent which is if anything even more conjectural.

If social choice is some, however contestable, inter-personal summation of strictly point-of-time preferences between no deficit and deficit, the deficit must always be chosen no matter how we do the sum, for no preference speaks against it. Only constraints having to do with public credit and interest rates would keep it within finite bounds.

There is, of course, much evidence that people's preference are not confined to goods at a single point of time, but have a pronounced time dimension. They save, or run up debts, or do both in some more or less intelligible combination, and what they choose to do is influenced at the margin by the 'price of time'. This finding, for all its intrinsic interest, achieves no more than to generalize choice among private goods over all relevant dimensions, including time. It puts exchanges between a present and a future good on a par with exchanges between two present goods, making equilibrium in both 'spot' and 'forward' (i.e. inter-temporal) exchanges a resultant of preference and price. Both kinds of exchange, however, concern private goods in an exchange regime regulated by ordinary contracts. They conform to the strict condition that each person 'gets what he pays for', the present value of his benefits being equal at the margin to that of his own contribution.

No such condition holds for public goods, present or future. Contract and exchange are inapplicable categories to free riding.

---

[6] A fine example of wordly-wise reasoning that predicts deficits is Buchanan and Wagner (1977).

Having laboured this point and its implications throughout this book with respect to goods distributed in space among persons, we need do no more than recapitulate it with respect to goods distributed over *both* space *and* time among persons today and persons in the future. Adding the time dimension does not bring private and public goods any closer, for it does not narrow down the smallest set of persons for which total benefits are a stable function of total contributions. If anything, it widens it, perhaps very considerably. Under the social contract, the *smallest* set which *must*, so to speak, 'break even' (its free rider members gaining what its sucker members lose) is the whole society. Prima facie, and failing specific knowledge to the contrary, any one person's incremental free-rider benefit is provided by the probable incremental contribution of every other. When this condition is generalized over time, 'every other' person includes all present and future members of society, the 'break-even set' stretching through all posterity. Specific knowledge about the incidence of future taxes, and of future interest rates and the evolving maturity distibution of the public debt, would make this conclusion more discriminating, but hardly in a manner to make much of an impression on the 'strategy' any rational public-goods 'player' would employ today to maximize both his free-rider benefit and the probability that others will not manage to free ride on him.

The admissibility of deficits under the rules of social choice offers the chance of free riding not only inter-personally, but also inter-temporally; benefit and contribution are now allowed to be *not only individually but also collectively unequal* at any one time, although they must still be collectively equal over time if the period considered is made long enough.

Any individual, however, can reasonably adopt the attitude today that *après lui, le déluge*. On probabilistic grounds, he has less cause to take account of the adverse repercussions of his free riding on his own (and his children's) contribution in an open-ended inter-personal *and* inter-temporal context than in the merely inter-personal one, when total benefits and contributions balance at a point of time. (When contributions are mandatory, the cost of enhancing his benefit is 'conventionally diluted' over the whole contributing set, which means that dilution increases as the set gets larger, since all in the set will together be made to match his enhanced benefit by their extra contributions. A set including both

THE RETURN OF THE FREE RIDER

present and future taxpayer members of society is, of course, larger than that including present taxpayers only.)

Needless to say, resources used up today must be provided today at the very latest. Whatever their accounting treatment, their production cannot be left to posterity. Taxing to spend and borrowing to spend are, on a physical view, merely different accounting treatments of one and the same 'real' phenomenon. Under certain and fairly exacting conditions, there is indeed 'neutrality' or 'equivalence'[7] between the two in that it makes no 'macro-economic' difference that the resources for a marginal increase of public goods are diverted from the production of private goods in one particular manner or another. There are obvious caveats when the economy is open and the debt is not 'owed to ourselves', especially if it is denominated in a currency that our own inflation cannot depreciate—as many hapless Latin American countries have discovered. Nor is it indifferent, even in a closed economy, that a deficit adds to the assets of the private sector and to the liabilities of the state[8]—an asymmetry which brings us back, by another path, to inter-personal and inter-temporal distribution problems.

It has been shown in the present section that when the social choice-rule permits members of society to influence both the public goods they shall get and the contributions they must make, rational interaction among them leads to an endemic deficit. For all its artificial abstractions, the 'Deficit' game offers a reasonably general explanation, independent of ideology and notions of social purpose, why states whose governments depend heavily on the consent of the governed tend to run deficits most of the time. (The rare phenomenon of a balanced budget invariably depends on some *ad hoc* circumstance.) An additional public good benefits above all those who have an intense preference (or 'need') for it. The resources that go into its provision are raised by mandatory contributions. Some contributors have a weak preference for the public good or would actually prefer private exchange goods instead. They gain less, or even lose. For reasons subsumed under the image of 'walking up the down escalator', social choice is biased towards producing more and more public goods without the least assurance that each successive distribution of benefits and burdens

[7] Barro (1974).
[8] Vanberg and Buchanan (1986).

generated in this process *would* be 'socially chosen' in preference to every previous one, if the choice clearly presented itself to the participants as one between distributions. In neither the 'Ask' nor the 'Deficit' game, however, do people choose a distribution as such. The latter is a somewhat indirect and temporally perhaps quite remote compound consequence of public-goods choices; even if it is foreseeable collectively, it is not individually.

The force of this argument is manifest if we suppose that from D-day all publicly required resources are raised by borrowing. The contributors voluntarily save (give up exchange goods) in return for public liabilities promising a future yield that makes the exchange attractive to them. They think they are better off; otherwise they would not have willingly traded private goods for public bonds. The beneficiaries of the public goods are likewise better off by definition. The solution 'additional public good by deficit' should therefore be unanimously and strongly preferred to 'no additional public good' as well as to 'additional public good by taxation'.

In the light of this simple choice, it is puzzling to hear deficits being blamed on the irresponsibility and demagoguery of 'politicians', and strange that the word has much the same connotation as 'lying cynical crook'. The intended implication is that if politicians were less crooked things would pass differently and less self-indulgent outcomes would be 'socially chosen'. However, if more 'honesty' were to produce some austere result, it might distress the critics even more than the state of affairs they now deplore. For if 'politicians' did not make the laws and shape the budgets that maximized (to put it summarily) their chances of being re-elected, they would in effect be frustrating the intent of the social-choice rules ('constitutions') that were designed to give the fullest effect to the preferences of society's members. Under most conceivable constitutions that had a chance of being respected, the normal and constitutionally intended consequence of their doing that would and indeed ought to be some form of electoral punishment. If, however, for argument's sake politicians *both* frustrated the preferences of their constituencies *and*, having done so, managed to stay in power, the social choices made by them (in such matters as spending and taxation) would be dictatorial. For real contractarians, such inherently non-democratic choices could never be legitimate.

For others, less taken with the prospect of democracy pushed to its logical conclusion, austere spending and budget-balancing decisions reached under such unlikely circumstances could be legitimate by virtue of their conformity to a norm, a standard incorporated in some manner in the social-choice rule, which had been agreed to override preference. 'We must pay our way' could well be such a norm. Its inclusion in the constitution would, as was noted in Chapter 5, violate what the literature of social-choice rules refers to as the Neutrality condition. Not that such violation is particularly disturbing, if it sticks: for what it amounts to is that under some constitutional rule society must sometimes renounce choosing what the 'sum of preferences' indicated as its best-liked choice. Renunciation cannot be condemned on general grounds; there is nothing *a priori* wrong with self-denial.

The problem is rather that the constitutional rule violating Neutrality in favour of a standard is, like any 'contract with one's self', unenforceable and unlikely to stick when it is inconvenient to respect it. In producing prevarication, fudge, and self-deception, it may have effects contrary to the intent of the rule. It is instructive to have, in this context, the authorized editorial voice of American liberalism on budget-making in the aftermath of the post-1985 Gramm–Rudman–Hollings deficit-reducing legislation, which, by making the dominant 'more public goods, fewer taxes' strategy of the 'Deficit' game illegal, was to have permitted American politicians to act responsibly without being electorally punished for it:

In the end, no procedure can make the members of Congress behave responsibly. They have shown that they can out-maneuver any rules they write to keep themselves honest.[9]

What the liberal critic is castigating, however, is that the elected representatives of the people are functioning as the political system has intended that they should, maximizing their and their friends' chances of re-election and, in so doing, reducing the gap between what is actually being 'socially chosen' and what would be socially chosen if the 'sum of preferences' prevailed. Why a consent-based, competitive political process should produce laws, budgets, and social choices in general that are morally superior, more virtuous, self-denying, and far-seeing than the preferences of the members of society, and why it is blamed for mirroring these preferences with as little distortion as it knows how instead of sublimating them into

[9] *New York Times*, reprinted in *International Herald Tribune*, 21 Dec. 1987.

statesmanship, is explicable only in terms of our evergreen
ambition of having it both ways.[10]

Free Riding on Fairness

In the last analysis, all arm's-length social coexistence and co-
operation that is not exchange under contract carries within itself
an element of potential abuse by free riding. This is so because
when benefits are not contractually tied to contributions both
contributors and non-contributors have access to the benefit. The
free rider can appropriate some part of it by taking advantage of
others (the suckers) who would rather produce the benefit and
share it with the free rider than go without it altogether. It tells
something of the human condition that room for free riding, and
the 'strategies' that give access to it, turns out to provide the most
basic explanation of the general principles of non-contractual social
co-ordination. Our organization is what it is because the opportunities
for free riding, offered by the provision of public goods, are what
they are.

In the state of nature, a person's decision to ride free is essentially
a utility-maximizing 'gamble' on the probability of everybody else's
voluntary decisions to contribute or to ride free, jointly producing
the outcome which makes free riding by the person concerned
feasible. The outcome, whatever it is, is blatantly 'unfair' in the
sense of conforming to no rhyme or reason in terms of the relation
beween contributions and benefits. Yet it has the singularly
interesting feature, which is far from devoid of significance in
another sense of 'fairness', that it is consistent with public-goods
provision by wholly voluntary contributions: it relies on no
command-obedience brought about by the surrender of individual
to social choice.

The social contract, which makes contributions to public
provision mandatory, is nothing more exalted than an anti-free-
rider device. It is an attempt at putting right the unfairness of a
voluntary system where contributions would be made by those who

---

[10] On this point, two maxims of F. H. Knight are worth recalling: 'The mystery is
not that representative institutions were discredited, but that any other result could
he been expected'; and 'To substitute competitive politics for competitive business is
to jump out of the frying pan into the fire'. Knight (1947), 36, 39.

wanted to insure against public provision failing if too few contributed to it, and free rides enjoyed by those who got away with running the risk of failure and exploited the prudence of others. But while the intent of the social contract is to suppress free riding, its actual effect is to open up an altogether new ground on which it thrives with impunity. For the deterrent to state-of-nature free riding is the falling probability of successful public provision of a good as abuse of it by free-riding increases. When the necessary contributions for successful public provision are assured by coercion, no such check operates and free riding is never too risky. Risk, in fact, enters people's calculations with the opposite sign: from a check upon free riding it turns into its spur.

All must now try and wrest free-rider benefits through the social-choice process, for if some do not others would presumably get away with securing bigger ones at their expense. Must pull who do not want to be pulled. Free-rider behaviour thus becomes preventive and defensive, a matter of prudence. Incremental public-goods provision little by little drives out contractual exchanges and the state tends to become 'maximal', without this result being 'chosen' in any proper sense of the word, and without anybody in particular being noticeably pleased by it.

One way or another, any human community must, for its peace of mind, end up with an ideology affirming that if something like its present social organization had not come about in history's occult ways, it would have been willed and, as such, it is legitimate. If the argument that without it there could be no public goods will not stand up to critical analysis, there is always the fallback position that without it there can at least be no fairness. We have probed both positions at length and found both precariously dependent on an element of self-delusion. The provision of public goods is in general not contingent on the surrender of free choice in the matter. Nor is there any convincing reason for believing that the associated distributions of benefits and contributions are less unfair when imposed by collective decision than when they emerge from individuals assuming or declining alternative social roles, and the attendant burdens and risks, as they see fit.

However, if there were some universally agreed standard of distributive justice, such that a political community could, at least in principle, impose upon its members a distribution under which all reasonable men felt fairly treated, its fairness could only be fleeting, glimpsed for a brief moment. Anyone not using the political process to modify it in his favour would be needlessly accepting the risk of its being modified by others to his detriment. (I am using 'risk' colloquially, to stand for a probability distribution with significant negatively valued outcomes.) The mechanics of free riding, giving rise to an expanding sphere of public provision, should normally ensure that distributions are continually undone and superseded by new ones.

The unending pursuit of fairness proves to be an altogether sufficient reason for the shrinking of the domain of contractual exchanges. The norms of commutative justice regulate exchange: that terms have been duly agreed matters more to the practice concerned than that they should be concordant with some consensus of moral opinion. In the nature of the case, distributive justice comes into its own in public provision, where no mutually agreed and contingent promises regulate who gives and who gets what, and where it is irresistibly tempting to impose fair shares in place of *ad hoc* ones. While it is dubious (and impossible to demonstrate) that the quest for fairness yields greater fairness considered as the measure of equitable distribution, it self-evidently leads to less fairness considered as the measure of immunity of each from the unrestrained will of all, and as the measure of the responsibility of each for the consequences of his own actions.

WORKS CITED

ALCHIAN, A. A., and DEMSETZ, H. (1977), 'Production, Information Costs and Economic Organisation', in A. A. Alchian (ed.), *Economic Forces at Work*.

ATIYAH, P. (1979), *The Rise and Fall of Freedom of Contract*.

AXELROD, R. (1984), *The Evolution of Co-operation*.

BARRO, R. J. (1974), 'Are Government Bonds Net Wealth?' *Journal of Political Economy*.

—— and HARDIN, R. (eds.) (1982), *Rational Man and Irrational Society*.

BARRY, B. M. (1986), 'Lady Chatterley's Lover and Doctor Fischer's Bomb Party: Liberalism, Pareto Optimality, and the Problem of Objectionable Preferences', in J. Elster and A. Hylland, (eds.), *Foundations of Social Choice Theory*.

BERNHOLZ, P. (1986), 'A General Constitutional Possibility Theorem', *Public Choice*.

BISPHAM, J. A. (1987), 'Rising Public Sector Indebtedness: Some More Unpleasant Arithmetic', in M. Boskin, J. S. Flemming, and S. Gorini (eds.), *Private Saving and Public Debt*.

BOSWELL, J. (1791, 1793), *The Life of Samuel Johnson, L.L.D.*, Navarre Society edn., (1924).

BOUDON, R. (1987), *L'Idéologie, ou l'origine des idées reçues*.

BRENNAN, G., and BUCHANAN, J. M. (1985), *The Reason of Rules*.

BUCHANAN, J. M. (1986), 'Better than Plowing', *Banca Nazionale del Lavoro Quarterly Review*.

—— and TULLOCK, G. (1962), *The Calculus of Consent*.

—— and WAGNER, R. E. (1977), *Democracy in Deficit*.

BURKE, E. (1757, *A Vindication of Natural Society*, F. N. Pagano edn. (1982).

CHAMBERLIN, J. (1974), 'Provision of Collective Goods as a Function of Group Size', *American Political Science Review*.

—— (1976), 'A Diagrammatic Exposition of the Logic of Collective Action', *Public Choice*.

COASE, R. H. (1960), 'The Problem of Social Cost', *Journal of Law and Economics*.

COLINVAUX, P. (1978), *Why Big Fierce Animals are Rare: An Ecologist's Perspective*.

COLLARD, D. (1978), *Altruism and Economy*.

CONYBEARE, J. (1986), 'Trade Wars: A Comparative Study of Anglo-

Hanse, Franco-Italian and Hawley–Smoot Conflicts', in K. A. Oye, (ed.), *Co-operation Under Anarchy*.

ELSTER, J. (1986*a*), 'The Market and the Forum: Three Varieties of Political Theory', in J. Elster and A. Hylland (eds.), *Foundations of Social Choice Theory*.

—— (1986*b*), *Rational Choice*.

—— (1986*c*), 'Utility, Duty and Fairness', Gareth Evans Lecture, unpublished manuscript.

FAMA, E. F., and JENSEN, M. C. (1983), 'Agency Problems and Residual Claims', *Journal of Law and Economics*.

FRANKFURT, H. G. (1971), 'Freedom of the Will and the Concept of a Person', *Journal of Philosophy*.

FRIED, C. (1981), *Contract as Promise*.

FROHLICH, N., OPPENHEIMER, J., and YOUNG, D. (1971), *Political Leadership and Collective Goods*.

GAUTHIER, D. (1985), *Morals by Agreement*.

GILMORE, G. (1974), *The Death of Contract*.

HAMPTON, J. S. (1987), 'Free-Rider Problems in the Production of Collective Goods', *Economics and Philosophy*.

HARDIN, R. (1982), *Collective Action*.

HARSANYI, J. C. (1975), 'Can the Maximin Principle Serve as a Basis for Morality? A Critique of John Rawls's Theory', *American Political Science Review*.

HART, H. L. A. (1955), 'Are there any Natural Rights?', *Philosophical Review*.

HAYEK, F. V. (1964), 'Kinds of Order in Society', *New Individualist Review*, 2.

—— (1979), *Law, Legislation and Liberty*, vol. iii.

HINTZE, O. (1975), 'The Pre-Conditions of Representative Government', in F. Gilbert (ed.), *The Historical Essays of Otto Hintze*.

HIRSHLEIFER, J. (1983), 'From Weakest-Link to Best-Shot: The Voluntary Provision of Public Goods', *Public Choice*.

HOBBES, T. (1651), *Leviathan*, ed. C. B. Macpherson (1968).

HOGUE, A. R. (1966), *Origins of the Common Law* (reprinted 1985).

HUME, D. (1739), *Treatise of Human Nature*.

—— (1748), 'Of the Original Contract', *Essays Moral and Political*, in Sir Ernest Barker (ed.), *The Social Contract* (1960).

KNIGHT, F. J. (1947), *Freedom and Reform* (reprinted 1982).

MACK, E. (1981), 'Nozick on Unproductivity: The Unintended Consequence', in J. Paul (ed.), *Reading Nozick*.

MANENT, P. (1987), *Histoire intellectuelle du libéralisme*.

MARX, K. (1875), 'Critique of the Gotha Programme' reprinted in K. Marx and F. Engles, *Selected Works* (1968).

MAY, K. O. (1952), 'A Set of Independent, Necessary and Sufficient Conditions for Simple Majority Decision', *Econometrica*, reprinted in B. M. Barry and R. Hardin, (eds.), *Rational Man and Irrational Society?* (1982).

NOZICK, R. (1974), *Anarchy, State and Utopia*.

OAKESHOTT, M. (1962), 'The Moral Life in the Writings of Thomas Hobbes', in *Rationalism in Politics and Other Essays*.

OLSON, M. (1965), *The Logic of Collective Action*.

PARETO, V. (1923), *Œuvres complètes*, vol. xii.

PARFIT, D. (1984), *Reasons and Persons*.

POSNER, R. (1980), 'A Theory of Primitive Society with Special Reference to Law', *The Journal of Law and Economics*.

RADNITZKY, G., and BERNHOLZ, P. (eds.) (1987), *Economic Imperialism*.

—— and BARTLEY III. W. W. (eds.) (1987), *Evolutionary Epistemology, Rationality and the Sociology of Knowledge*.

RAMSEY, F. P. (1931), 'Truth and Probability' in *The Foundations of Mathematics and Other Logical Essays*, reprinted in H. E. Kyburg and H. E. Smokler (eds.), *Studies in Subjective Probability* (1964).

RAWLS, J. (1972), *A Theory of Justice*.

ROUSSEAU, J. J. (1755), *The First and Second Discourse*, ed. and trans. R. D. Masters and J. R. Masters (1964).

—— (1762), *The Social Contract*, ed. Sir Ernest Barker, *The Social Contract* (1960).

RYAN, A. (1983), 'Hobbes, Toleration and the Inner Life', in D. Miller and L. Siedentop (eds.), *The Nature of Political Theory*.

SAMUELSON, P. A. (1954), 'The Pure Theory of Public Expenditure', *Review of Economics and Statistics*.

SCHELLING, T. (1963), *The Strategy of Conflict*.

SCHOECK, H. (1970), *Envy: A Theory of Social Behaviour*.

SCHUMPETER, J. S. (1949), 'Science and Ideology', *American Economic Review*.

SEN, A. K. (1976–7), 'Rational Fools', *Philosophy and Public Affairs*, reprinted in F. Hahn and M. Hollis (eds.), *Philosophy and Economic Theory* (1979).

—— (1955), 'Social Choice and Justice: A Review Article', *Journal of Economic Literature*.

—— (1986), 'Foundations of Social Choice Theory: An Epilogue', in J. Eslter and A. Hylland (eds.), *Foundations of Social Choice Theory*.

SIMON, H. A. (1976), 'From Substantive to Procedural Rationality', in S. Latsis (ed.), *Method and Appraisal in Economics*.

SUPPES, P. (1984), *Probabilistic Metaphysics*.

TAYLOR, M. (1969), 'Proof of a Theorem on Majority Rule', *Behavioural Science*.

—— (1976), *Anarchy and Co-operation.*

—— and WARD, H. (1982), 'Chickens, Whales and Lumpy Goods: Altenative Models of Public Goods Provision', *Political Studies.*

ULLMAN-MARGALIT, E. (1977), *The Emergence of Norms.*

VANBERG, V., and BUCHANAN, J. M. (1986), 'Organisation Theory and Fiscal Economics: Society, State and Public Debt', *Journal of Law, Economics and Organisation.*

WARD, B. (1961), 'Majority Rule and Allocation', *Journal of Conflict Resolution.*

INDEX